Witchy Watercolor

75+ Easy Projects for Enchanting Art

Lizzy Gass

PAGE STREET
PUBLISHING CO.

*To my husband, Zach—
thanks for always listening and
being so supportive of my wild ideas*

PAGE STREET
PUBLISHING CO.

First published in 2025 by
Page Street Publishing Co.
27 Congress Street, Suite 1511
Salem, MA 01970
www.pagestreetpublishing.com

Distributed by Macmillan, sales in Canada by The Canadian Manda Group.

29 28 27 26 25 1 2 3 4 5

ISBN-13: 979-8-89003-276-8

Library of Congress Control Number: 2024945340

Edited by Krystle Green
Cover and book design by Emma Hardy for Page Street Publishing Co.
Artwork by Lizzy Gass

Printed and bound in China

Page Street Publishing protects our planet by donating to nonprofits like The Trustees, which focuses on local land conservation.

Witchy Watercolor

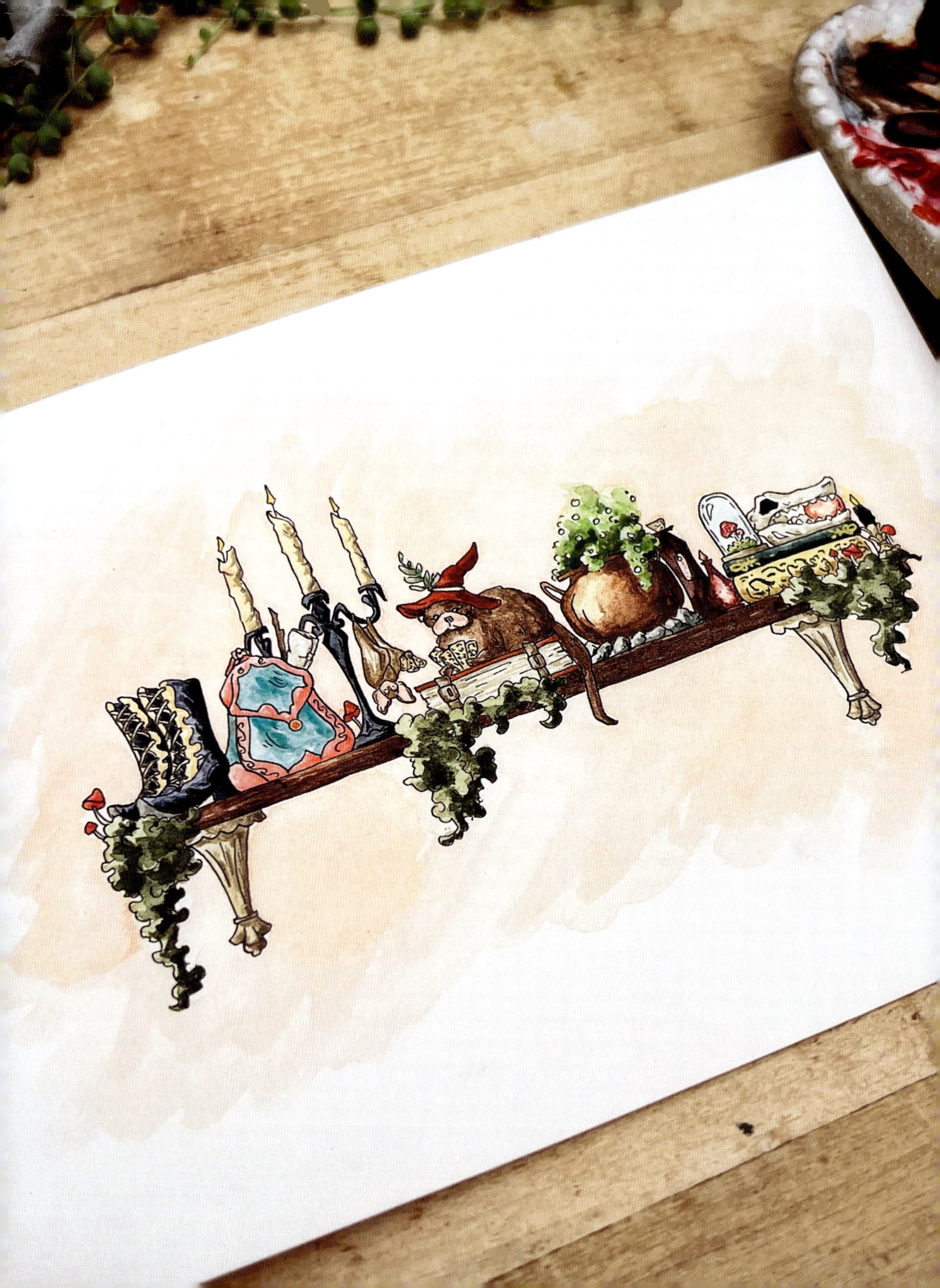

Table of Contents

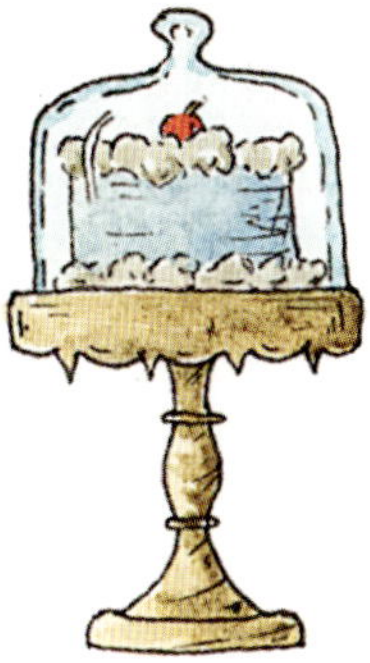

Introduction 9

Supplies 11

Watercolor Techniques and Paints 12

Tips and Tricks for Creating Your Shelves 14

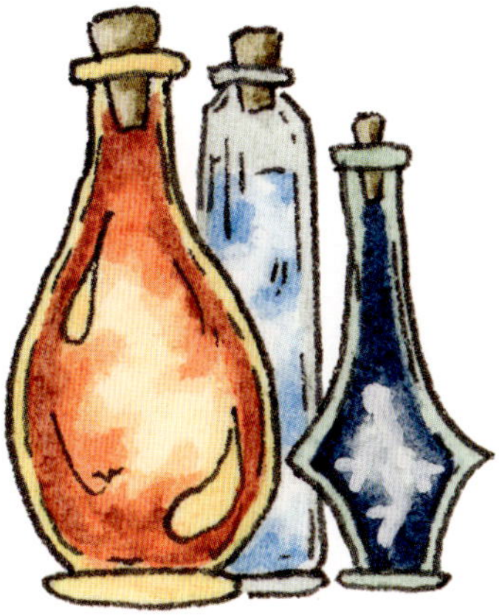

Kitchen Witchery 17

Feline Familiar Napping in a Mixing Bowl 18

Mysterious Cauldron 20

Colorful Stained-Glass Lamp 22

Delicate Dried Herbs and Flowers 25

Charming Potted Basil 28

Shining Copper Teakettle 30

Enchanted Hourglass Timer 32

Cherry Pie in a Red Pan 33

Witchy Cookbooks 34

Magical Frosted Cake 36

Enchanted Kitchen Utensils 38

Magic Potion Bottles 40

Blue and White China Teacup 41

Decorative Tea Towel 42

Climbing Potted Vine 44

Hand-Carved Wood Storage Rack 46

Mortar and Pestle with Spelled Herbs 48

The Kitchen Witchery Shelf 49

Assembling Your Kitchen Witchery Shelf 51

Cottage Witchery 59

Cat Napping with Spelled Knitting 60
Magical Springtime Flowers in a Tea Tin 62
Cozy Stained-Glass Lamp 64
Pumpkin from the Witch's Garden 65
Cozy Witch's Hat 66
Three-Tier Tower of Treats 68
Mysterious Crystal Ball 70
Wellies for Traipsing in the Garden 71
Delicate China Teapot 72
Clever Mouse Hiding from the Cat 73
Books of Magic Spells and Recipes 74
Wooden Trinket Shelf 76
Floral Teacup 77
Magical Crystals 78
Tiny House for Fairy Visitors 79
Romantic Paperback Books 80
The Cottage Witchery Shelf 82
Assembling Your Cottage Witchery Shelf 84

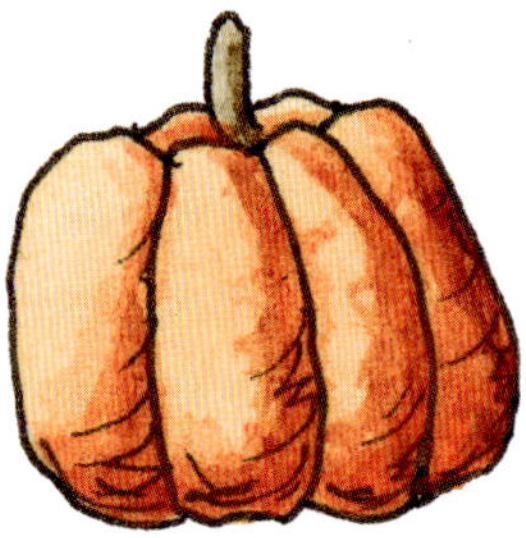

Sea Witchery 91

Octopus Familiar in a Magical Cauldron 92
Distinguished Seagull with a Witch's Hat 94
Magical Ship in a Bottle 96
Enchanted Spellbooks 97
Sturdy Boots for Seaside Adventures 98
Fishbowl with a Brightly Colored Fish 99
Bottled Weather Spells 100
Shelf with Stained-Glass Details 102
Stargazing Telescope 104
Warm and Gooey Chocolate Chip Cookie 105
Enchanted Always-Warm Teacup 106
Silver Filagree Teapot 107
Candle for Late-Night Reading 108
Weathered Moon Phases Chart 109
Inkwell with Phoenix Feather Quill 110
Armillary Stargazing Sphere 111
Bright Red Coral 112
Beautiful Seashells 113
Crystal Ball with a Driftwood Stand 114
Mysterious Treasure Box 115
The Sea Witchery Shelf 116
Assembling Your Sea Witchery Shelf 118

Celestial Witchery 125

Cauldron Full of Moonlight 126

Haunted Skull with Sunglasses 128

Enchanted Pocket Sundial 130

Ever-Glowing Lantern 131

Ancient Spell Mirror 132

Essence of Starlight 134

Liquid Sunshine 136

Midnight-Colored Familiar 138

Delicate Orrery Solar System 140

Spellbooks of Dubious Origin 142

Moonlight-Infused Amethyst Crystal 143

Maidenhair Fern that Grows in Moonlight and Sunlight 144

Terrarium with an Ever-Blooming Moonflower 146

Drawers for Bits and Bobs 148

The Celestial Witchery Shelf 149

Assembling Your Celestial Witchery Shelf 150

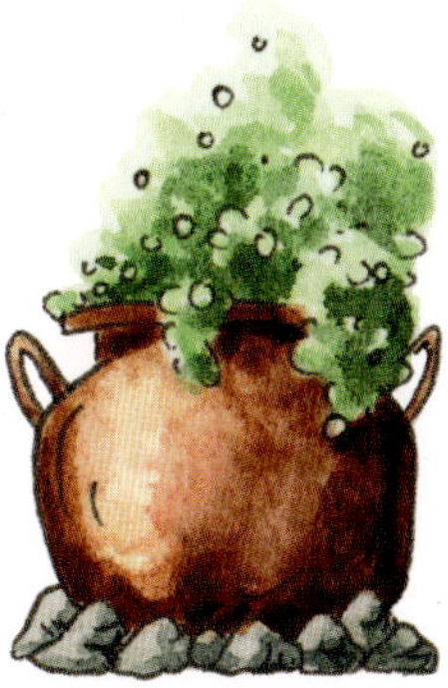

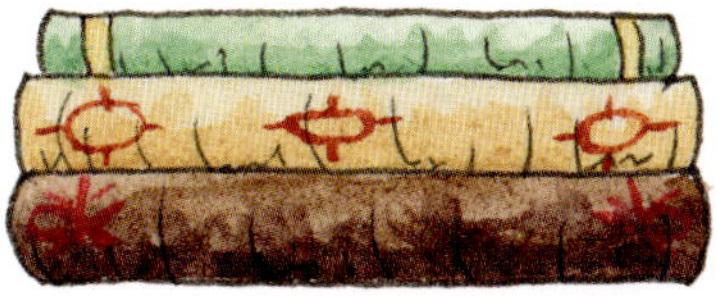

Swamp Witchery 157

Talkative Otter in a Pointed Hat 158

Pointed Boots for Traipsing in the Swamp 160

Inquisitive Bat Playing Cards 162

Gothic Candelabra 163

Talking Alligator Skull with a Crystal Ball 164

Long-Lost Book of Perilous Spells 165

Cauldron with a Bubbling Potion 166

Glass Terrarium with Poison Mushrooms 168

Sturdy Adventuring Knapsack 170

Mesmerizing Potion Bottle 172

Enchanted Pink Potion 174

Dark Candle on a Golden Candlestick 175

Enchanted Books 176

Delicate Moss and Mushrooms 178

The Swamp Witchery Shelf 180

Assembling Your Swamp Witchery Shelf 182

Acknowledgments 187

About the Author 188

Index 189

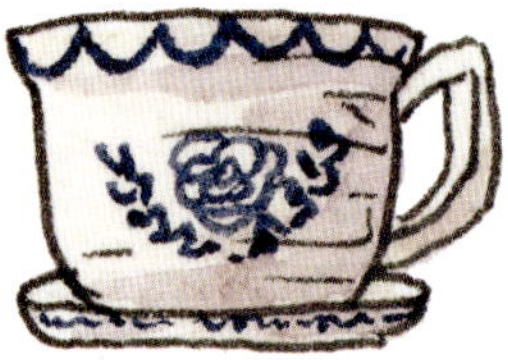

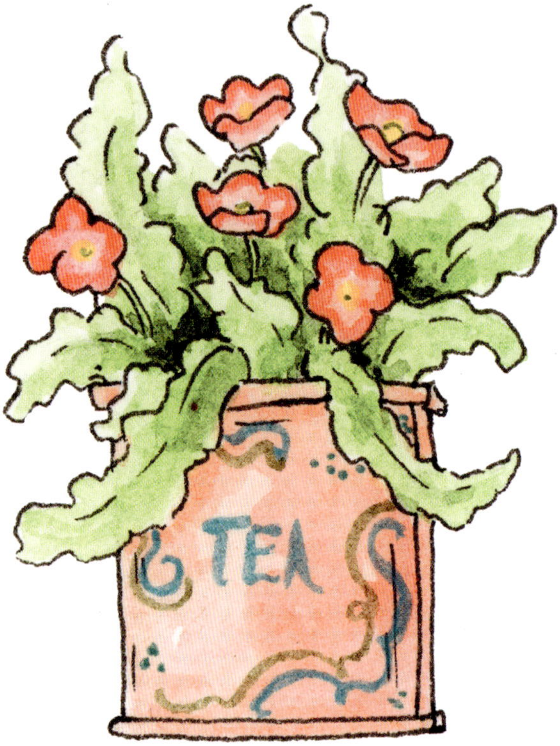
TEA

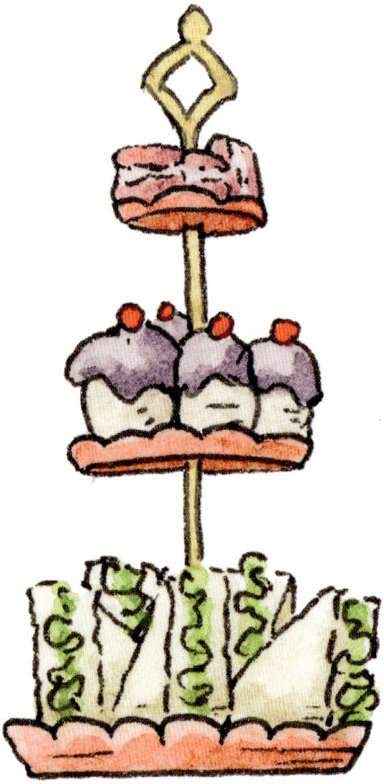

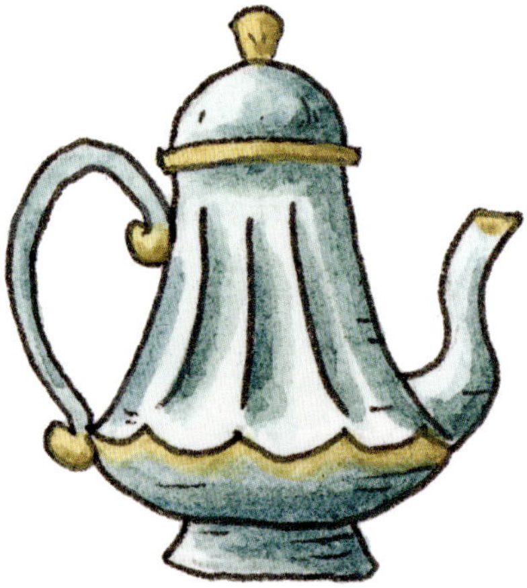

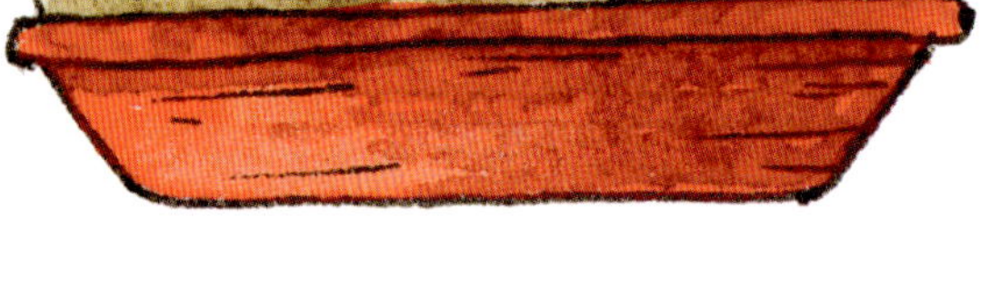

Introduction

Hello, and welcome to *Witchy Watercolor*! I hope you find some magical inspiration in these pages and that you use these tutorials and (occasionally wacky) advice to create art that you truly love.

I first started creating shelf paintings back in 2019, inspired by my love of detailed illustrations and my background in science. The series slowly grew from there, branching out into various occupations and whimsically delightful witches.

My hope with every shelf I paint is to bring a smile and a sense of wonder, reminiscent of all your favorite childhood stories, and I hope we've captured some of that magic in this book. Rather than simply including the instructions for you to paint a whole shelf, you'll find each project split up into individual tutorials. This, of course, will help each part of the shelf feel less overwhelming, since you won't be staring at a single tutorial that spans an entire chapter (yikes!).

My hope is that you'll be able to mix and match the projects like a choose-your-own-adventure story to make a shelf that's representative of all your favorite things. You can also use the individual tutorials to decorate a journal, a letter to a friend, a notebook, or anything else that could use a bit of magic and whimsy! I hope you love this book, and I can't wait to see the magic you create!

Happy painting!

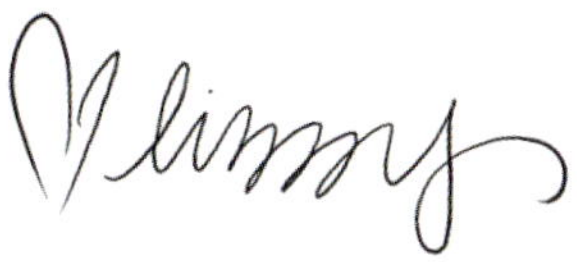

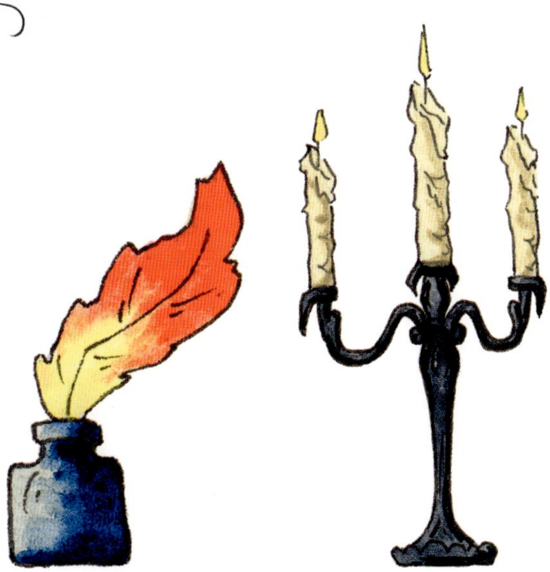

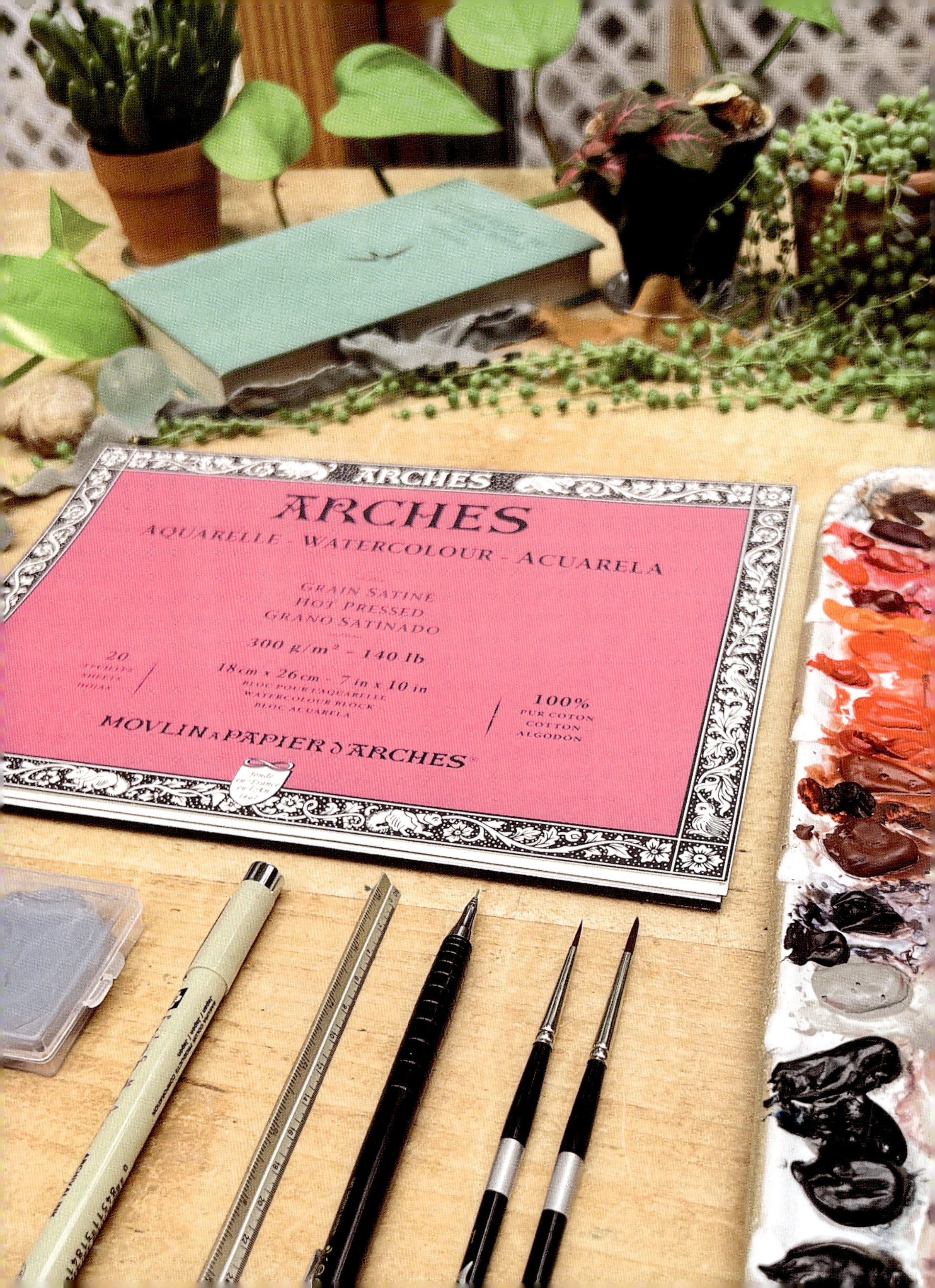
ARCHES
ARCHES
AQUARELLE - WATERCOLOUR - ACUARELA
GRAIN SATINÉ
HOT PRESSED
GRANO SATINADO
300 g/m² - 140 lb
20
18 cm x 26 cm - 7 in x 10 in
BLOC POUR L'AQUARELLE
WATERCOLOUR BLOCK
BLOC ACUARELA
100%
PUR COTON
COTTON
ALGODÓN
MOVLIN A PAPIER D'ARCHES

Supplies

You can always create beautiful art with anything you have on hand, but it can be easier to make art that looks the way you've envisioned it with supplies that work well for you. Peek into any art supply store and you'll find a dizzying array of mediums, options, and tools—and no two artists will give you exactly the same list of supplies, since no two people are exactly the same. I've included a list here of what I've found works the best for me, but please don't feel like you have to purchase any or all of these supplies—they're suggestions designed to minimize frustration, not firm requirements.

Pens

I've used a waterproof size 01 Sakura Micron® pen throughout the book for both outlines and shading; however, you can switch to a smaller size (such as an 005 pen) for the shading if you prefer.

Pencil

You can, of course, use any easily erasable pencil you already have, but I've found that a 0.2mm drafting pencil works well since you can draw delicate lines that erase cleanly.

Brushes

My go-to brushes for shelves are round, size 3 (the "larger brush") and size 5/0 (the "smaller brush"). An additional small brush, such as a 10/0 or 20/0 (the "smallest brush") can be useful for tiny details, but you should always experiment to see what works best for you. I use Trekell and Da Vinci Paint Co. brushes, and both brands hold up well over time, which is important for painting crisp lines and nice details. The brush sizes you need will, of course, depend strongly on personal preference and the size you choose for your painting, so experiment and see what works best for you. Throughout the book, I've included suggestions on what size brush to use, but, in general, you'll be using the larger brush (the size 3) for almost all of the painting and just grabbing the small brush for tiny details or fiddly little areas.

Paper

The best paper for these shelves will be a smooth, hot-press watercolor paper, such as Arches® hot-press paper. It can be difficult to get the details and lines to look the way you want if you use a textured, cold-press paper, but it's certainly possible if that's your preferred kind of paper.

Paint

There are so many lovely watercolor paint options, but my favorite, which I've used throughout these paintings, are Daniel Smith watercolor tubes. The books on The Celestial Witchery Shelf (page 149) will require white paint, and I'd recommend white gouache or Dr. Ph. Martins® Bleedproof White™. White gouache is very handy to have around, since you can mix it with any color of watercolor to fix mistakes, since the gouache will then make your watercolor opaque.

Watercolor Techniques and Paints

Let's talk about water. It may seem obvious, but watercolor painting involves a lot of water, and it will end up being one of the most important factors to consider when you're painting the *Witchy Watercolor* tutorials. You may be familiar with beautiful wet-on-wet painting techniques, where watercolors are used with a great deal of water to blend the colors together and make flowing, loose artwork. Throughout this book, however, we'll be utilizing two main skills: wet-on-dry and glazing. You can find wonderful books and videos with tons of detail on these techniques, so I'll give more of a bird's-eye view here.

Wet-on-dry refers to painting on dry paper (instead of wet), and it allows you to control exactly where the paint goes on the page. This is particularly useful for the projects you'll find on the following pages, where you'll be painting within an ink outline and don't want the paint ending up in unexpected places.

Glazing refers to building up several semi-transparent layers of paint of the same or varying colors to achieve a deep, rich hue. Both of these require you to pay attention to how much water you're using—if you hold up your brush and water drips off the tip, you'll have trouble controlling exactly where the paint goes since too much water (and therefore paint) will come off your brush at once. However, if you don't have enough water on the brush, you'll end up with paint that moves down onto the paper unevenly or not at all when you try to paint. There's no hard-and-fast rule for the perfect amount of water—it's something you'll develop a feel for quickly.

My recommendation is to always have several paper towels on hand, and gently dab your brush on the paper towel every time after you pick up more paint on your brush. If it makes a small spot of evenly distributed color, you're good to go! If a large amount of water rushes off the brush onto the paper towel, there's too much water. If nothing happens, there's not enough water.

Next, let's chat about color. You can, technically, mix any color from the primary colors, but it's not a technique I personally enjoy (at all), so we're not going to do that in these tutorials. As a general rule, the fewer colors you use in a given painting, the more likely they are to match. My favorite way to choose colors for a painting is to swatch them individually on small pieces of paper (and label the swatches). I then pick a color or two that I absolutely love and want to use (often quinacridone coral and deep sap green), and then I choose colors that go nicely with those. I often find that the colors straight out of the tube (or pan) are a bit too saturated for me, so, if you're going to buy one new color, I'd 100 percent recommend Daniel Smith's German greenish raw umber. It's like magic—you can mix it with almost any other color to give it a mellower, earthier hue, which I love.

You'll find throughout the tutorials that we'll be mixing a lot of colors together—often three or four to make a single color in the final painting. If that doesn't sound fun (which I completely understand), you can use whichever color in your palette is closest or that you prefer. This book is meant for you to enjoy, so once you pick up a brush to begin painting, feel free to customize the colors to your liking! Color mixing is one of those interesting (and occasionally maddening) things where you can arrive at the same end result in any multitude of ways, and oftentimes the colors you end up with on accident are the best ones. I've tried to include details on how much of each color I've used, and if I don't specify, that means I used more or less equal quantities of each color. Don't fret if your colors don't turn out exactly the same as the ones on the page; focus on mixing colors that you enjoy and that look nice together. I always keep a piece of scrap paper (ideally the same kind of paper that you're doing the actual painting on) to test colors before I use them because sometimes a color will look wildly different on the palette versus on paper, and it's nice to know that ahead of time, since watercolor isn't erasable!

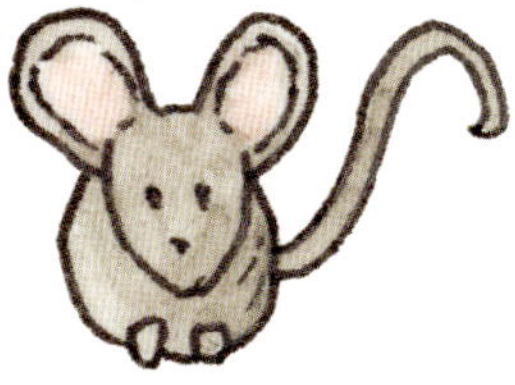

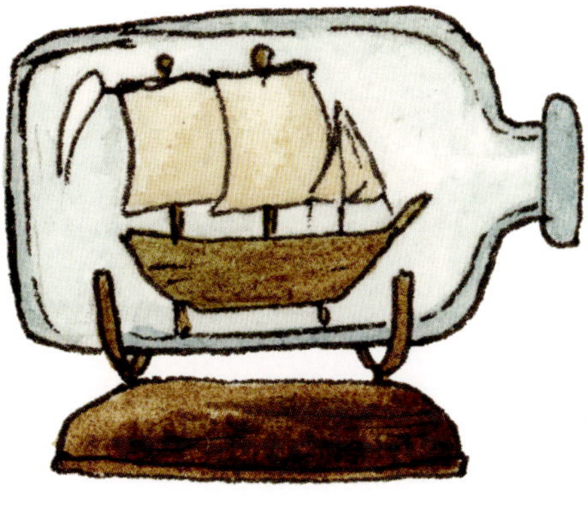

Tips and Tricks for Creating Your Shelves

As you flip through this book, you'll find tutorials for more than 75 individual witchy elements that go together to make five witchy shelves. You can use the examples provided for each witch, or mix and match the items to make a shelf that incorporates all your favorite items. You can also use the individual tutorials to practice new techniques, to decorate journals and cards, or to create individual pieces of art. If you'd like to make the shelves as described in the tutorials, here are my best tips and tricks for assembling your finished shelf:

1 Start off with a pencil sketch of the whole shelf before you add any ink. You want to see how everything overlaps before you add ink to an area that'll be covered by something else.

2 Begin with the shelf itself, and then sketch the various items on it so you can make sure everything is in proportion (and in a line, so you don't end up with a wiggly shelf).

3 You can use a ruler to get perfectly straight lines or embrace the slight imperfections of freehand outlines. It's always fun to experiment and see what works best for you.

4 When you start your ink outline, begin with the items that are closest to the front, gradually working your way back until you finish with the outline of the actual shelf. If you're having trouble getting delicate ink lines, it can help to leave the cap off your pen for a few minutes so it dries out a bit—just don't forget about it or it'll dry all the way.

5 If you'd like to mix and match to make your own shelf, I've found that sketching layouts in a digital drawing program such as Procreate® can be very helpful. This allows you to fine-tune the design so you can adjust the sizes and locations of the items to your heart's content. Also, if you erase repeatedly on watercolor paper, you'll damage the paper fibers, and the texture will be pilly in that area, so it's best to do any troubleshooting and adjustments on something other than your final watercolor paper.

6 If you're stuck deciding what colors should go where, you can take a picture of your painting at whatever stage it's at, and color it in digitally before you go in with actual paint. This lets you try out different colors to see what the best fit will be.

7 If you prefer not to draw digitally but still want to test out colors, there are a few options. You can cut out a piece of watercolor paper in the shape of the item you're testing, paint it, and lay it on top of the actual painting to see how the colors look. If you have another kind of paint (gouache or acrylic work best), you can also paint over a clear layer of plastic such as a sheet protector, and then lay that on top of your painting to compare the colors.

8 You'll see that the example shelves in each chapter have been painted with colored backgrounds. Whenever paper comes into contact with water, it may warp and bend a bit as it dries, and if you paint the colored background on your shelf, you may find that your paper has warped—this is very common, but don't fret, we have a solution! Flip your paper over and paint a thin layer of water over the entire back. (Some people use a small spray bottle, but I prefer painting on the water.) Let the paper dry. It should be much flatter now, and when you're finished with the whole painting, you can always pop it between two books like you're pressing flowers to help get rid of the last of the wiggles in the paper.

9 Ultimately, the order in which you choose to paint the assembled shelf is completely up to you—you should always make art in whatever way feels best. I've included the steps in the book in the order that I find to be the easiest, but if you're particularly excited about painting a particular section or just want to leave an area unpainted and choose its color later in the process, it's totally fine to paint things out of order. The main reason I've chosen this order is to keep two simultaneously wet edges from being next to one another, since it's easy for them to bleed together, and then your colors wander around to unexpected places.

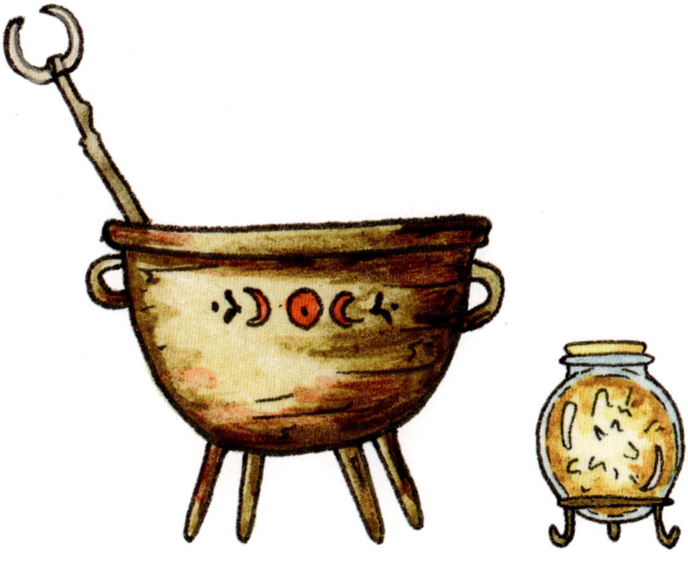

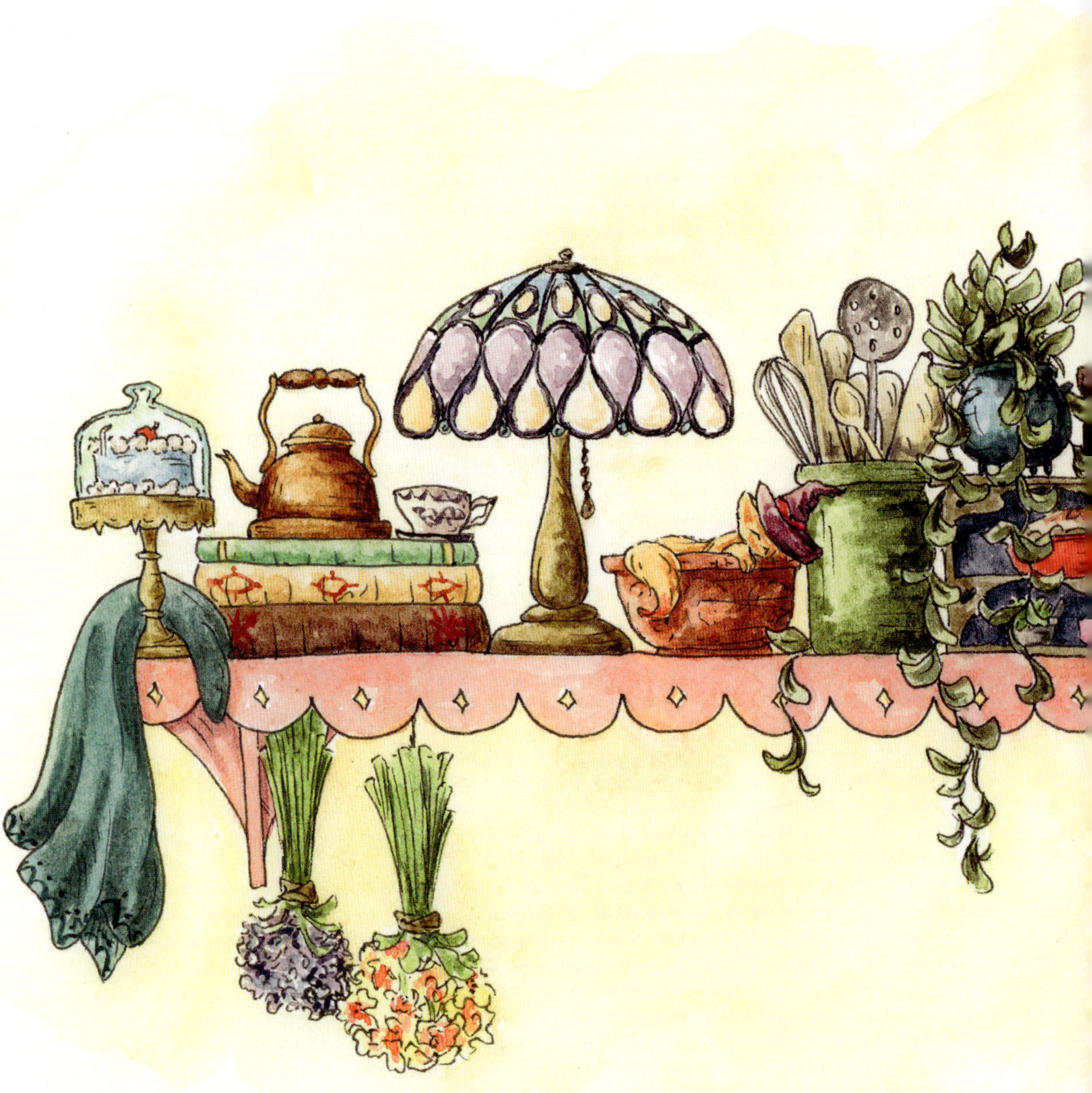

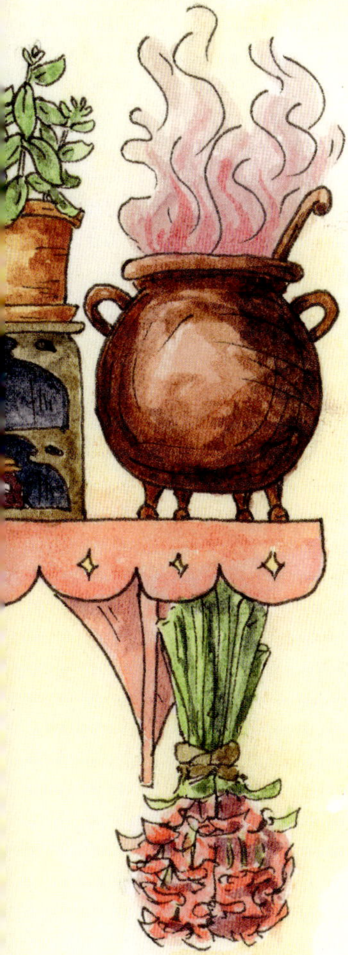

Kitchen Witchery

Friendly and inviting, the kitchen witch's shelf is full of mysterious potions, thriving houseplants, and a plethora of knickknacks. This shelf has so many fun opportunities to incorporate elements from your life, such as a favorite mug or beloved pet, and there's always room for more plants! Whether you prefer to bake delicious desserts (and use magic to wash all the ensuing dishes) or throw all the veggies in a cauldron to make stew, you'll find plenty of projects in this chapter to fill a kitchen witch's shelf! Let's get started!

Feline Familiar Napping in a Mixing Bowl

Every kitchen witch needs a familiar, and ours enjoys the company of a precocious cat, currently napping happily in a mixing bowl in preparation for later shenanigans. Subtle pink highlights add whimsy to this adorable feline, matching its vibrant personality. You'd better keep an eye on your tea and snacks, since I'm sure the cat will be looking for a treat when it wakes up!

Colors Used

- Raw sienna
- Cadmium red medium hue
- Rose madder permanent
- Moonglow purple
- Buff titanium
- Naples yellow
- Mayan yellow

1

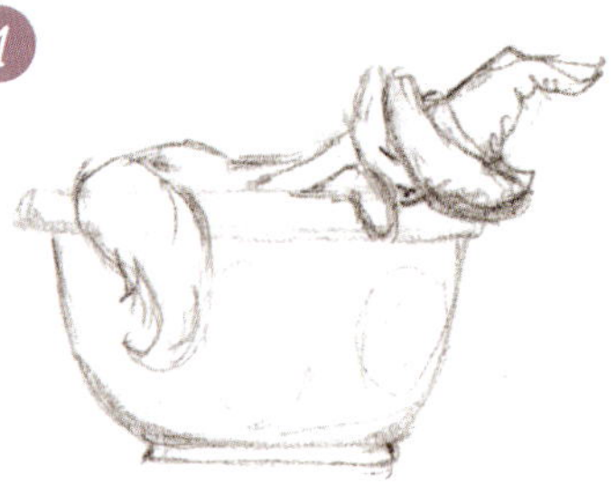

2

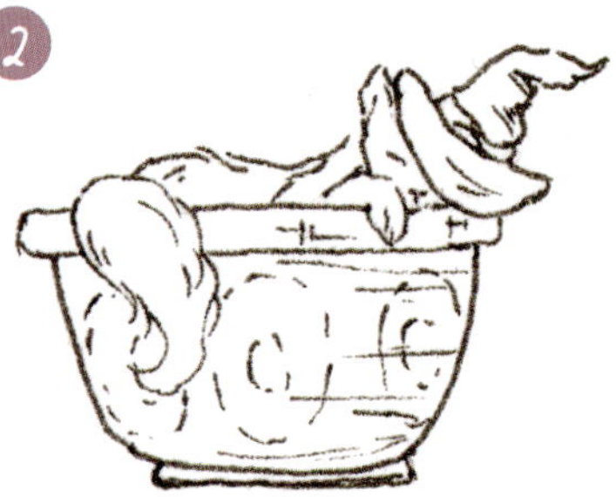

1 Start off with a light pencil sketch of a mixing bowl, adding some concentric circles for a subtle embossed design. Then add the cat's tail and head at opposite ends of the bowl, fill in the rest of the body and paw, and finally, add the jaunty hat.

2 Using your waterproof pen, add ink to the hat, cat, and mixing bowl (in this order). I find it helpful to work front to back like this, since it helps avoid accidentally adding ink to areas that are covered by other things, but there are also times when it's best to work in the opposite order, so experiment and see what works best for you! Once the ink is dry, gently erase the pencil layer.

3

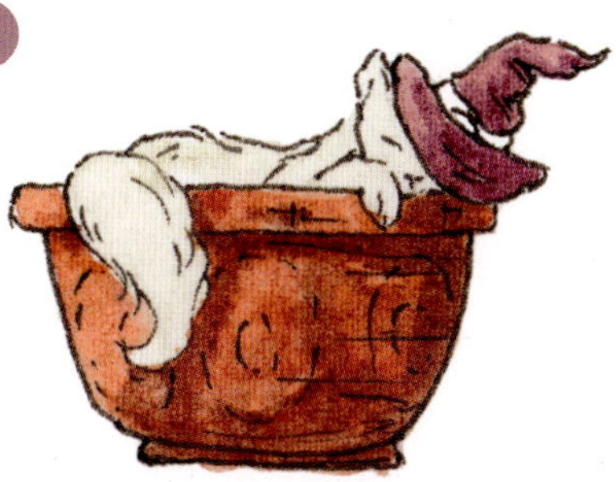

4

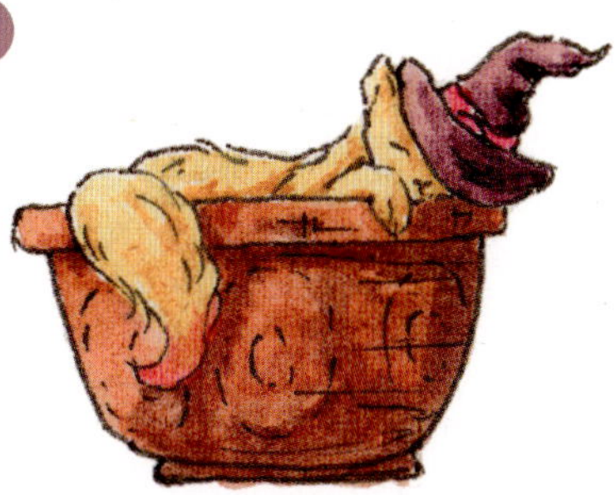

3 Let's add the first layer of color to the mixing bowl! Using your larger brush, mix together some raw sienna, cadmium red medium hue, and rose madder permanent to get a nice, light, orangey-pink color, and then go lightly over the whole mixing bowl with it. On your palette, add a bit of moonglow purple, and then use this slightly darker orange towards the bottom right of the bowl and just to the right of the cat's tail for shadows. Let the bowl dry, and then fill in the whole cat with a layer of buff titanium, which will show through for the lightest highlights on the cat's fur later on. Finally, for the hat, combine moonglow purple, rose madder permanent, and Naples yellow, and fill in the hat (except for the band around the middle), while also adding more to the areas where there'll be shadows.

4 Using your bowl shadow color, add a bit more texture and shadow to the bowl until you love the way it looks. Then use three to five light layers of raw sienna to fill in the cat's fur, using a bit more color on the areas where we'll find shadows (anything that's down and to the right). Mix together some cadmium red medium hue, Mayan yellow, and raw sienna, and paint the darkest bits of fur, especially on the edges of the cat's belly and face. While the paint on the tail is still wet, use your smaller brush to place a tiny amount of rose madder permanent at the very tip and blend it up into the main part of the tail. This'll add a fun pop of color but can be omitted if you'd prefer a more realistic cat. Use that same rose madder permanent and your smaller brush to paint the middle band on the cat's hat. Finally, mix together moonglow purple and rose madder permanent and use that to add the very darkest shadows of the hat. Now you have a precious little feline familiar napping in a mixing bowl, resting up for future mischief!

Mysterious Cauldron

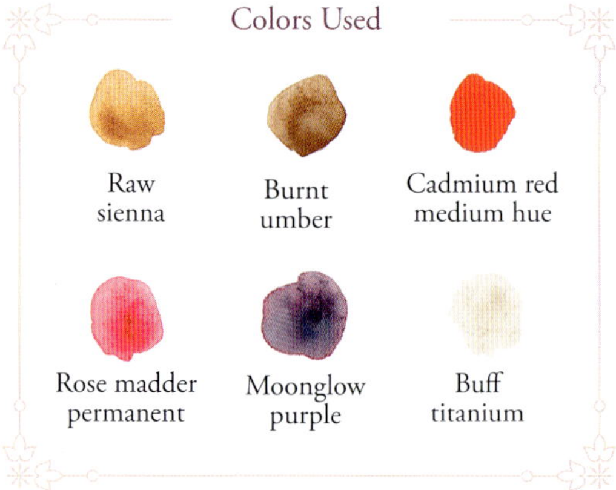

Every kitchen witch needs a cauldron—an indispensable tool for potions, soups, stews, and brewing up mischief. The cauldron is enchanted to keep the contents at exactly the right temperature, so you'll never need to worry about the contents boiling over or cooling too quickly. Mysterious pink smoke is rising from this cauldron, perhaps from a magical potion or a warm winter beverage.

1

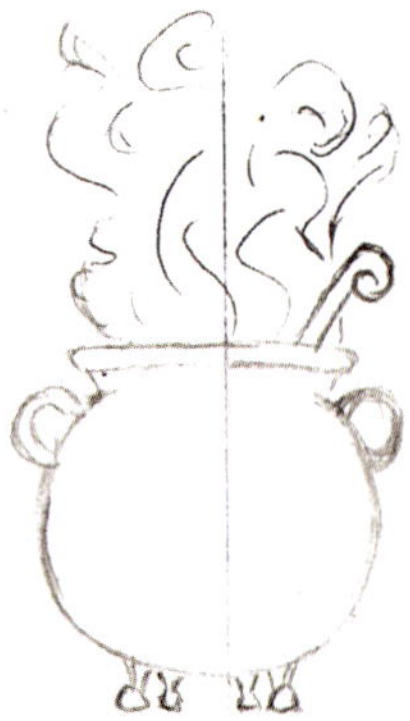

2

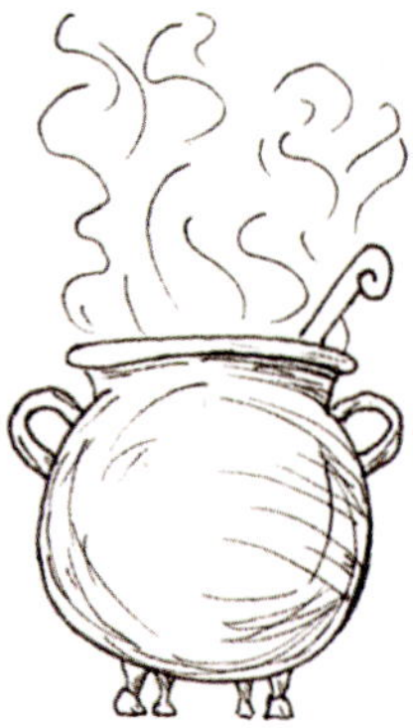

1 As always, we're going to start off with a light pencil sketch. Since the cauldron is symmetrical, it can help to draw a center line and build the rest of the cauldron out from that, beginning with a rounded oval for the main cauldron shape, and then adding the feet, handles, ladle, and smoke.

2 Using your waterproof pen, carefully trace the outline of the cauldron, and add extra lines for shading. This is the perfect place to add decorative designs and patterns on the cauldron, perhaps some carvings or filigree, if you like a bit more decoration. To achieve the translucent look of smoke, don't fully outline it, but use the lines to hint at the edges and shading. Once the ink is dry, gently erase the pencil layer.

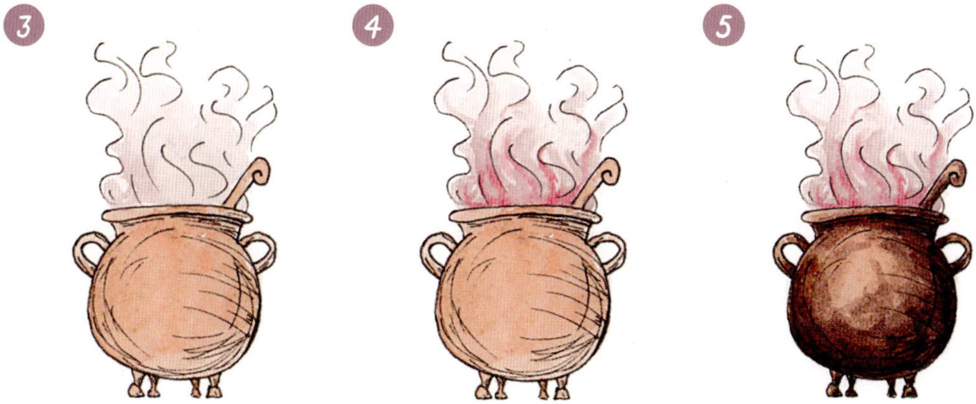

3 Mix together some raw sienna, burnt umber, and cadmium red medium hue, and then use this warm brown and your larger brush to lightly fill in the whole cauldron and ladle. While that's drying, go over the smoke with a very light layer of watered-down grayish-purple made with a mixture of rose madder permanent, moonglow purple, and buff titanium, adding a second layer closer to the cauldron where the smoke would be denser.

4 Once that layer of smoke is dry, go over it with a third layer of the same color in the areas closest to the cauldron. While that's still wet, mix up some slightly more concentrated pink (I used pure rose madder permanent), and add some highlights in the densest portions of the smoke.

5 Now for the best part—the shadows! To give the cauldron a nice, rounded appearance, add some moonglow purple to your warm brown from step 3, and use your larger brush to add more color where there would be shadows on the cauldron. Around the bottom and underneath the lip of the opening of the cauldron are perfect places to add shadow to get this realistic effect! Don't forget; you can let it dry and come back and add more shadows any time, so don't worry about getting it perfect on the first try. Go over the ladle handle with a bit of your purply-brown shadow color, and then enjoy your new cauldron. I'm sure you can practically smell whatever pink potion the witch is brewing up!

Colorful Stained-Glass Lamp

The kitchen witch needs plenty of light for late-night baking, since ancient recipes written in cursive on chocolate-stained pages can be difficult to decipher without a brightly glowing lamp. Stained glass is one of my favorite things to paint, and stained-glass lamps are extra delightful since you can make them in all sorts of whimsical shapes and sizes. Feel free to tinker with the shapes in the design and the colors to suit your particular tastes—you can make the lamp glow with your own unique personality!

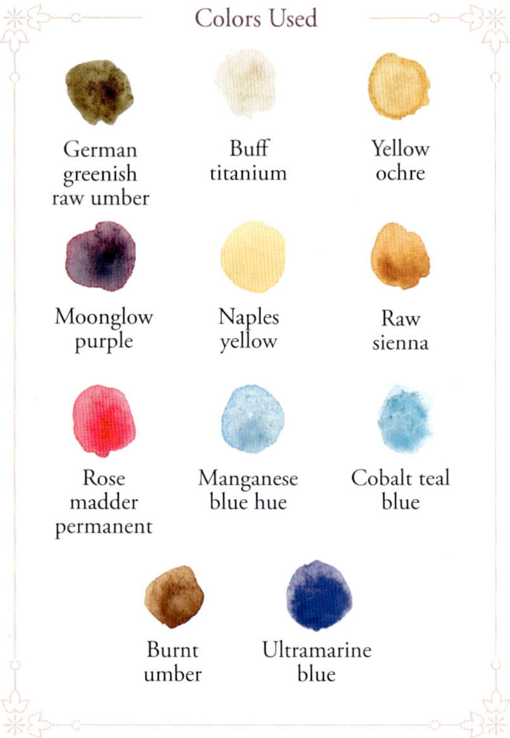

1

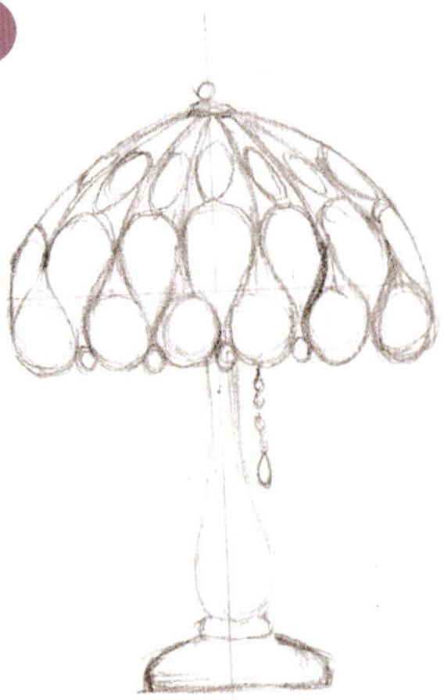

1 Use your pencil to draw a very light vertical line through the center of where you'd like your lamp to be, and a horizontal line three-quarters of the way down from where you'd like the bottom of the lampshade to be. Then sketch the outline of the lampshade and base, and fill in the details of the stained-glass design. If you'd like to make your own design, circles, gently swooping lines, and interconnected shapes will give a classic stained-glass lampshade look, or you can find lots of beautiful examples of different styles online. This is a fun place to play with the design and shape of the lamp, so feel free to change the lamp any way that makes you happy!

2

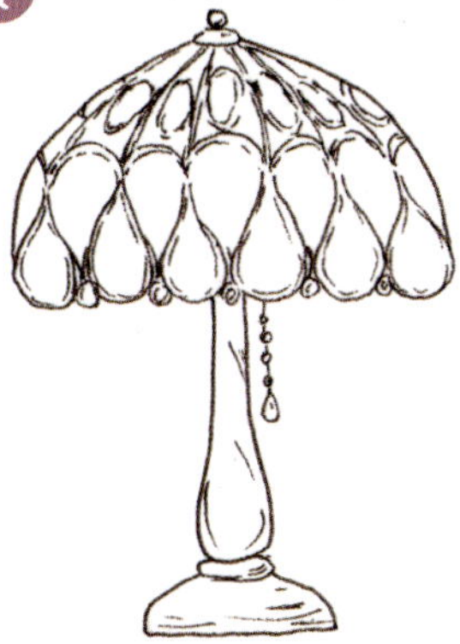

2 Using your waterproof pen, go over your pencil outline, adding some shading to the lamp base along the lower right edges. You have two options for the welds (the bits of metal between the glass pieces) holding the bits of stained glass together. Here, I've outlined both sides of the welds, so we can paint them a dark gray later on, but depending on the size you've chosen for the lamp and your personal preference, you can also use the ink lines themselves as the welds. If that's what you want to do, draw a single line for each weld instead of the double lines shown here. Once the ink is dry, gently erase the underlying pencil sketch.

3

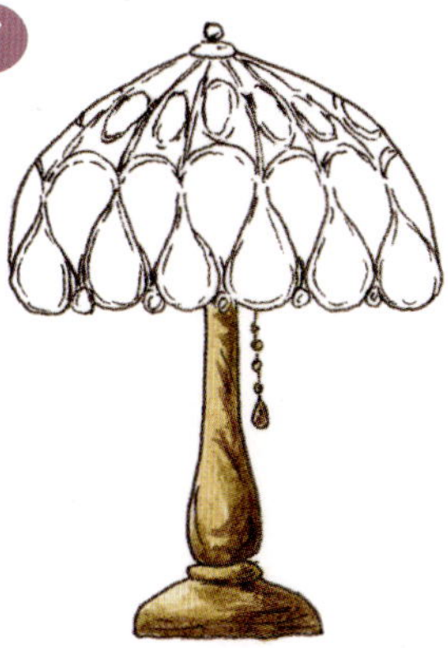

3 Let's start with the base, where we'll be making a progressively darker golden-bronze color. First, with your larger brush, mix up some German greenish raw umber, buff titanium, and yellow ochre, and then go over the whole base, including the pull-string. While that's still wet, add more German greenish raw umber to the mixture on your palette, and paint in some lovely shadows on the right-side edges of the base. Then add a smidge of moonglow purple to the mix, and go over the very darkest sections of the shadows. Now, on to the stained glass!

4

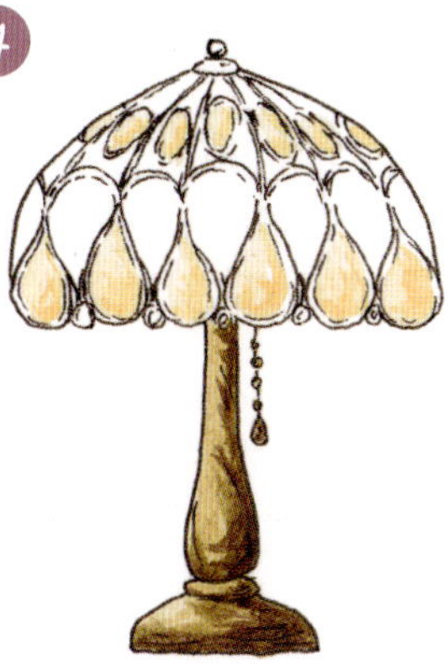

4 To keep the colors from bleeding together, we'll do this in two sections. First, still using your larger brush, mix up some Naples yellow and raw sienna, and go very, very lightly over the bottom teardrop shapes and the upper circles on the lamp. Second, using that same color, dab your brush near the right edges of those areas to add some texture to the glass.

(continued)

5

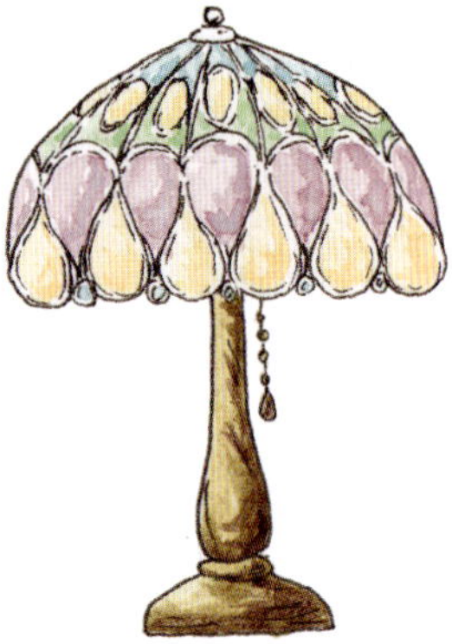

5 Let the yellow areas dry, and then let's add the rest of the colors! For the purple teardrops, mix together moonglow purple, buff titanium, and rose madder permanent, and fill in the teardrop shapes like you did with the yellow, adding a second layer towards the right edge of each teardrop. While that dries, since it's always a good idea to keep the wet edges as far away from one another as possible, combine manganese blue hue, buff titanium, and cobalt teal blue, and fill in the tiny circles at the bottom of the lampshade as well as the pieces at the very top. Finally, once the other colors have dried, let's mix up a nice green color with Naples yellow and cobalt teal blue, and use that to fill in the last empty spaces, again adding a bit more color on the right edge.

6

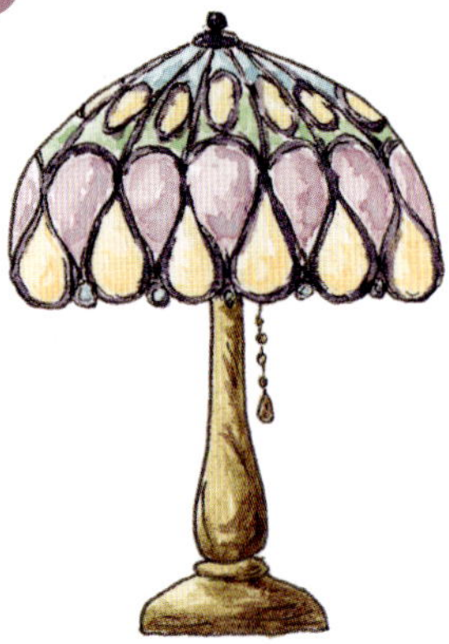

6 Once the stained glass is completely dry, use your smaller brush to fill in all the welds between the glass pieces with a mixture of burnt umber, ultramarine blue, and moonglow purple. The less water you use when combining the colors, the more control you'll have over where the paint goes when you place the brush on the paper. If you feel like there's too much paint or water in your brush, dab it gently on a paper towel, and then move forward with the painting. I hope you're positively glowing with excitement about how amazing your lamp looks!

Delicate Dried Herbs and Flowers

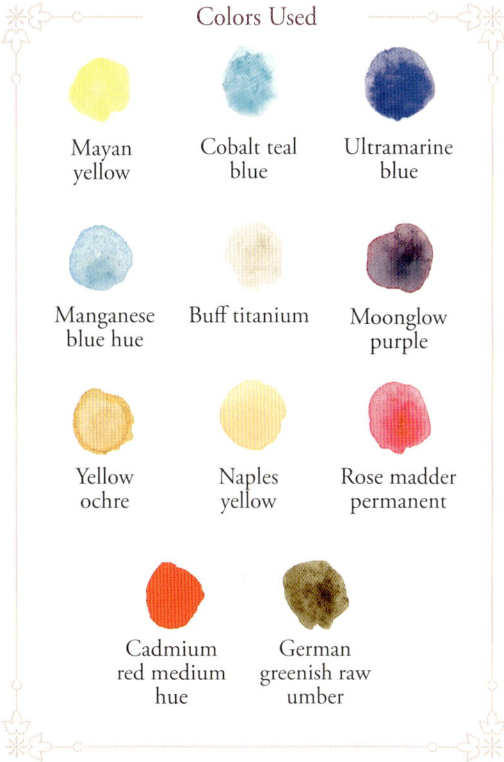

The kitchen witch's shelves are always full of sunshine and beautiful things, and these bundles of delicate dried herbs and flowers are the perfect addition to bring in some extra pops of color all year round, even when the flowers aren't blossoming. We'll go over how to paint three different bundles of foliage, but this is a wonderful opportunity to adjust the shelf to include your favorite flowers, or add more!

1

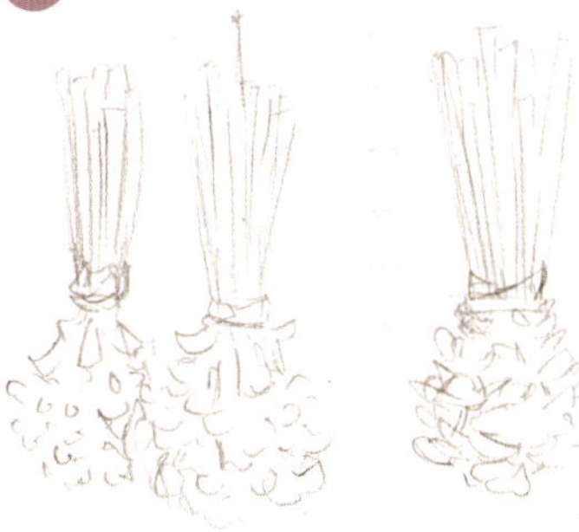

1 Once you've decided on the perfect locations for the bundles of dried herbs and flowers, use a pencil to lightly sketch the outlines of the stems, flowers, and cords holding the bundles together. You can move the bundles to wherever works best on your shelf, depending on how you've chosen to arrange the items, or use the locations I've shown in the example here—it's totally up to you! Since the flowers are relatively small, we don't need to outline every single flower or petal—just enough to give the impression of flowers. Also, we'll add more detail with the paint, so focus more on the outline and overall shape here.

(continued)

2

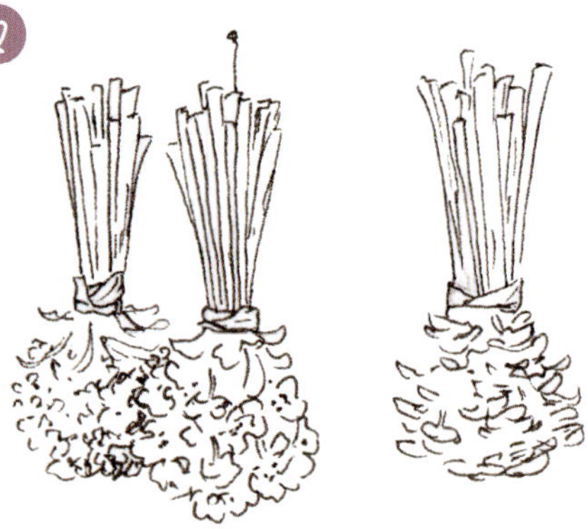

3

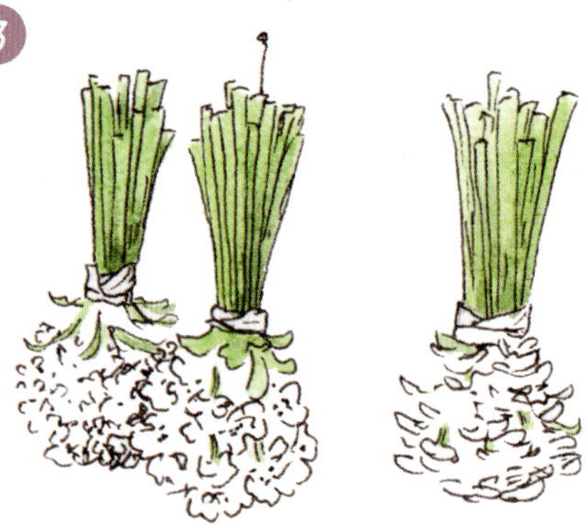

To differentiate the bundles of flowers, use small fluffy circle shapes for the ones on the left, subtle petal outlines for the middle flowers, and sideways ovals for the ones on the right, or swap out any of the shapes for your favorite spring blooms.

2 Use your waterproof pen to go over the pencil outlines, adding a bit of shading on the right sides of the flowers and stems where we'll find shadows. Once the ink is dry, gently erase the pencil layer.

3 Let's start with the stems of the flowers. I used the same colors for all three bundles, but you can vary the greens however you please. Use your larger brush to combine Mayan yellow, cobalt teal blue, and ultramarine blue, and then fill in the stems, leaves, and a few bits within the bouquets where the stems might peek through. While this is still wet, add a bit more ultramarine blue to the mixture, and add some shadows toward the right sides of the stems and towards where they're bundled together, keeping in mind we'll add another layer of shadows in the last step.

4 We'll add two layers of color to each bundle of dried flowers in this step. The idea here is to make layers of lightly overlapping shades to give the impression of petals and depth, without having to paint every flower individually—which would take way too long! For the bundle of flowers on the left, use your larger brush to combine manganese blue hue with buff titanium and a hint of moonglow purple, and then fill in the whole bundle of flowers. Switch to your smaller brush and add some more moonglow purple to the mixture, and add some small dots of this slightly darker purple shade to make shadows and petals.

4

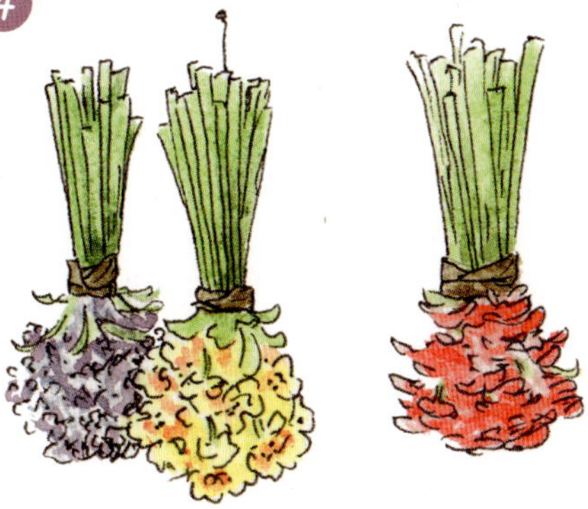

5

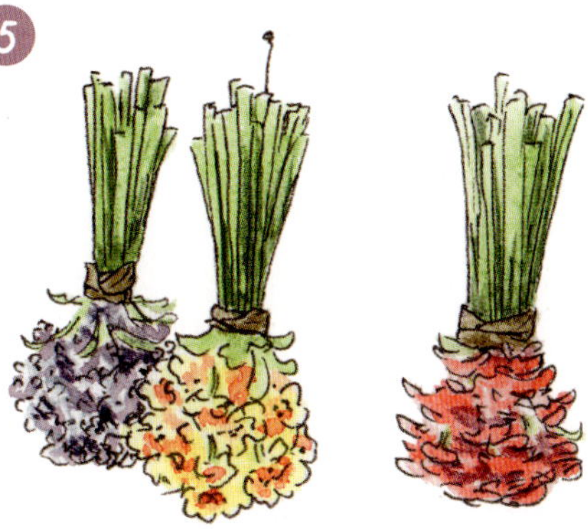

Now, for the middle bundle of flowers, combine Mayan yellow, yellow ochre, and Naples yellow with your larger brush and fill in the whole bouquet. Once that's dried for a few moments, add a second layer towards the right to make shadows. While that's drying, combine rose madder permanent, cadmium red medium hue, and buff titanium to make an orangey-pink color, and use your smaller brush to place that at the centers of your flowers. For the bouquet on the right, use a mixture of rose madder permanent, cadmium red medium hue, and buff titanium and fill in all the flowers. Then combine rose madder permanent with some cadmium red medium hue to add shadows and texture to the flowers.

Finally, using your smaller brush and a small amount of German greenish raw umber, fill in the cords holding the bouquets together, adding an extra layer or two to make shadows towards the right side.

5 Now let's add another layer of shadows to really make these flowers pop! Using the darkest green you mixed up for the stems, add some final shadows to the stems along the right edge and just above where each bundle is wrapped. For the left and middle bouquets, use the darkest color you mixed for each one to add some delicate shadows. Finally, combine rose madder permanent, cadmium red medium hue, moonglow purple, and Naples yellow, and add the last shadows to the bouquet on the right using your smaller brush. Now sit back and enjoy your beautiful flowers!

Charming Potted Basil

A kitchen witch's shelves are always full of plants for cooking, potion making, and decor, so let's paint a basil plant, which can be small and tucked away on a stack of books, or it can be a large and verdant plant that draws the eye. You can, of course, include any herb or plant of your choice, but we've got basil here so the kitchen witch can make homemade pizza on a whim. After all, what could be more magical than pizza, except maybe cookies, but since there's no cookie plant, we'll make do with this charming little basil.

Colors Used

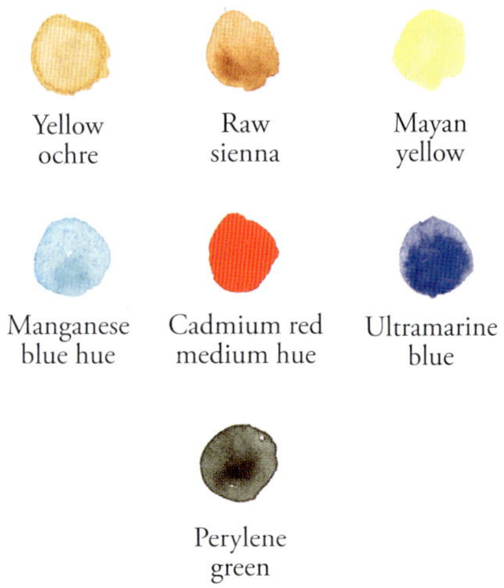

1

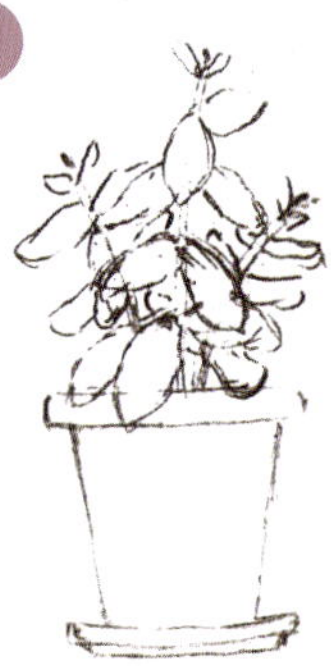

2

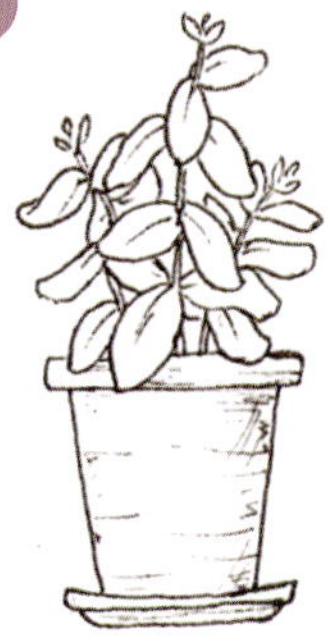

1 Start off with a light pencil sketch of a pot, and then draw three gently curving stalks and start adding pairs of leaves. Do you see how some of the leaves will overlap with the pot and with each other? That's great! It'll add a lot of depth and interest to our finished painting, but you'll want to carefully erase the bits of the sketch that are now covered by a leaf so you don't end up adding ink to those areas.

2 Now it's time to add some ink! Use your waterproof pen to trace the pencil drawing, keeping in mind it's often a good idea to start off with the part of your sketch that's the farthest forward. In this case, it's the leaves on the center stalk of our basil plant since you know those lines won't be interrupted by anything overlapping with them.

3

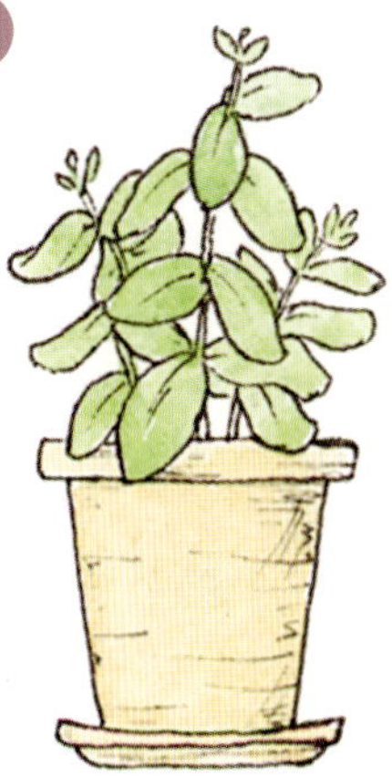

4

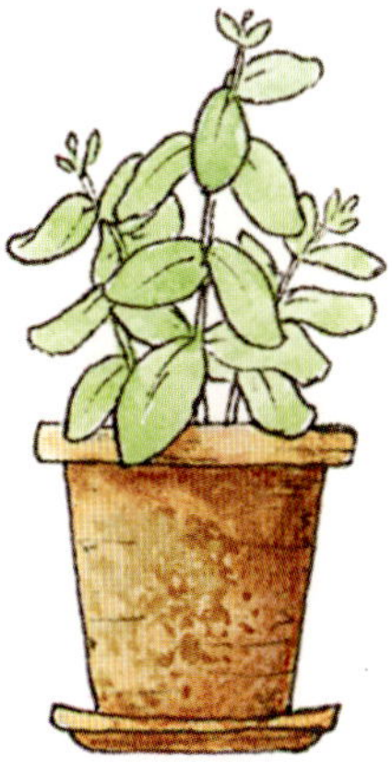

5

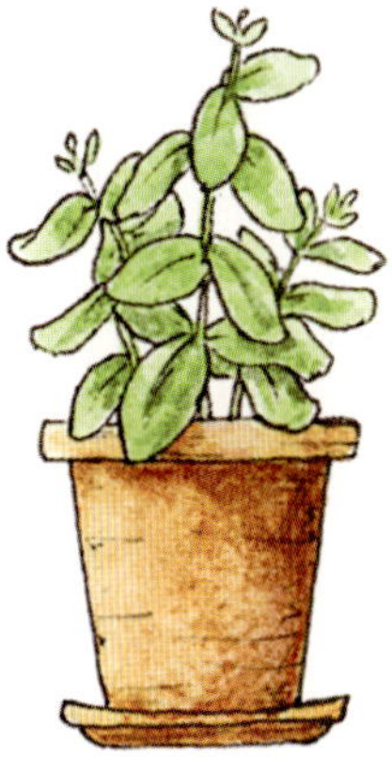

3 In this example, the light is coming from the upper left corner of the page, so the shadows will be on the lower right side of the plant. Just keep in mind that we'll add more shading with the watercolors, so it doesn't have to be perfect here. Once the ink is dry, it's time to gently erase your pencil drawing and make any last-minute adjustments. Using your larger brush, add a thin layer of yellow ochre and raw sienna over the whole pot. Then, mix up a bright, happy green color (a combination of Mayan yellow and manganese blue hue), and go very lightly over the entire plant.

4 While the paint on the pot is still wet (you can go over it with a tiny bit of water if it's dried), mix up a darker shade of raw sienna, cadmium red medium hue, and ultramarine blue, and use your larger brush to add shadows along the right edge and under the lip of the pot. You could also add a bit of brown, such as burnt sienna or sepia, if you want to add a deeper shadow.

5 Now it's time to go in and add some lovely shadows to make the basil leaves pop. Add a bit of perylene green to the green from earlier, and then use your smaller brush to build up darker areas of shadow on the right side of the plant, making sure to leave some highlights from the first layer of light green. That's it! Now you have a charming little basil plant!

Shining Copper Teakettle

Our kitchen witch needs a teapot, since it's important to have a nice cuppa tea while you're working. Old copper teapots have always felt very magical, with their gentle shine from years of use and polishing. They come in tons of different shapes and sizes, so you can have a lot of fun with this one. Copper teapots are one of my favorite things to paint, since it's always amazing to see how much depth and detail you can get with just a few colors. In fact, you'll use raw sienna for almost all of this painting!

Colors Used

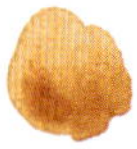

Raw sienna

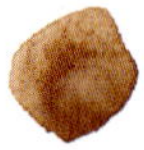

Burnt umber

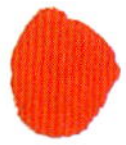

Cadmium red medium hue

Ultramarine blue

1

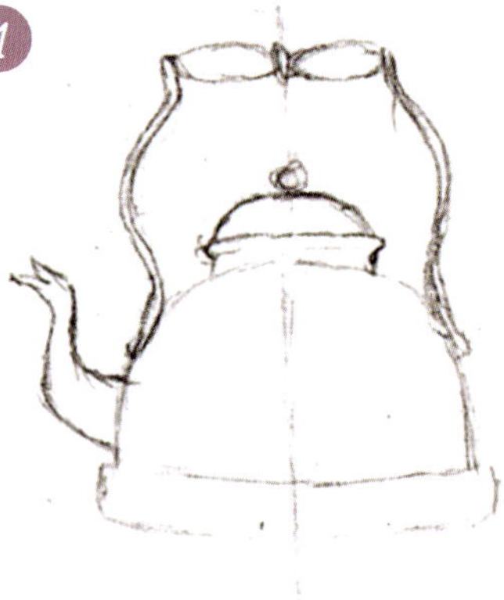

2

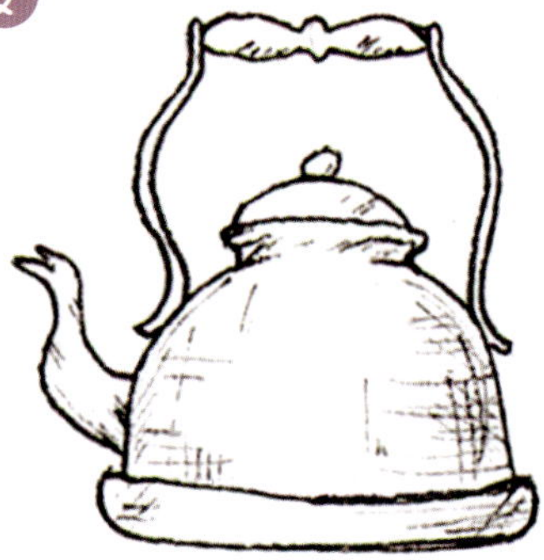

1 Start off with a light pencil sketch, making sure to get the overall shape as symmetrical as possible. It can help to begin with two lightly curved lines for the base. Mark the center of those lines, draw a very light line up from there through the center of the teapot, and then draw the sides down from that mark.

2 Now it's time to add the ink with your waterproof pen. Teapots are the perfect place to add lots of rich contrast and shading, so don't be afraid to add some nice shadows! You can use hatched or wiggly lines to add some initial shadows as part of the ink outline, making sure to add more towards the lower right side of the kettle. Once the ink is dry, gently erase the pencil layer.

3

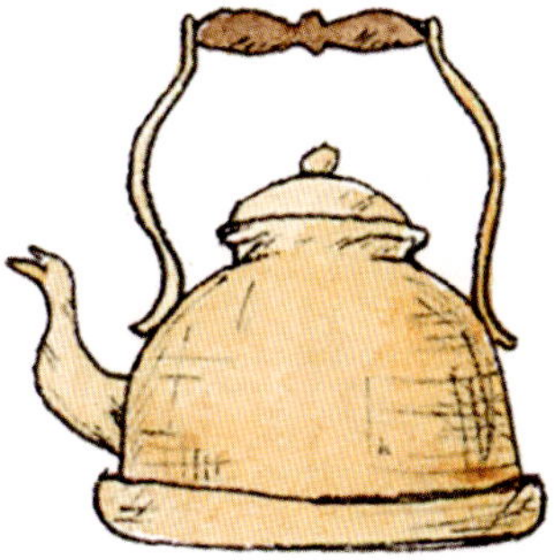

4

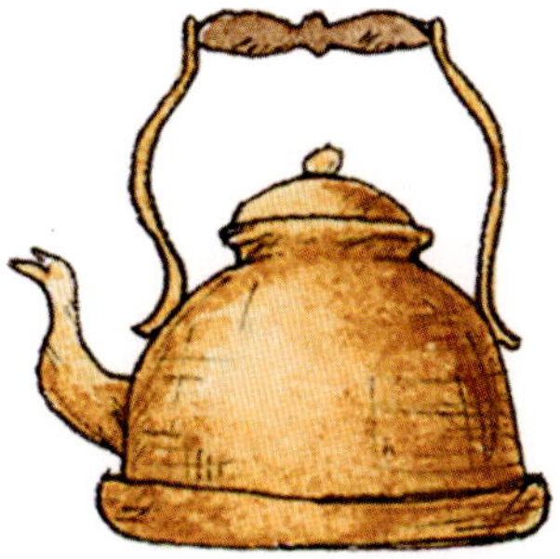

5

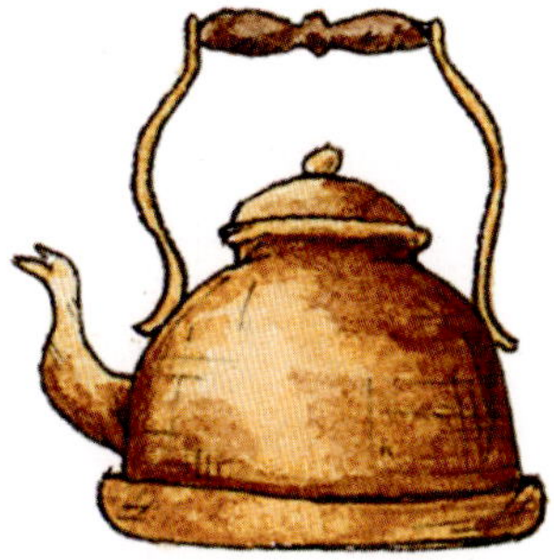

3 Use your larger brush to fill in the whole sketch with a very light layer of raw sienna, and then add burnt umber to the handle using your smaller brush.

4 Start adding thin layers of raw sienna, building up the contrast slowly. Building these layers will make deep color with lots of subtle variation, perhaps reflecting a candle or firelight in the witch's kitchen.

5 Now for the best part, the final shadows. Mix some cadmium red medium hue and ultramarine blue with your raw sienna, and add a few thin layers of this shadowy color to the darkest areas on your teapot, which will be towards the edges and base, particularly the lower right edges. This'll make the highlights pop and add extra depth to the painting. Add some more burnt umber to the lower surfaces of the handle, since there'll be shadows there as well. And there you have it, a shining copper teapot!

Enchanted Hourglass Timer

Since our kitchen witch probably has something delicious baking in the oven or bubbling happily on the hearth, she'll need an enchanted hourglass timer to keep track of everything. What makes it enchanted? Well, a normal hourglass could only time one thing, and this one is spelled so the kitchen witch can have as many reminders as she needs so nothing ever burns or bakes too long.

Colors Used

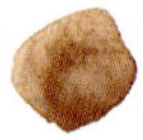
Burnt umber

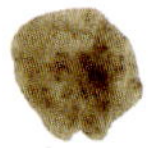
German greenish raw umber

Moonglow purple

Naples yellow

Cobalt teal blue

Buff titanium

1

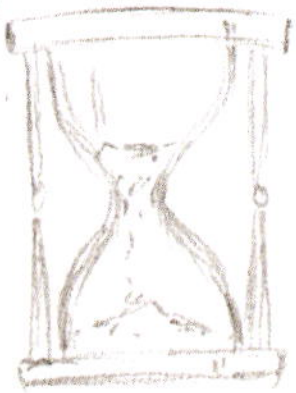

2

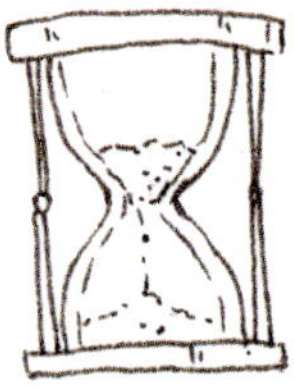

3

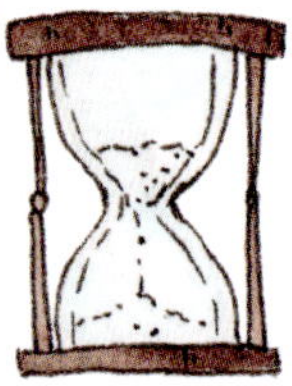

4

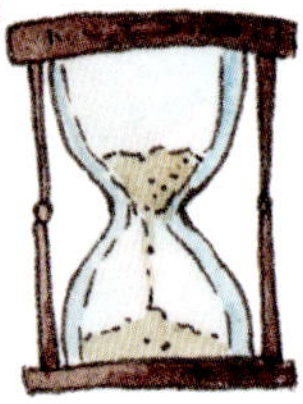

1 Using your pencil, sketch two short cylinders for the base and top of the timer, and then add a small circle in the middle on each side. Add some delicate spindles between the circles and the top and bottom, and then draw two sets of curved parallel lines that almost come together in the middle and then curve back out to make the hourglass shape, and add some delicate lines for the falling sand.

2 Use your waterproof pen to go over the outline, adding some small ink dots to show the texture of the sand. Once the ink is dry, gently erase the pencil layer.

3 Using your smaller brush, combine burnt umber, German greenish raw umber, moonglow purple, and Naples yellow, and fill in the whole stand, adding a bit more color along the right edge. Let that dry completely, and then fill in the hourglass portion with a very, very light layer of cobalt teal blue.

4 Using the same brown and blue colors from the prior step, add more shadows along the right edge of the stand, and fill in the narrow space between the edges of the hourglass. Then make a light, sandy color with a combination of buff titanium and German greenish raw umber and fill in the sand, and your timer is ready to be used!

Cherry Pie in a Red Pan

There's nothing quite like the magic of a freshly baked pie, still piping hot from the oven, so let's include a vibrant, cherry pie on our kitchen witch's shelf! You can use a bright, cherry red for the pie pan like in this example, incorporate a vintage china pattern, or include a pan from your own kitchen.

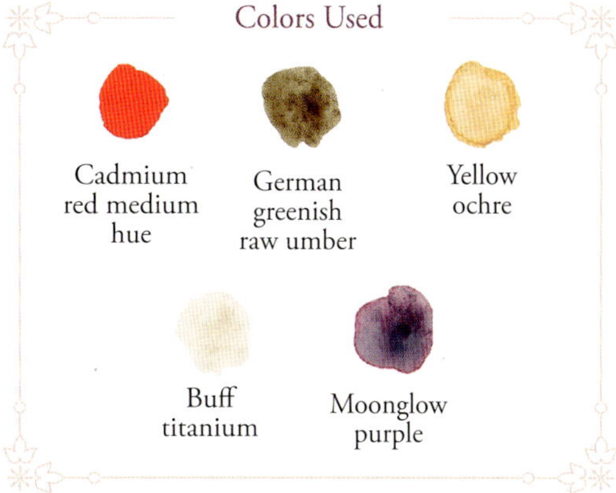

1

1 Let's start off with the pencil sketch, beginning with the pie pan, and then adding the little scallops along the bottom of the piecrust, and finally a curved dome shape with three small cutouts for the top of the crust.

2

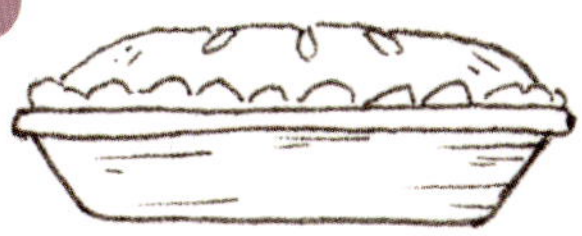

2 Trace your pencil outline with your waterproof pen, adding some shading along the right edge of the pan and a bit of texture to the crust. Once the ink is dry, gently erase the pencil layer.

3

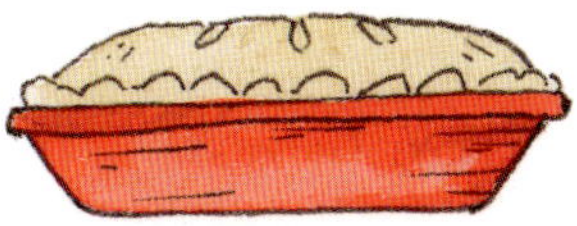

3 Using your larger brush, add a light layer of cadmium red medium hue to the whole pie pan, building up two or three subtle layers to make shadows under the edge and towards the right of the pan. Once that layer dries completely (we don't want the edges to bleed together here), mix up German greenish raw umber, yellow ochre, and buff titanium to make a light tan piecrust color, and then use that to fill in the whole piecrust.

4

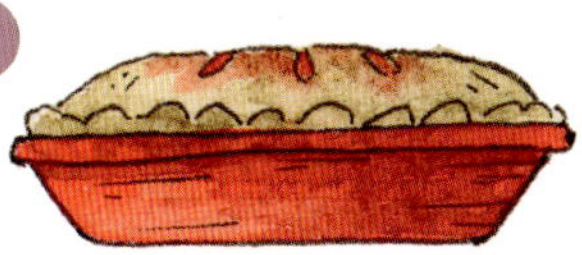

4 Now on to the fun little details! Add some more shadows to the pie pan with a mixture of cadmium red medium hue and moonglow purple, and then use some pure German greenish raw umber to place some shadows on the crust at the base of each scallop and towards the base and right edge of the domed part. While the piecrust is still wet, use a bit of cadmium red medium hue to add a bright cherry red to the cutouts in the top of the pie, allowing the red to bleed together with the piecrust color. Nice work! That looks good enough to eat!

Witchy Cookbooks

No kitchen is complete without a cookbook or two, and these magical books are full of delicious recipes that always adjust to the ingredients in the pantry—no more running to the store because you're out of baking powder! I love adding different designs to the spines, and vintage book covers are a wonderful source of inspiration if you'd like to make your own decorative designs or add more books.

Colors Used

- Cobalt teal blue
- Olive green
- Naples yellow
- Buff titanium
- Raw sienna
- Burnt umber
- German greenish raw umber
- Moonglow purple
- Yellow ochre
- Cadmium red medium hue
- Rose madder permanent

1

2

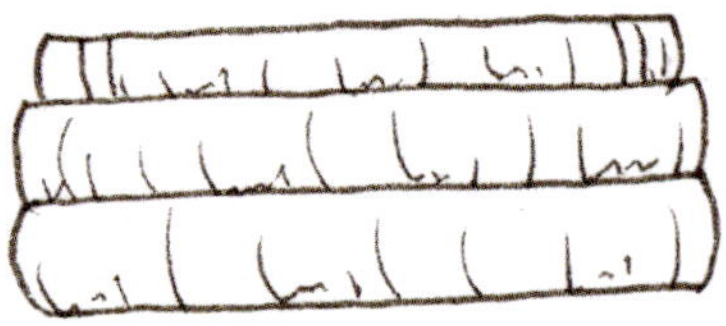

1 This step is nice and easy. With your pencil, draw three stacked rectangles with rounded edges on the right and left sides!

2 Go over the outlines of your books with your waterproof pen, and then add some shading by drawing gently curved lines up from the bottom edge of each book. For the top book, add two lines near each of the right and left edges so we can paint decorative stripes later. Once the ink is dry, gently erase the pencil layer.

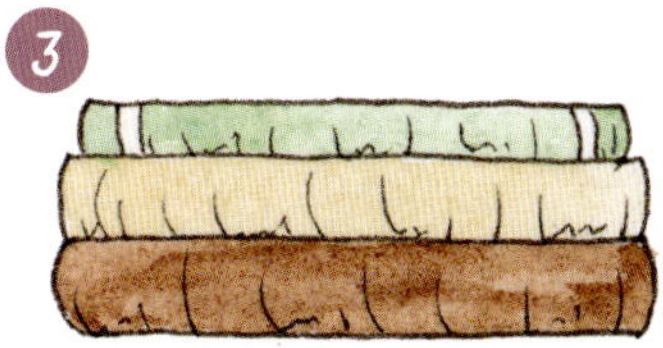

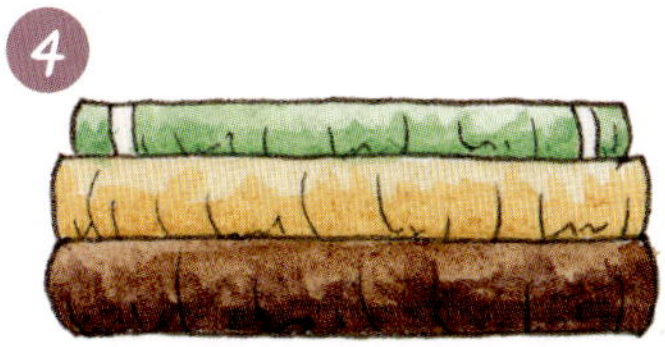

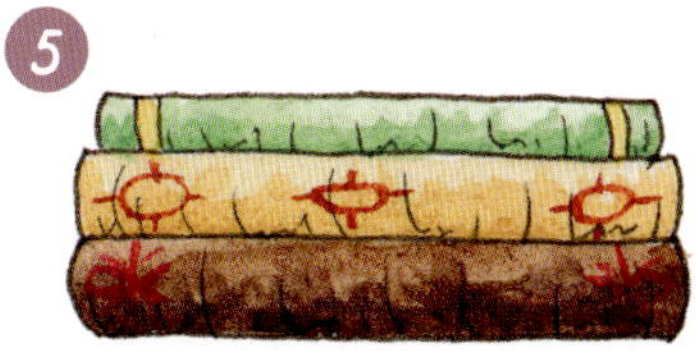

3 Now let's add some color! The trick here is to let each book dry before working on the next one so the edges won't bleed into one another. This is a great time to switch back and forth between projects, so you have something to do while you wait for each section to dry! For the top book in the stack, mix up a combination of cobalt teal blue, olive green, Naples yellow, and buff titanium to make a dusty green color. Move part of that mixture off to the side to use as a shadow in the next step, and add additional buff titanium to the half you'll use first, to make the lighter base layer for the book. Use your larger brush to go lightly over the entire cookbook with the new, lighter color, avoiding the two stripes we drew in the last step. Follow that same process, mixing half of each set of colors with buff titanium for this step, with a mixture of Naples yellow and raw sienna for the middle book and a mixture of burnt umber, German greenish raw umber, moonglow purple, and Naples yellow for the bottom book.

4 Remember the darker colors you saved in the last step? Let's use those now! Take a bit of the darker dusty green for the top book (the part you set aside in the prior step and didn't mix with buff titanium), and use your larger brush to add it just along the lower edge of the book, since the rounded edge of the spine will cause a shadow towards where it's resting on the other books. Use that brush to feather the edges of your wet paint up slightly towards the top of the book to make a gradual shadow. Do the same thing with the darker colors for the remaining two books, and let it all dry completely before moving to the next step. This is a great time to grab a snack or go for a quick walk—you really want the layers to be dry so the colors don't bleed!

5 For the top book, use your smaller brush to add yellow ochre to the two stripes. Now, mix together cadmium red medium hue, German greenish raw umber, and moonglow purple, and use your smallest brush to paint three ovals equally spaced along the spine of the book. Then add four lines coming off of each oval. Finally, using your smallest brush and a strong mixture of rose madder permanent (or pink gouache if you have it), paint a stripe near each end of the bottom book, followed by a teardrop shape facing away from the stripe and an "X" centered around the narrow end of the teardrop. Then add two more lines outside the base of the "X." Now you're ready to whip up some witchy recipes!

Magical Frosted Cake

You just know that nobody can bake a cake quite as well as a kitchen witch, since the cakes are guaranteed to be magically delicious. However, since the kitchen witch also has a feline familiar, the cake needs to be kept in a stand where it can be safe from inquisitive paws. We'll add some lovely, vintagey blue frosting, white details, and a cherry on top for the most magical cake you've ever painted.

Colors Used

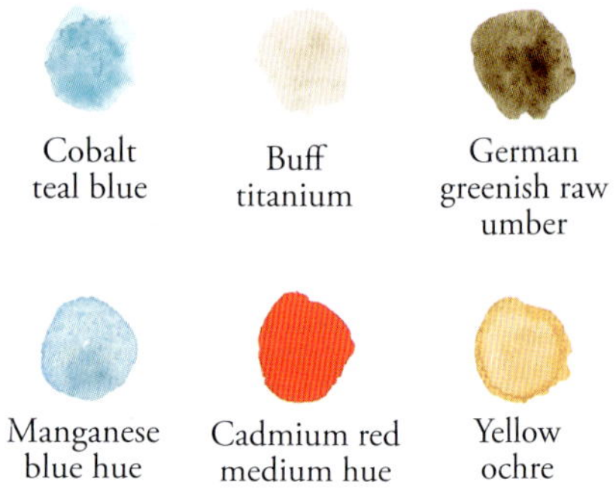

1

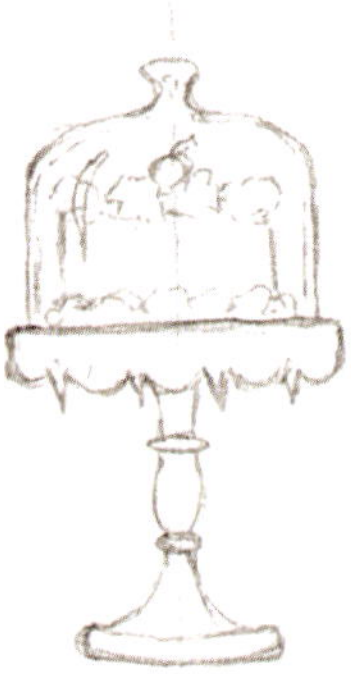

2

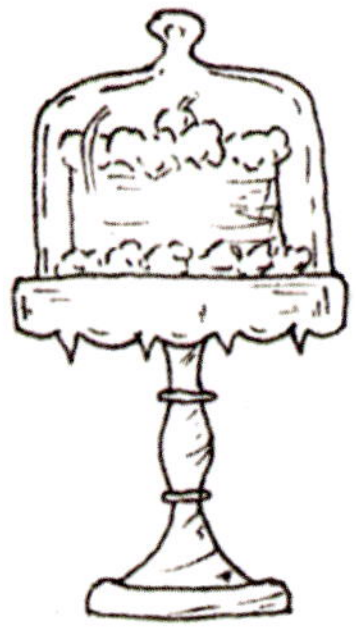

1 The first step is to grab a snack, since you're sure to get hungry while painting tasty treats. Once that's sorted, find your pencil and sketch out the stand, which you can think of as a capital T that's all dressed up for a fancy party—add some swoops and curves, and it's ready to go! Then, add the glass top, which can have any shape you'd like, and add two lines for the edges of the cake, making sure to leave plenty of space for frosting. Now, on to the frosting (my favorite part), which you can make as simple or complex as you'd like, depending on the size of your cake. I've added some bubbly swooping frosting shapes here, along with a shining cherry on top.

2 Using your waterproof pen to go over the pencil layer, start with the outline of the glass top, since you'll want to add extra lines there to show some reflections on the curve near the top. Then follow the rest of your pencil outline, making sure to include some shading. If you'd like to have a completely black cake stand, you can fill in most of it at this step, leaving a few highlights, but I've left it this way so we can add a gold color. Once the ink is dry, gently erase the pencil layer.

3

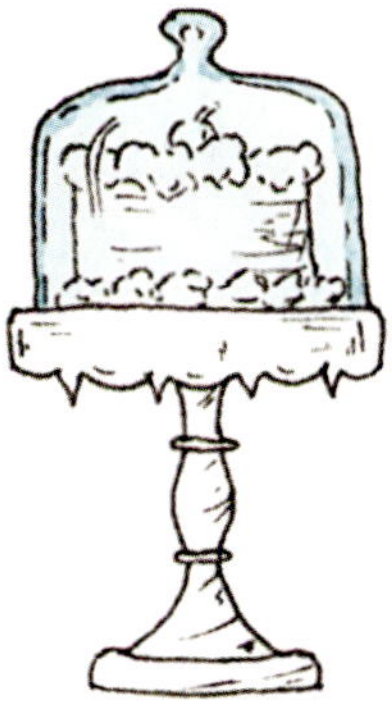

4

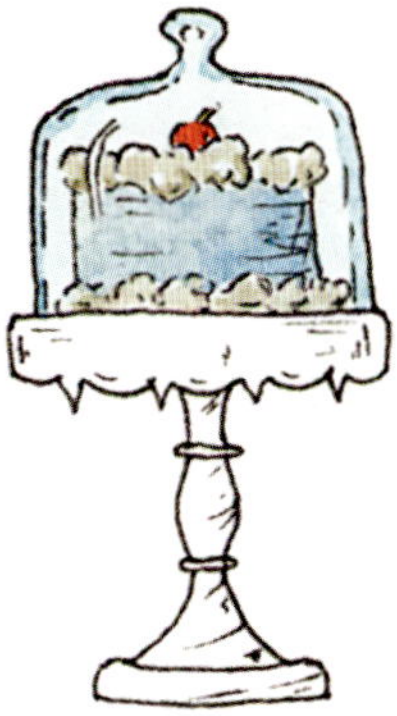

5

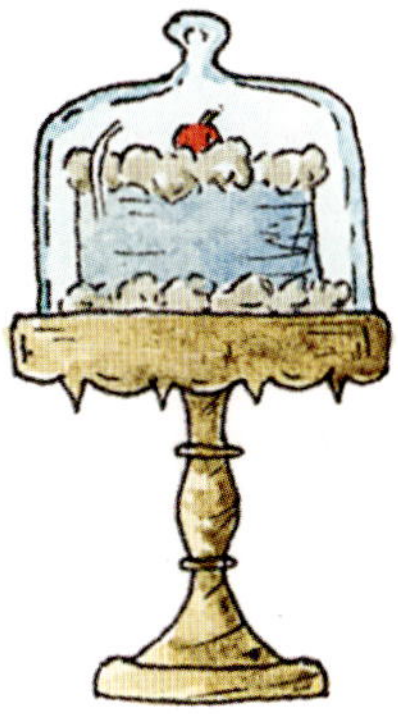

3 Use your larger brush to add a very thin, almost translucent layer of cobalt teal blue to the whole glass top (including the cake). Let that dry a bit, and then use your smaller brush to add a slightly more concentrated outline of that same blue to the edges of the glass, just inside your ink outline, so it looks three-dimensional.

4 Let that layer dry, and then, using your smaller brush and a light layer of buff titanium, or whichever other color you'd like the frosting to be, add some color to the frosting, making any areas that would have shadows a bit darker with a touch of German greenish raw umber. Then switch to your larger brush, and go over the whole cake with a mixture of manganese blue hue and buff titanium, using more buff titanium on the left and more manganese blue hue towards the right to demonstrate shadows. Using your smaller brush again, add some bright red (I've used cadmium red medium hue here) for the cherry.

5 Once your delicious-looking cake is dry, we can finish the stand! Start by mixing yellow ochre and a touch of German greenish raw umber, and then use your larger brush to go over the whole stand. Then grab your smaller brush and, with a little more German greenish raw umber in the mix, add some shadows to the stand. If you want to make it look reflective, you can use some buff titanium or white gouache to add highlights along the left edges. And now your magical frosted cake is ready to enjoy!

Enchanted Kitchen Utensils

You may have heard of witches wielding wands to cast spells, but our kitchen witch uses a lovely assortment of enchanted kitchen utensils to work her magic, including a whisk and an assortment of wooden spoons. These handy tools need to be corralled to make them easy to find, so they're all arranged in a green ceramic jar of kitchen utensils. The jar is a great place to add more personality to your shelf by switching up the color or adding a decorative design to match your own kitchen or favorite mug!

Colors Used

- Naples yellow
- Cobalt teal blue
- Olive green
- Ultramarine blue
- German greenish raw umber
- Yellow ochre
- Buff titanium
- Gray titanium
- Burnt umber

1

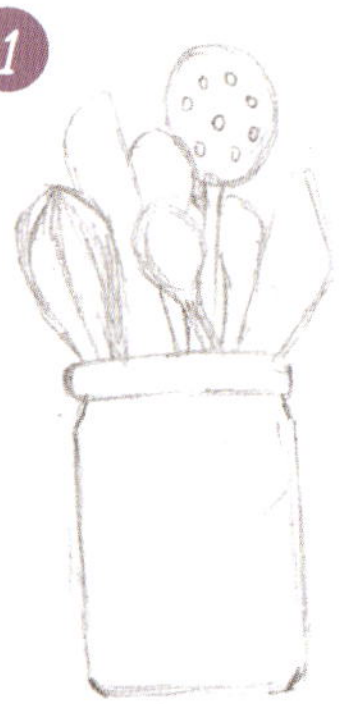

2

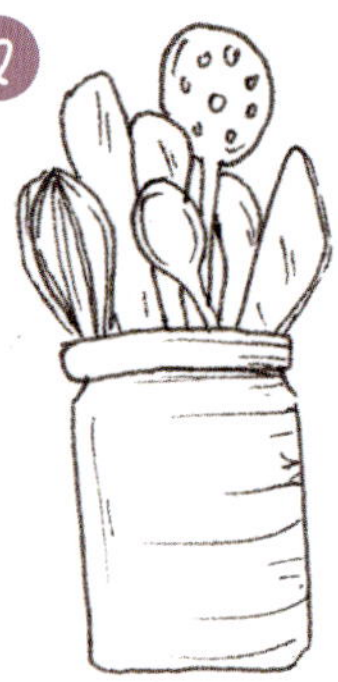

1 Use your pencil to sketch a cylinder for the main body of our utensil jar, and then shape the corners, and add a rim around the top with a small oval. Then add the utensils, working front to back in the jar—start with the whisk, spoon, and spatula, and then outline the pasta spoon and remaining utensils.

2 Go over your pencil sketch with your waterproof pen, adding some nice shading towards the right side of the jar and each utensil using light hatch lines. If you're ever unsure of what shape or location will be best for shading hatch lines, you can test them out in pencil and make any adjustments before you commit to shading with ink. Once the ink is dry, gently erase the pencil layer.

3

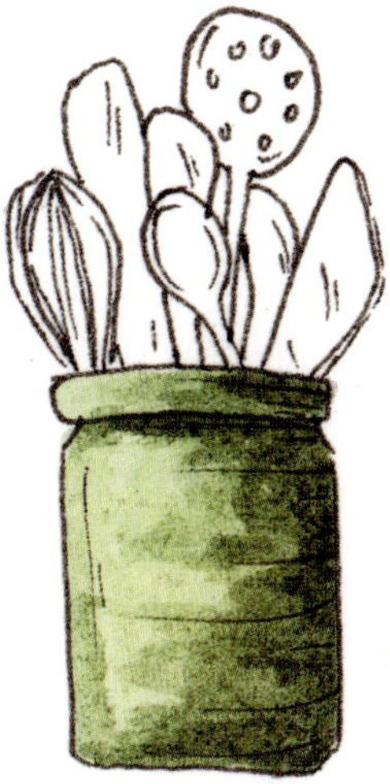

4

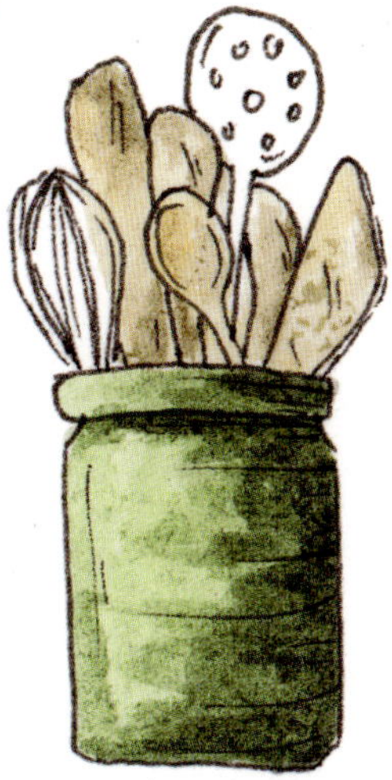

5

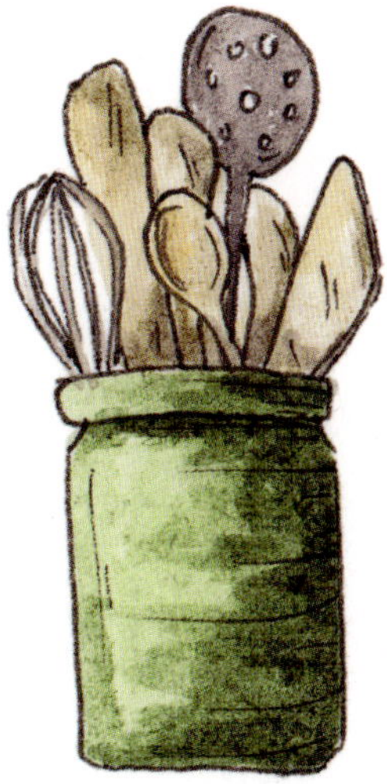

3 Using your larger brush, fill in the whole jar with a mixture of Naples yellow, cobalt teal blue, and olive green. Mix together Naples yellow, cobalt teal blue, olive green, ultramarine blue, and German greenish raw umber to make a nice shadow color, and build up several layers towards the right side of the jar, gradually adding more ultramarine blue as you darken the shadows closest to the right edge and just under the rim.

4 Using your smaller brush, go over all the wooden utensils with a light mixture of yellow ochre and buff titanium. Then use German greenish raw umber to add shadows and texture.

5 Using your smaller paintbrush, go over the wires of the whisk with gray titanium, and then use that same brush and a mixture of gray titanium, ultramarine blue, and burnt umber to fill in the pasta spoon. Using that same dark gray color, add a few more shadows to the darkest areas of the wooden utensils and the pasta spoon. Now the kitchen witch is ready to make some magically delicious cakes and cookies!

Magic Potion Bottles

In this tutorial, we'll be making three cute little magic potion bottles, but this is a great time to have fun playing with the sizes, shapes, and colors of the bottles! You never know what useful potions you'll find on the kitchen witch's shelf—perhaps one makes herbs grow for cooking supper and another might make sunshine on a cloudy winter day.

Colors Used

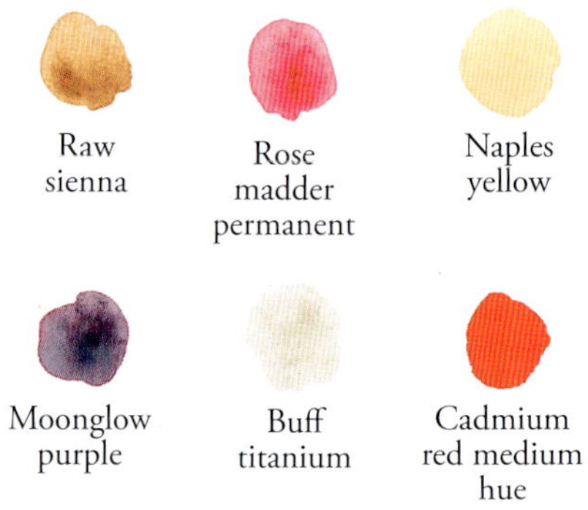

1

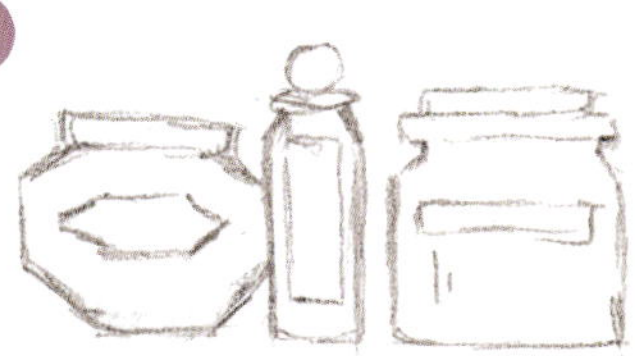

2

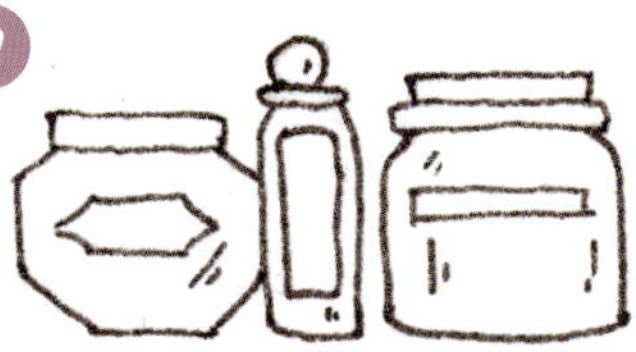

3

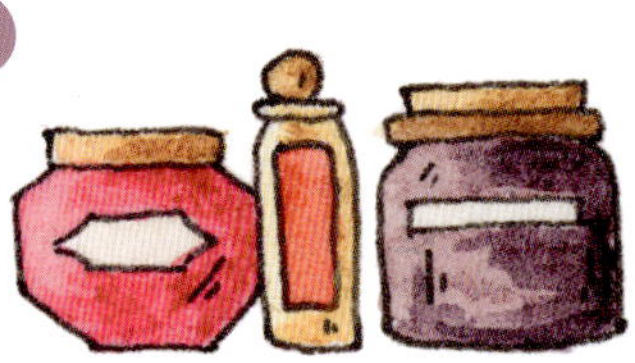

1 As always, start off with a light pencil sketch for each of your bottles, arranging them however you think they look best. Don't forget to add labels so the kitchen witch can make sure to use the correct potions.

2 Go over the pencil outlines with your waterproof pen, adding extra lines to indicate reflections on the glass. Once the ink is dry, gently erase the pencil layer. It's time to add watercolor!

3 Using your smaller brush, add a layer of raw sienna to the lids of all three potion bottles, and let that dry. Then paint the left bottle with a thin layer of rose madder permanent, the middle bottle with Naples yellow, and the right bottle with moonglow purple. Allow those initial layers to dry for a few moments before layering those same colors again to add some shadow and texture to the glass bottles and lids. To get slightly darker shadows on the middle bottle, use a bit of raw sienna on your smaller brush along the right edge of the bottle. Then still using your smaller brush, use buff titanium to fill in the paper labels on the left and right bottles, and fill in the label on the middle bottle with cadmium red medium hue. Now these mysterious bottles of potions are ready to adorn the shelves of your kitchen witch!

Blue and White China Teacup

There's nothing quite like a warm cup of tea while you're baking desserts and brewing potions, so let's add a blue and white china teacup to the kitchen witch's shelf! If blue and white aren't your cup of tea, you can use any combination of colors that appeal to you.

Colors Used

Buff titanium | Moonglow purple | Prussian blue

1

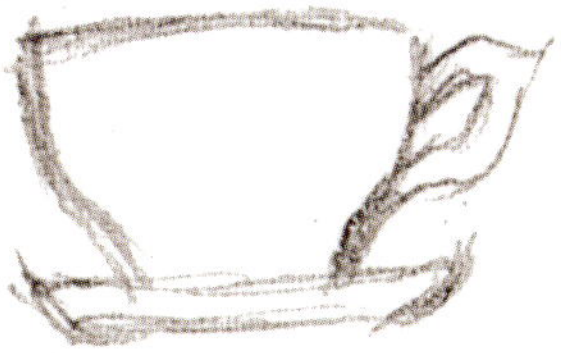

2

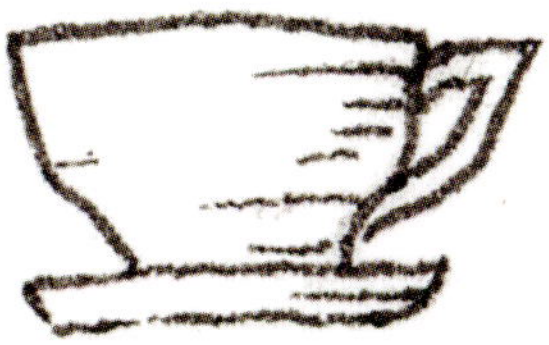

3

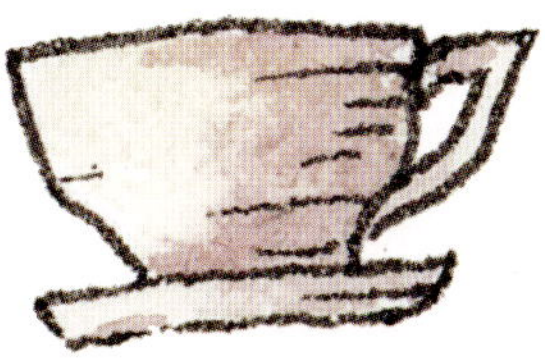

4

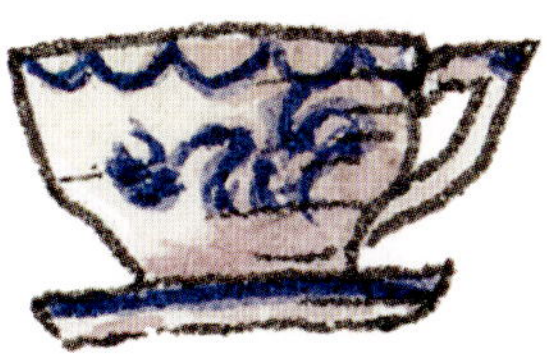

1 Start off with a pencil outline for the teacup and saucer, and then add the curving lines for the handle.

2 Add the ink outline with your waterproof pen, including some shading along the edges of the teacup and saucer. Once the ink is dry, gently erase the pencil layer.

3 To make the white base color pop, use your smaller brush to go over the whole teacup with a light layer of buff titanium, and then use moonglow purple to add shadows where you placed the shading in the previous step. Now is a great time to take a break or work on another project for a few minutes, since this layer needs to be completely dry before you add the decorative blue designs.

4 Once the cup is dry, mix up some Prussian blue with just a bit of water until you have a very solid and vibrant color. Using your smallest brush, add a stripe of blue along the top edge of the saucer, a dollop of color at the corner of the teacup handle, and a scalloped edge along the top of the teacup. Depending on the size you've chosen to draw your teacup, it'll be hard to get much detail for the design in the center, but here the cup is fairly small so you can add some curving lines in the overall shape of a flower, and then your teacup is finished and ready for a magical brew!

Decorative Tea Towel

A beautiful towel is a staple in any kitchen—always handy for drying dishes and tidying up spills. This lovely, decorative tea towel is tucked around the cake stand, ready to be grabbed at a moment's notice, but you can place it wherever you like on the shelf. Just keep in mind where the shadows will end up based on the way it drapes. This example shows a scalloped design on the edge of the towel, but it's also a great place to add a whimsical design or incorporate a color or detail from your own kitchen.

Colors Used

Cobalt teal blue

Buff titanium

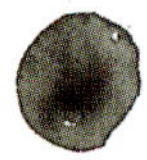
Perylene green

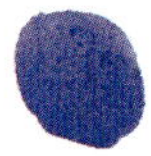
Prussian blue

1

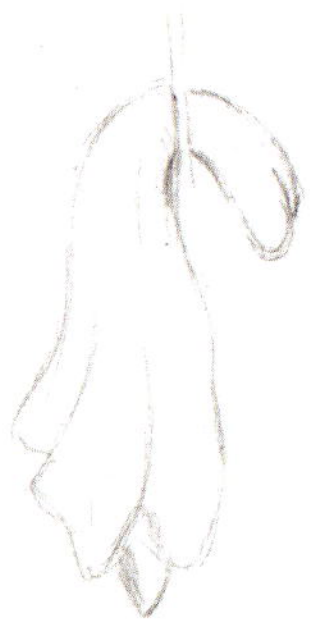

2

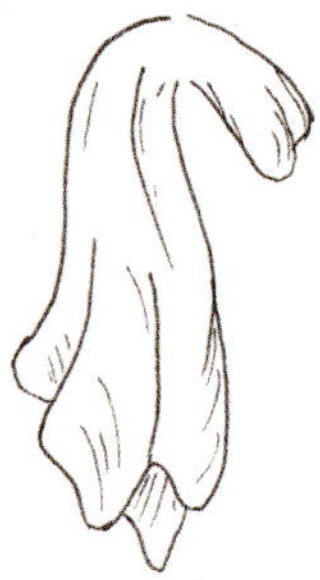

1 As always, let's begin with a pencil sketch! Start with long, swooping lines for the left and right edges of the towel, which connect in a rounded end at the top, and then add another pair of swooping lines between those, to give the impression that the towel is draping gracefully. Connect those lines with some gentle curves, and then add a lightly curving corner behind one of the draping curves to give the towel some depth.

2 Go over that outline with your waterproof pen, making sure you don't add ink to any areas that'll be covered by another item, such as the cake stand. (Turn to Assembling Your Kitchen Witchery Shelf on page 51 to see an example of how the towel can be positioned.) Then add some shadows to the towel using gently swooping hatch lines towards the lower right side of each curve to give the fabric a natural, draped appearance. Once the ink is dry, gently erase the pencil layer.

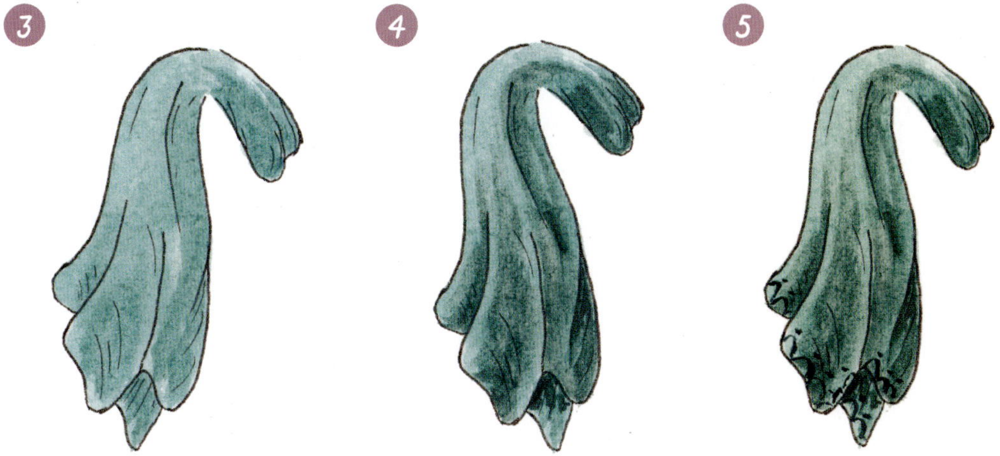

3 Using your larger brush, combine cobalt teal blue, buff titanium, and a little bit of perylene green, and then fill in the whole towel, adding a light second layer to the areas you shaded in the last step.

4 Here's where it really starts to come together: the shadows. Mix some cobalt teal blue and perylene green, and then use your larger brush to build up gradual layers of shadows in the folds and towards the right edge of the towel. This is a great time to take a quick break, since you want the towel to be completely dry before moving on to the decorative details so the edges don't bleed.

5 Once your towel is completely dry, use your smaller brush to mix up a strong combination of cobalt teal blue, perylene green, and Prussian blue. Use just a bit of water when mixing the colors so you can have more control over how the paint moves. Add a series of scallops along the bottom edge of the towel, and then add some fun dots just above those scallops. Now your towel is finished and ready for some kitchen magic!

Climbing Potted Vine

Because our kitchen witch can use magic, she's able to keep all her houseplants alive and healthy—a power I'm sure many of us could use! This climbing potted vine is planted in a tiny cauldron, and its tendrils snake in and out throughout the kitchen witch's shelf, looking for the very brightest patches of sunlight.

Colors Used

Cobalt teal blue

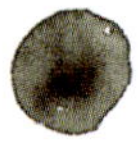
Perylene green

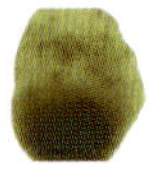
Olive green

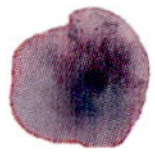
Moonglow purple

1

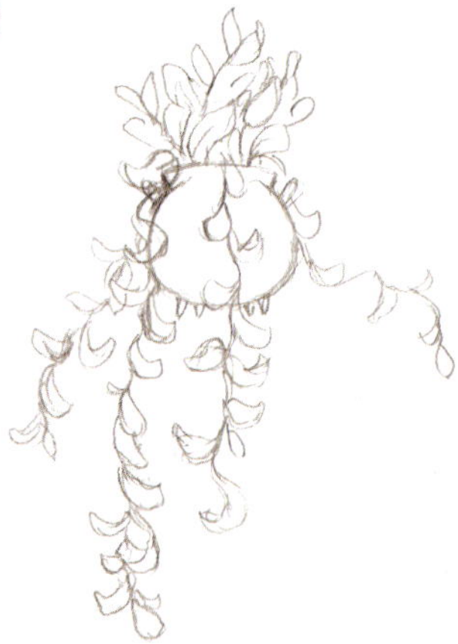

2

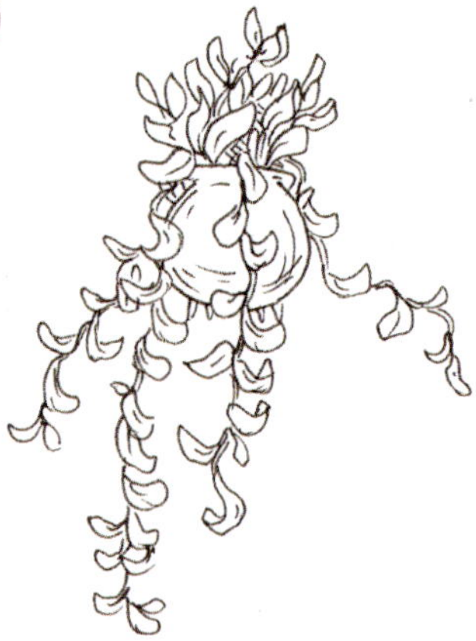

1 Start off by sketching the cauldron with your pencil, making a nice rounded shape with short little legs. Now, use the lightest pencil lines you can possibly make to draw some gently wiggling lines wherever you'd like to find trailing pieces of the vine, and then outline each leaf, making sure to vary the shapes and sizes a bit so it looks natural.

2 Now, use your waterproof pen to add ink to your vine, adding a bit of shading and texture to the leaves and the tiny cauldron. Once the ink is dry, gently erase the pencil layer.

3

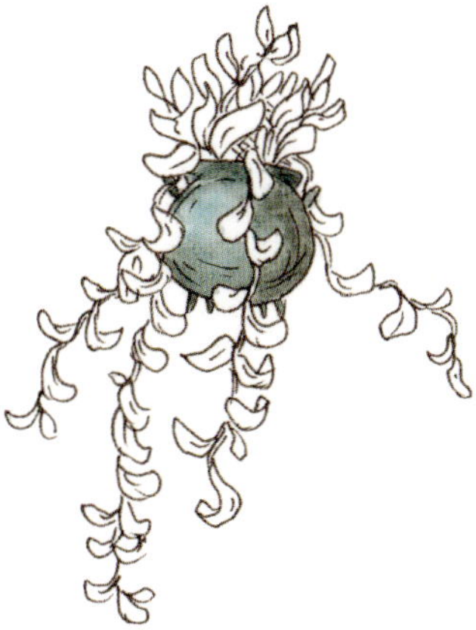

4

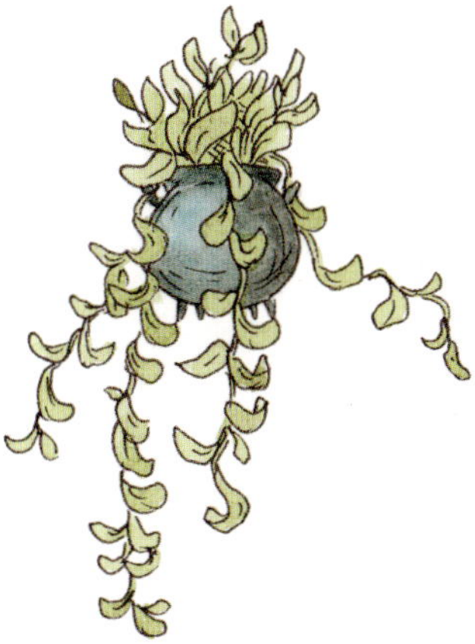

5

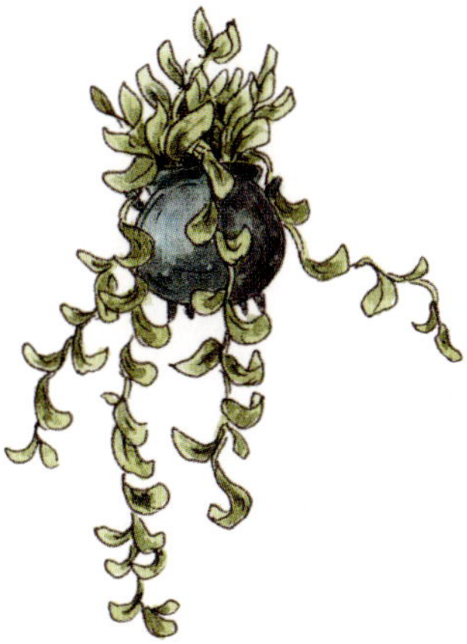

3 Using your smaller brush, lightly go over the whole pot (except the parts covered by the leaves) with a mixture of mostly cobalt teal blue with a touch of perylene green. While that layer is still wet, add a bit more perylene green to the mixture and place some shadows on the lower right edges of the pot. Keep in mind the rounded shape of the pot, placing the shadows in almost a crescent shape instead of going straight across. It doesn't need to be perfect yet as we'll go back and add more shadows after this layer has dried.

4 Using your smaller brush, fill in the whole vine with a light layer of olive green. The trick here is to use a very small amount of water, since you don't want the paint wandering outside the lines. It can help to mix together your water and olive green to make a small puddle of paint, completely dry your brush on a paper towel, and then dip just the tip of the brush in the paint so you can have just a tiny bit of paint on your brush. This is my favorite way to paint tiny areas, especially the narrow vines.

5 Now for the best part, the final details! Add some moonglow purple to the color you used for the pot, and use your smaller brush to add the very darkest shadows along the right edge and just to the right of any leaves that overlap the pot. Then combine olive green and perylene green, and use your smaller brush to add shading to the leaves. Finally, using pure perylene green, add the very darkest shadows to the vine, just above the top of the tiny cauldron. Beautiful work! Your vine looks ready to climb right off the page.

Hand-Carved Wood Storage Rack

We all know you can never have enough cute storage, and this hand-carved wood storage rack is the perfect place for your kitchen witch to stash odds and ends, as well as keep cooling baked goods away from overly inquisitive pets! This shelf is a great place to experiment since you can use so many different colors for the wood—maybe your witch needs a pop of red, a moody walnut color, or polka dots! You can also have a lot of fun choosing and arranging trinkets and items on the shelf, and it's a fun way to incorporate a favorite teacup, crystal, or other item that's special to you.

Colors Used

German greenish raw umber | Moonglow purple | Prussian blue

1

2

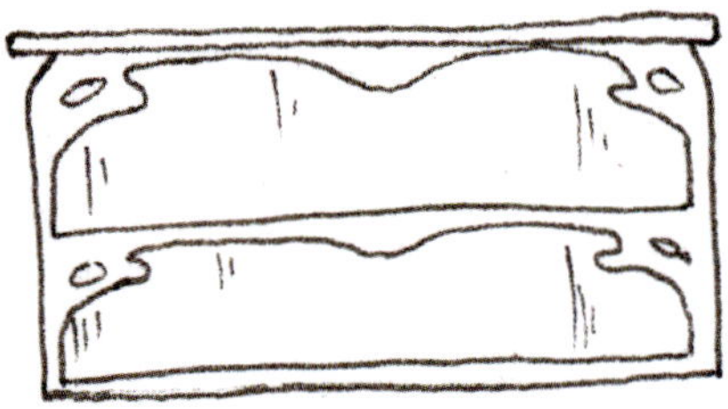

1 Start off your pencil sketch with a narrow rectangle for the top surface of the storage rack, and then add the sides and middle shelf. Add the decorative, carved edges, including the small oval cutouts in the corners. It's important to note here that, if you're going to put items on the shelf, you don't want to paint shadows where those items need to go. So you'll need to add the outlines for those items before adding the shadow! (For an example of this, see Assembling Your Kitchen Witchery Shelf on page 51.)

2 Go over the pencil sketch with your waterproof pen, and then add some shading inside the shelf, since that area will be darker. Once the ink is dry, gently erase the pencil layer.

3

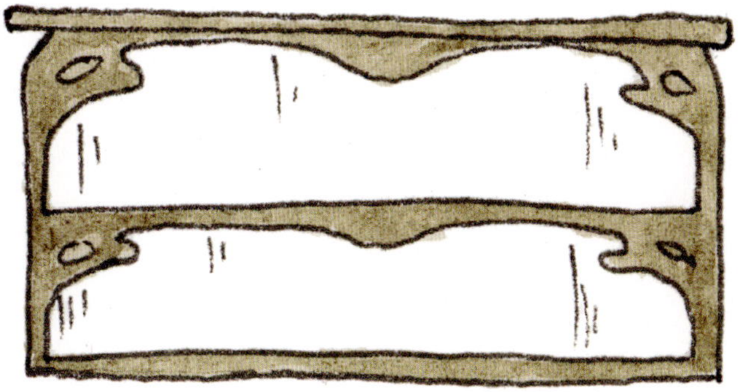

4

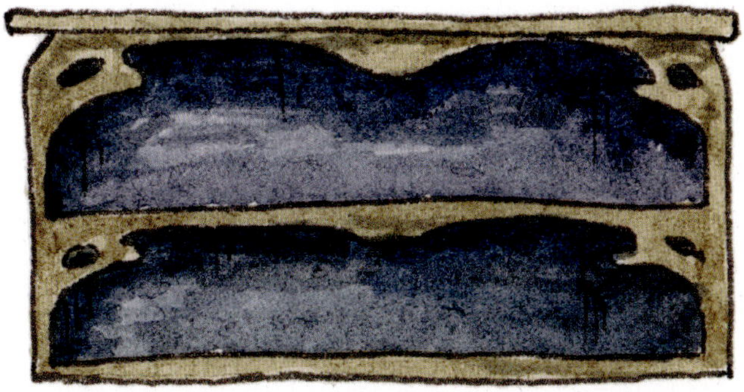

3 Now it's time to paint the shelf! Mix up some German greenish raw umber or a light brown color you're partial to, and grab your smaller brush. Go lightly over the whole shelf, except for the "inside," which we'll need to paint with a darker shadow color.

4 Mix together some moonglow purple, Prussian blue, and German greenish raw umber to make a rich blue shadow, and use your smaller brush to fill in the "inside" of the shelf, making sure you add the shadows to the cutouts near the edges of the shelf. Now that you've got the edges all nice and neat using your small brush, switch to your larger brush, and go over the areas of the shelf that would have the darkest shadows again in order to add a little more contrast. Finally, use a very small amount of this shadow color to make some wood-grain wiggles under the lip of the shelf and on the sides. And now you have a beautiful shelf, with some rich color contrast that'll really make the items you put on the shelf pop!

Mortar and Pestle with Spelled Herbs

No magical kitchen is complete without a mortar and pestle, and our kitchen witch grows spelled herbs like her potted basil and other plants for magically delicious snacks and spells. This example includes sage leaves, but you can switch them out for any herb or combination of herbs that you prefer.

Colors Used

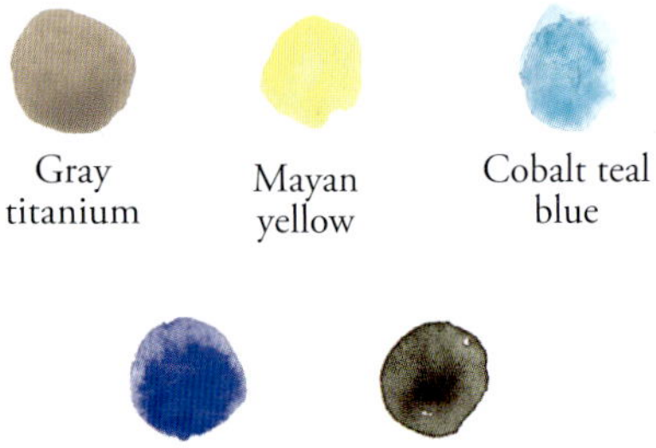

- Gray titanium
- Mayan yellow
- Cobalt teal blue
- Ultramarine blue
- Perylene green

1

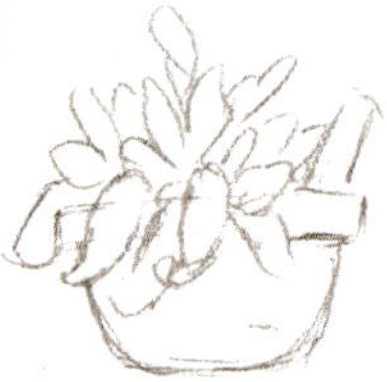

2

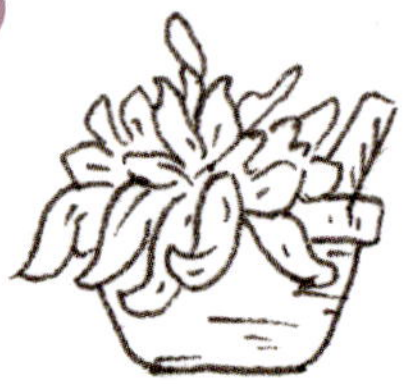

3

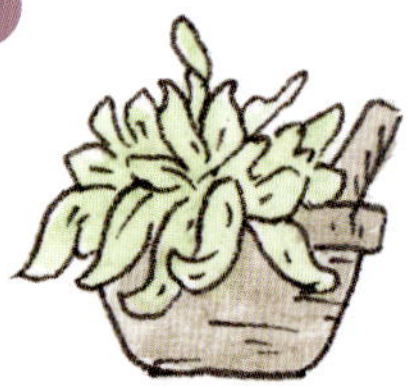

4

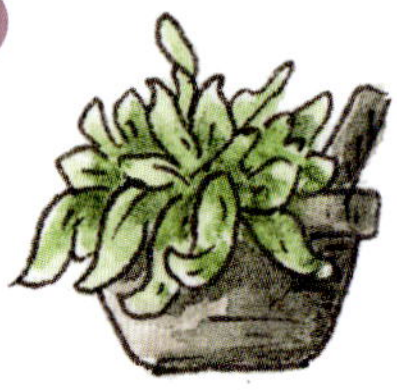

1 Start off the pencil sketch with the bowl shape of the mortar, and then add a rim around the top and the pestle leaning on the side. Next, add the spelled herb leaves, some of which will be draping over the rim of the mortar.

2 Go over your pencil outline with a waterproof pen, making sure to start with the leaves instead of the mortar so you don't accidentally ink the parts of the mortar that are covered by the leaves. Add some shading to the edges of the mortar and pestle and some texture and shading to the leaves. Once the ink is dry, gently erase the pencil layer.

3 Using gray titanium, fill in the whole mortar and pestle using your smaller brush. Then combine Mayan yellow, cobalt teal blue, and ultramarine blue to make a nice green color for the leaves, and fill them in with a light layer.

4 Now for the shadows, and you'll be amazed how much a little more color will make everything pop! Combine gray titanium and perylene green to make the darkest shadow colors for the mortar. Then use your smaller brush to add this along the lower right edge of the mortar and pestle and just to the right of the leaves that overlap with the mortar, since they'll cast shadows there. Add more ultramarine blue to the green from the prior step, and then use that to add shading on the leaves near where they all overlap and towards the right side. Well done!

The Kitchen Witchery Shelf

Now that we've covered how to paint all the kitchen witchery items, we need a shelf to put them all on! This happy little shelf, with its pink color and yellow highlights, is the perfect complement to the whimsical, magical items we've covered so far. Let's get started!

Colors Used

- Naples yellow
- Mayan yellow
- Rose madder permanent
- Cadmium red medium hue
- Moonglow purple

1

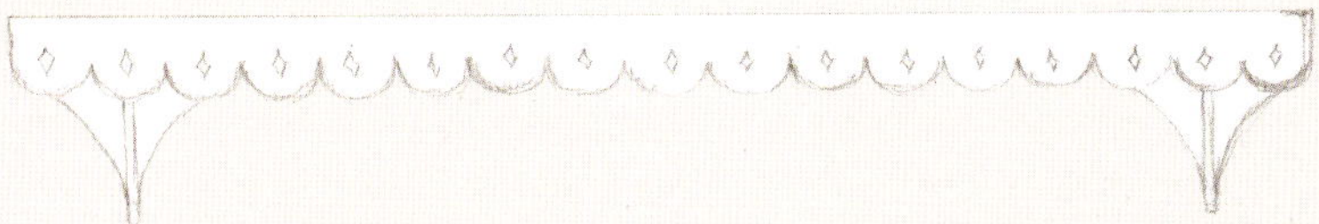

1 Start off your pencil sketch with a horizontal line—you can use a ruler if you want it to be straight or freehand it for a more organic look. Then add a scalloped edge below that line with a little diamond shape in the center of each scallop. Now, add the shelf brackets with their curving side braces.

2

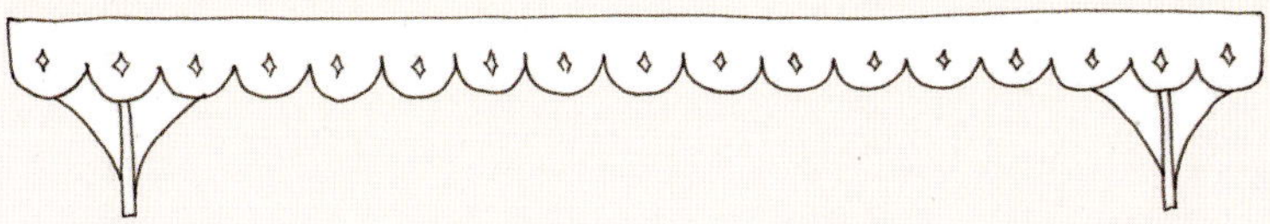

2 Before adding any ink, decide where you'll place the items on your shelf—some of them may overlap with the shelf itself, so you don't want to add ink to those areas. Once you know where not to add ink, go over that pencil outline with your waterproof pen. Once the ink is dry, gently erase the pencil layer.

(continued)

3

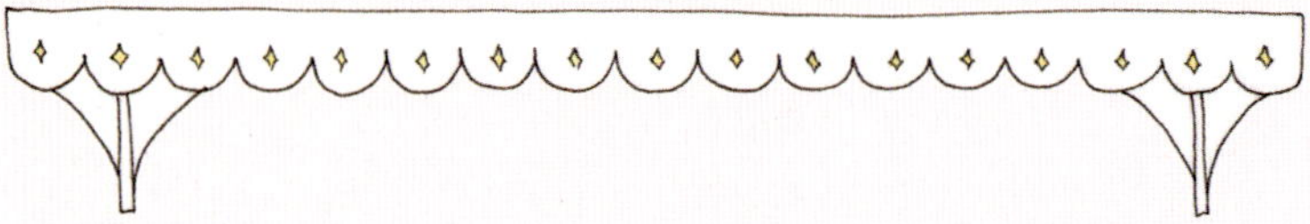

3 Combine Naples yellow and Mayan yellow to make a bright, happy yellow, and then fill in each of the diamond shapes with your smaller brush. Let these dry completely before moving on to the rest of the shelf, since we don't want the yellow and pink to bleed together.

4

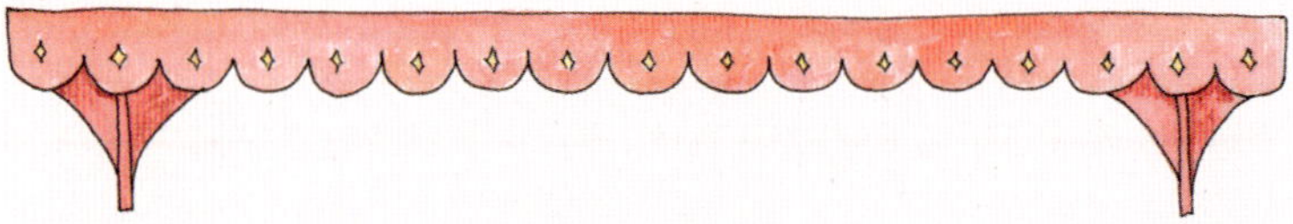

4 Using your larger brush, combine rose madder permanent, Naples yellow, and cadmium red medium hue to make a peachy pink, and fill in the whole shelf (avoiding the yellow diamonds). While that's still wet, add some moonglow purple to the pink color and add shadows on the shelf brackets, since those'll be a bit darker than the top part of the shelf. Now you have a beautiful shelf ready for all sorts of kitchen witchery!

Assembling Your Kitchen Witchery Shelf

It's finally time! Now that you know how to paint all the individual items, let's put it all together to paint the kitchen witch's shelf! While the overall project may seem daunting, take it one step at a time and you'll be done before you know it!

Colors Used for the Background

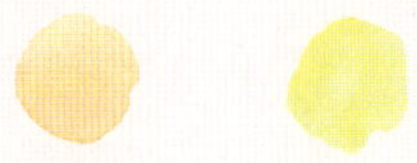

Naples yellow | Mayan yellow

1

1 Start off with a pencil outline for the shelf, and then gently mark the edges where you'll place each item on the shelf. I find this step helpful since it ensures you've allocated sufficient space for each item. You don't want half the cauldron hanging off the edge because another item ended up being too wide! Refer to The Kitchen Witchery Shelf (page 49) for tips on sketching the shelf, and refer to each project's tutorial for details on sketching each item.

2

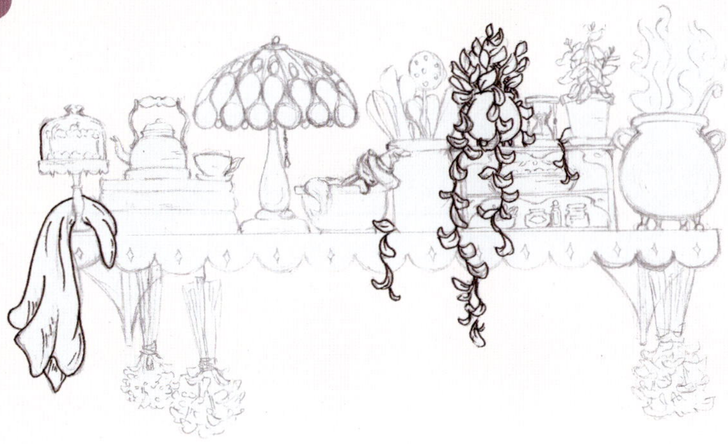

3

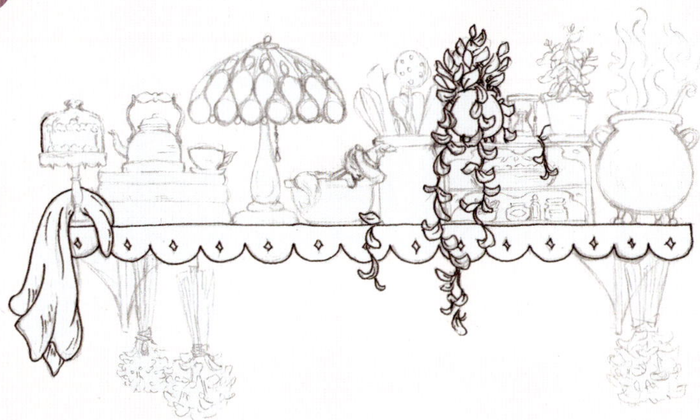

2 We're going to break up adding ink into several steps, since it's easy to add ink to an area that's actually covered by another item, and we'd like to avoid that! You'll notice that the Decorative Tea Towel (page 42) and Climbing Potted Vine (page 44) both overlap with the shelf, so let's start off by inking those with your waterproof pen.

3 Now, carefully fill in the outline for the top, scalloped edge, and little diamonds on the shelf.

4

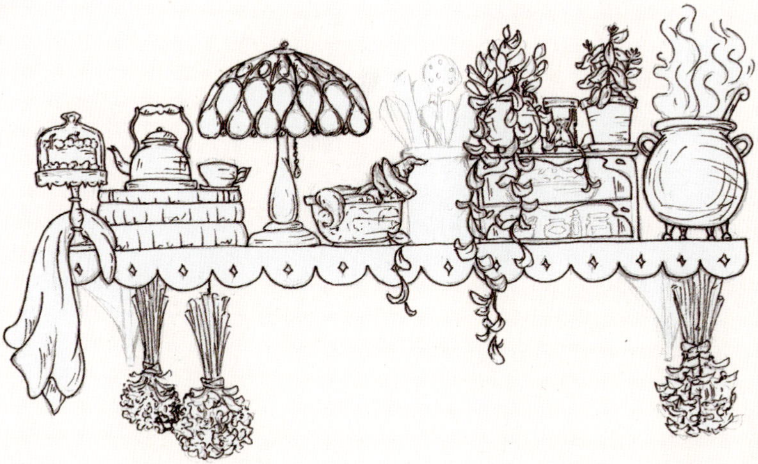

5

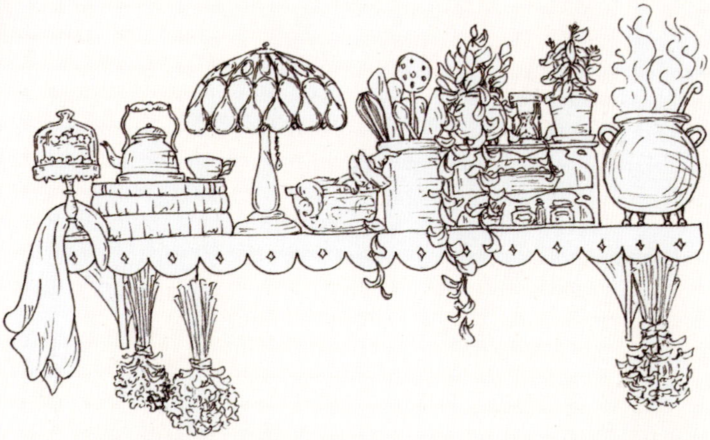

4 Now that we have the shelf to use as a base, fill in the ink outlines for everything except the shelf brackets, Enchanted Kitchen Utensils (page 38), and the small items on the Hand-Carved Wood Storage Rack (page 46).

5 Almost there! Fill in the ink for the remaining items, and then once the ink is dry, gently erase the pencil layer.

6

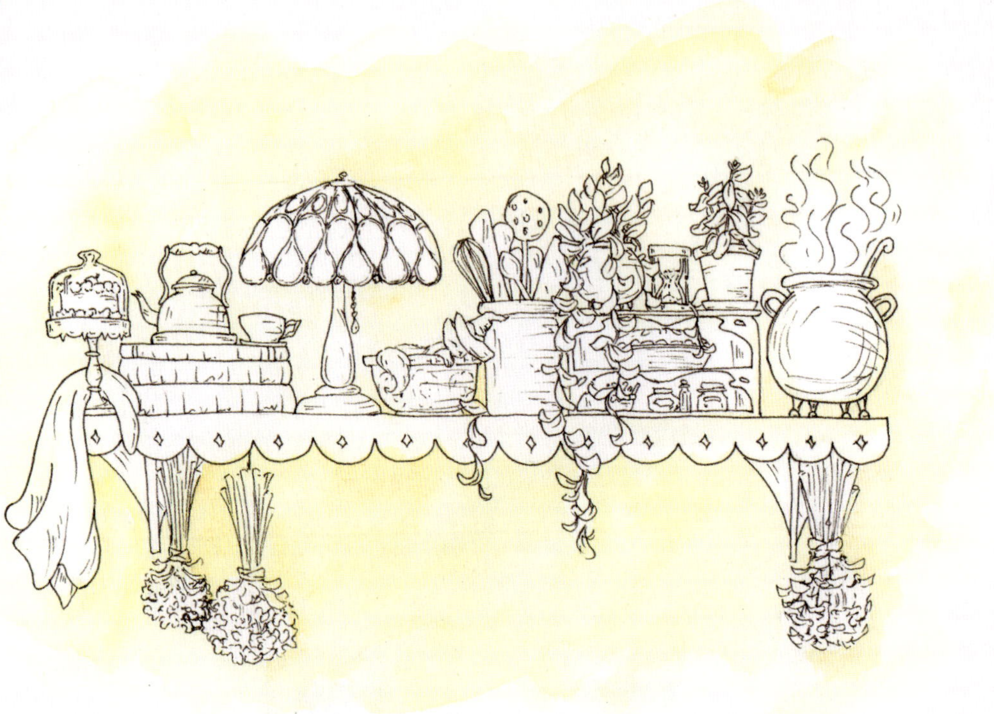

6 If you'd like to add a colored background like the one in the example, do so now. Start off by using your larger brush and trace the whole ink outline with water. The idea here is to make a slightly damp surface (no puddles!) on the whole area we want to add background color to, without that color bleeding into the areas we'll paint in the next steps. Once you've got the water layer just outside all the ink, use an extra-large brush (if you have one—otherwise you can use your large brush) to add water to the rest of the area you'll want colored. Then use that brush to add a very light layer of Naples yellow combined with Mayan yellow, building up two to five successive layers until you're happy with how it looks. Keep an eye on the edges as they dry, particularly the edges adjacent to your ink outline, and nudge them with a slightly damp brush if they start to dry with odd lines. (Watercolor can dry in strange ways, and if you like the added texture, that's great, but you may not want it to surprise you!)

7

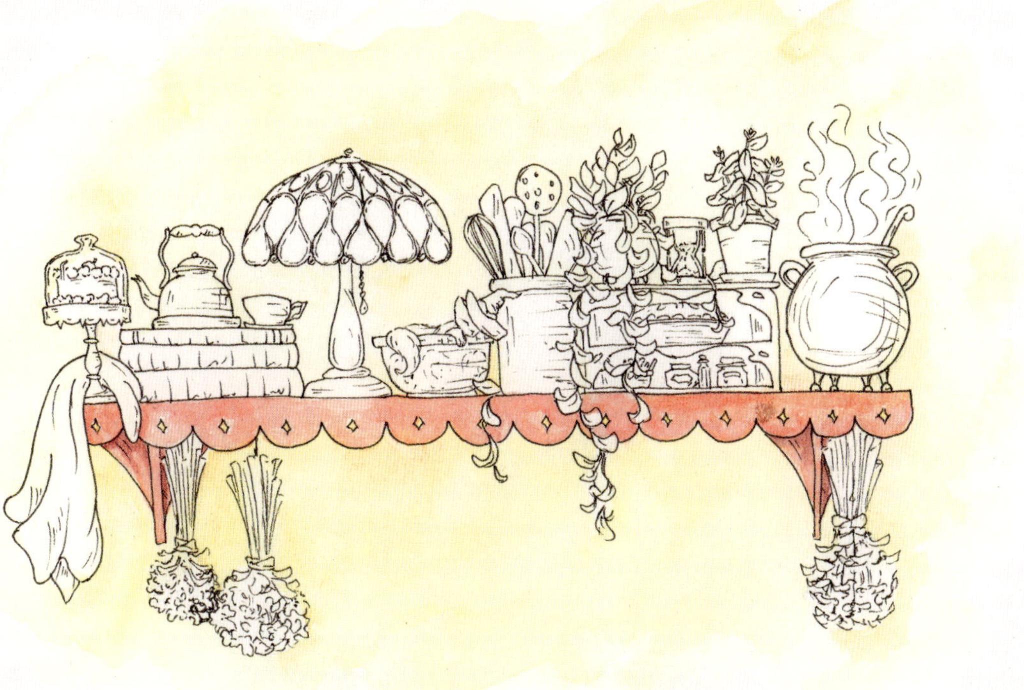

7 In general, it's a good idea to paint background to foreground, so we'll start off with the items farthest back on the shelf and finish with things closer to the front. The exception to this is the actual shelf, which is the first thing we'll paint so we can make sure all the other colors match it. Refer to The Kitchen Witchery Shelf (page 49) for full instructions, and add some beautiful pink to your shelf, making sure to add some gentle shadows just to the right of where the Decorative Tea Towel (page 42) and Climbing Potted Vine (page 44) overlap with the shelf. Congratulations! It looks awesome already!

8

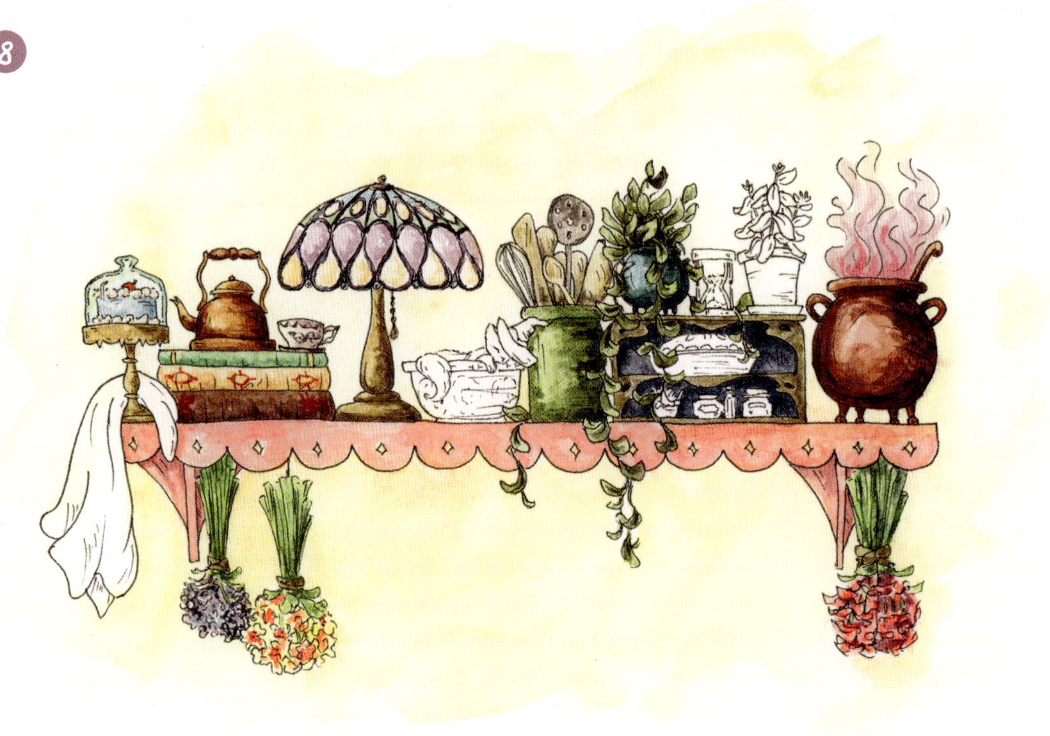

8 This step might feel like a lot, but you can swap between items as the various layers of paint dry, and you'll be done before you know it! Here you'll paint the Magical Frosted Cake (page 36), Shining Copper Teakettle (page 30), Colorful Stained-Glass Lamp (page 22), Witchy Cookbooks (page 34), Blue and White China Teacup (page 41), Enchanted Kitchen Utensils (page 38), Hand-Carved Wood Storage Rack (page 46), Climbing Potted Vine (page 44), Delicate Dried Herbs and Flowers (page 25), and Mysterious Cauldron (page 20).

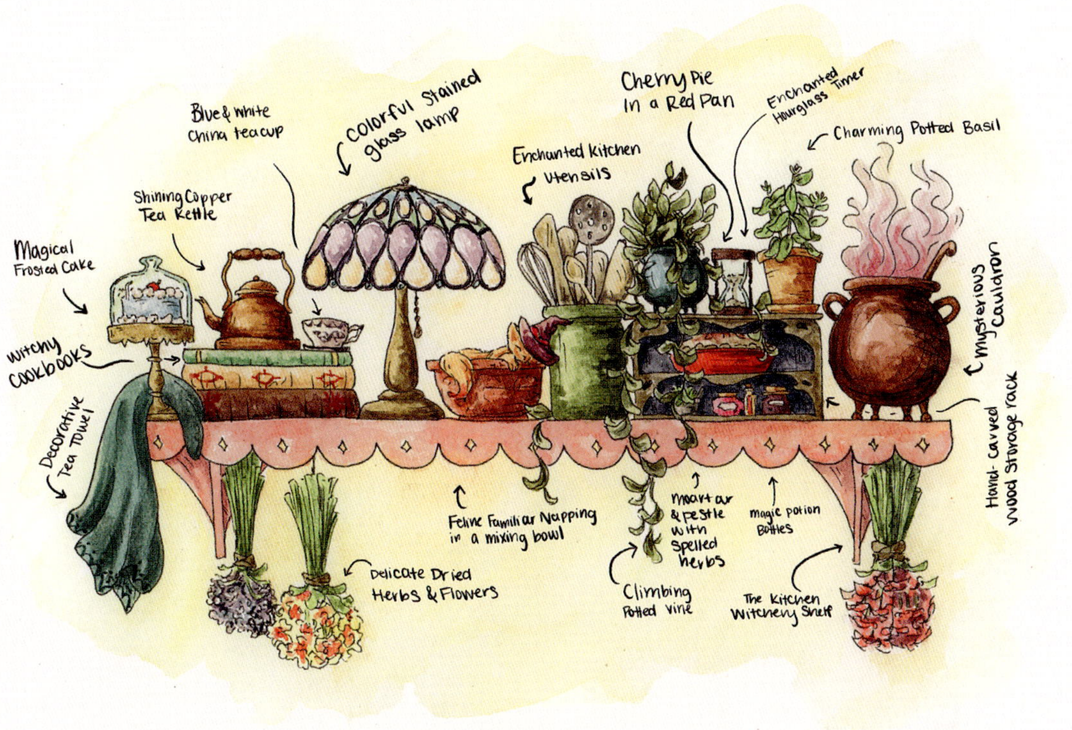

9 You're so close to the finish line—just a few more items! Now it's time to paint the Decorative Tea Towel (page 42), Feline Familiar Napping in a Mixing Bowl (page 18), Magic Potion Bottles (page 40), Mortar and Pestle with Spelled Herbs (page 48), Cherry Pie in a Red Pan (page 33), Enchanted Hourglass Timer (page 32), and Charming Potted Basil (page 28). Whew, you did it! Pat yourself on the back and admire your beautiful new witchy creation!

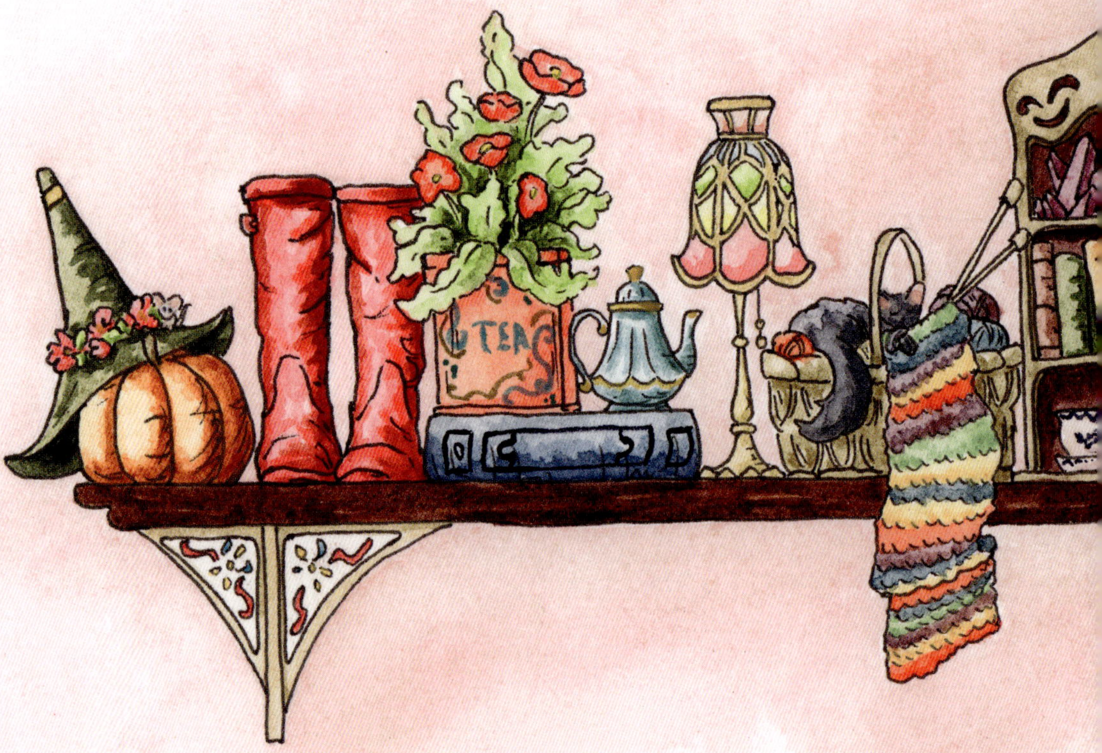
TEA

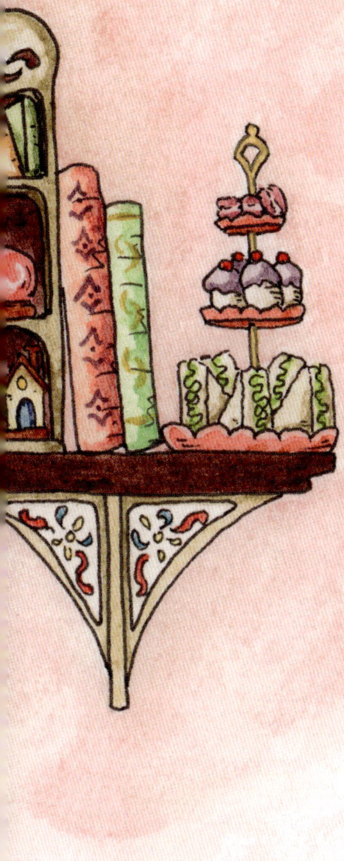

Cottage Witchery

The cottage witch's shelf is cozy and warm, somewhere you'll definitely want to rest and curl up with a good book and a warm cuppa tea. Her cottage is probably nestled somewhere idyllic, surrounded by blossoming fields of flowers and well-tended gardens, and you'll find wellies for traipsing the forest paths and a pumpkin from the witch's own garden on this fun shelf. There's even a tiny house, tucked away safely next to some books, for visiting fairies that the cottage witch has befriended while exploring the gardens and wildflowers. This whimsical shelf is such a joy to paint, so let's grab some art supplies and get to work!

Cat Napping with Spelled Knitting

What could be more magical than a basket of spelled knitting? A basket of spelled knitting with a napping cat, of course! After all, the cottage witch sits by the fire in the evenings with her familiar kitty nearby, waving the knitting needles and muttering "knit two, purl one," to herself. After a few hours, a colorful scarf appears, warm and cozy, ready for walks in the winter snow!

Colors Used

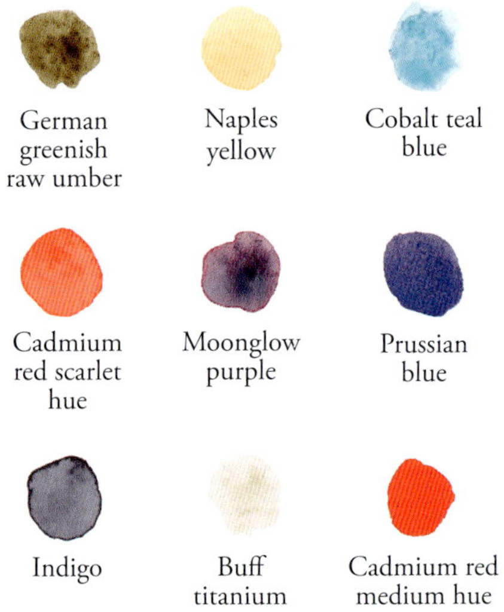

1

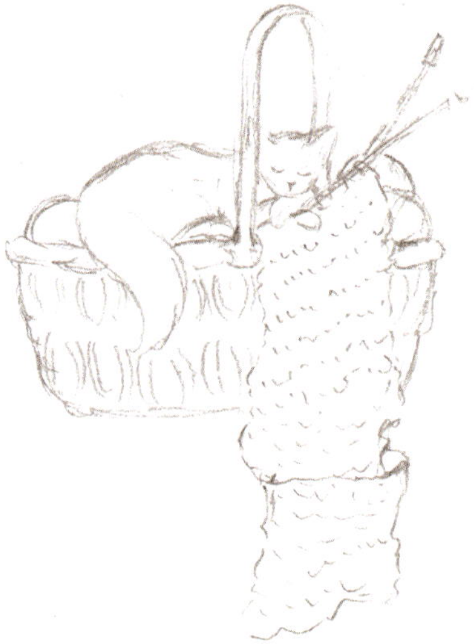

1 Begin with a light pencil sketch of a basket, including a gentle arch for the handle. Then add some circles to be the balls of yarn, and finally add some knitting needles and wiggling lines for the scarf. Sketch the adorable napping kitty, erasing any parts of the basket that are now covered so you don't accidentally add ink to those parts in the next step. Draw a very, very light oval for the cat's body, and then add two curving lines for the tail, an upside-down triangle for the head with two triangles on top for the ears. Finally, sketch the rest of the cat-shaped details around that base sketch, like a sleeping face or perhaps one eye open to keep an eye out for potential snacks.

2

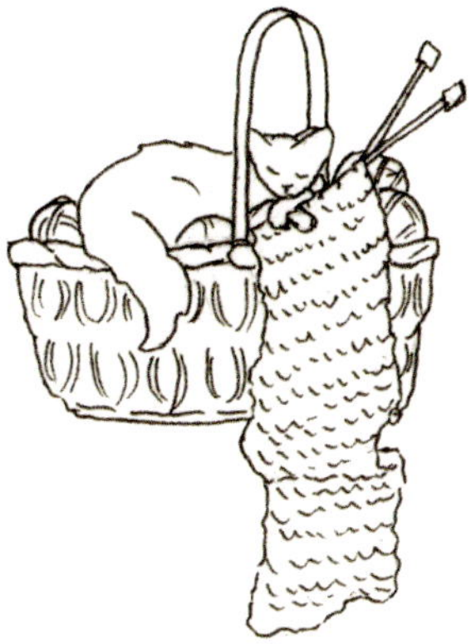

3

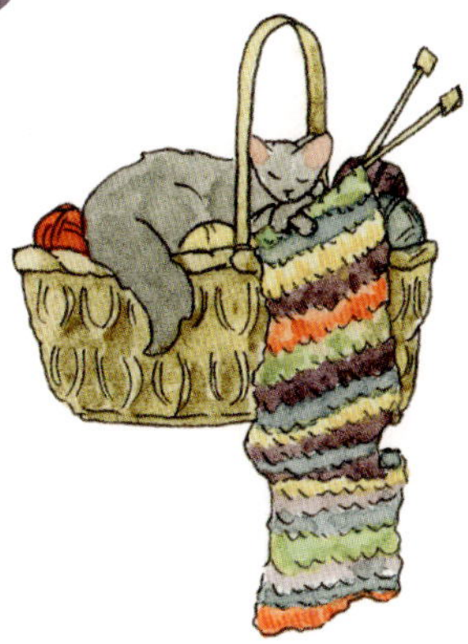

4

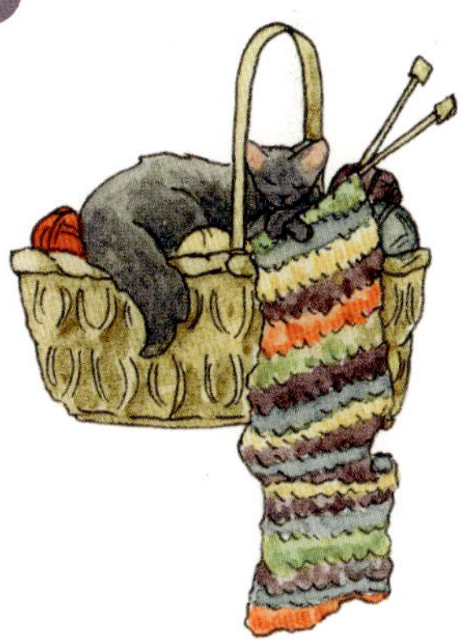

2 Carefully go over the pencil outline with your waterproof pen, using sections of parallel lines on the yarn balls to give the impression of the wound yarn. Once the ink is dry, gently erase the pencil layer.

3 Using your larger brush, go over the basket and knitting needles with some German greenish raw umber and Naples yellow, adding shadows and texture with some pure German greenish raw umber. Now add some fun colors to the scarf! The stripe colors will be reused for the yarn balls, so this is a great place to incorporate any favorite colors you enjoy. To keep the scarf colors from bleeding together, let each stripe dry before painting the ones directly adjacent to it. I used Naples yellow combined with cobalt teal blue; pure Naples yellow; Naples yellow combined with cadmium red scarlet hue; Naples yellow combined with moonglow purple; and Naples yellow combined with Prussian blue, building up layers to add shadows on the balls and in the stripes. Now let's paint the first layers on our cat! We'll build up the color in a few layers, so start off by mixing some indigo and Naples yellow with your larger brush and filling in the whole cat except for the ears. Use your smaller brush and a mixture of buff titanium and cadmium red medium hue to fill in the ears.

4 Almost there! Mix up some more indigo and Naples yellow, and then add a few more layers to the cat's fur to really build up the shadows. Make sure to allow each layer to dry for a few minutes so you can get the very deepest colors. Go back and add any additional shadows and texture that the scarf and yarn balls need, and then you're done! It looks magically amazing! You made a beautiful scarf and an adorable cat!

Magical Springtime Flowers in a Tea Tin

Springtime flowers and tea are both pretty wonderful on their own, but enchanted blossoms that make flowers all year round, planted in a colorful tin? That sounds like the perfect addition to the coziest of cottage witch shelves! This is a great place to customize your shelf. Include some wildflowers native to your area, favorite flowers that remind you of a cherished place or memory, or a design on the tea tin that reminds you of your favorite book or place!

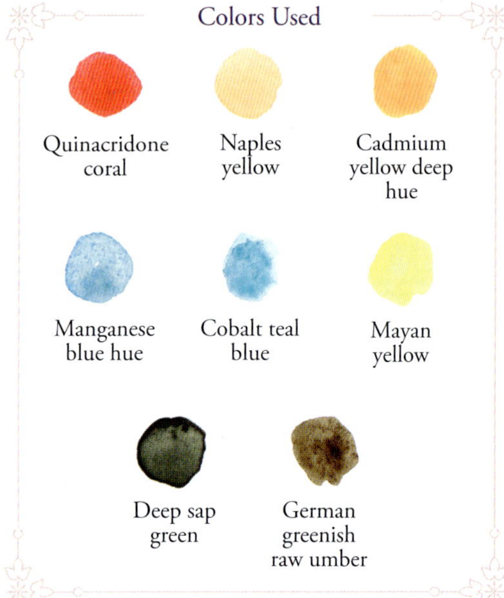

1

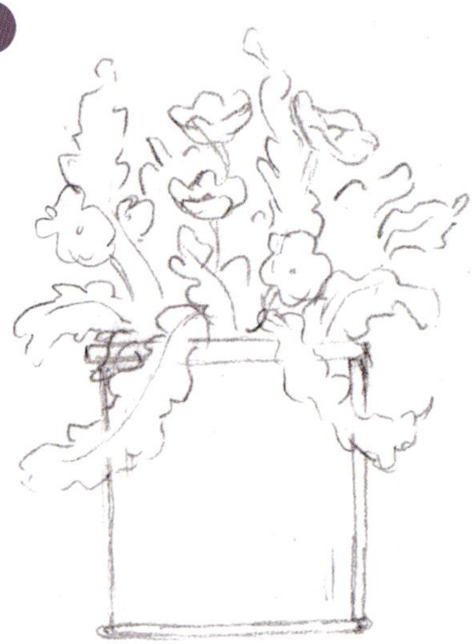

1 As always, let's start off with a pencil sketch. The tea tin is super easy: Draw a rectangle with a small lip on the top and bottom. Next, add some gently curving lines for the general shape of the flower stalks, and add some leaves and subtle flower shapes.

2

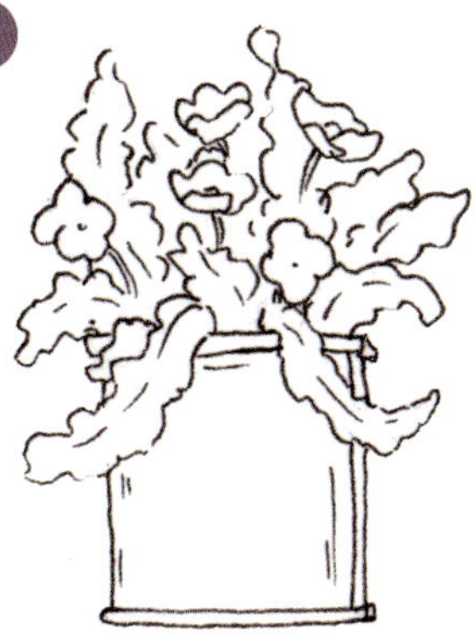

3

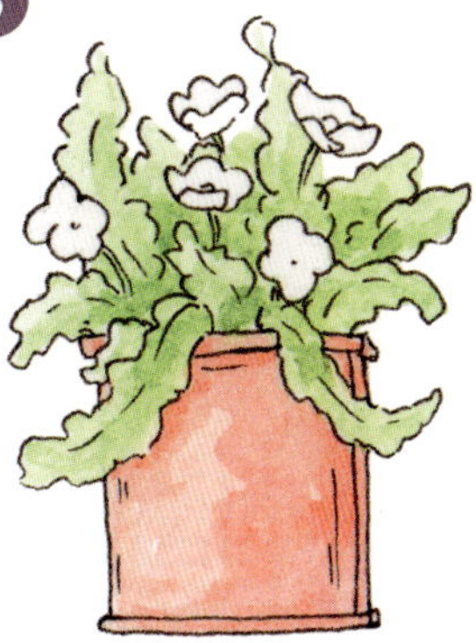

4

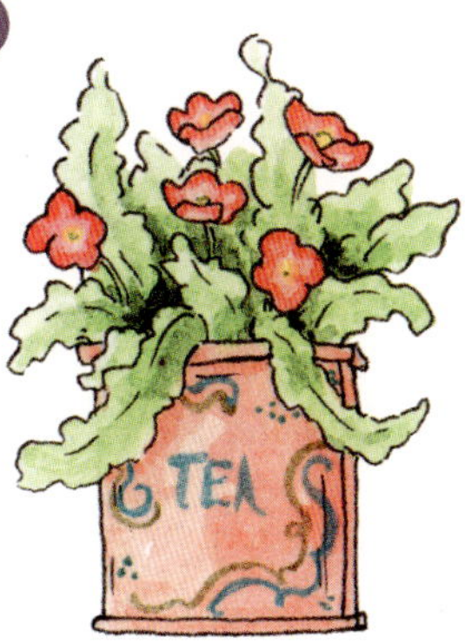

2 You'll notice that the flowers overlap with the tea tin, so let's ink those first with your waterproof pen. The idea here isn't to draw every leaf or petal; we're looking more for the general shapes and feeling of vibrant movement. If you're getting bogged down in the details, it can help to either hold your pen towards the back instead of near the tip or to use a very small reference photo where you can't see the tiny details. Once the ink is dry, gently erase the pencil layer.

3 Use your larger brush to combine quinacridone coral with Naples yellow, and fill in the whole tea tin with two to three light layers. While that dries, mix up a bright, springtime green by combining cadmium yellow deep hue with manganese blue hue, and fill in the greenery, leaving space for the flowers. Build up a few layers of the green to add depth and shadows to the leaves. This is a great time to take a quick break, because the pink base of the tea tin needs to be completely dry before we go in and add all the magical details.

4 Once the pink layer on the tea tin is totally dry, mix up some concentrated cobalt teal blue, using as little water as possible so you'll have the most control over where the paint goes. Paint some swooping lines in the upper left and lower right corners, and then write "TEA" in the center of the tin. Then use Mayan yellow mixed with deep sap green and German greenish raw umber to add more decorative lines. Add some final details using cobalt teal blue combined with deep sap green. Combine quinacridone coral with Naples yellow to make a happy pink color for the flowers, and then use that to fill in the spaces you left in the greenery earlier. Then using a small amount of cadmium yellow deep hue on your smaller brush, add some yellow to the center of each flower. While that dries, use deep sap green to add shadows to the darkest parts of the greenery, which will be towards the lower right side of each leaf and down between the leaves and flowers. Finally, build up more layers of quinacridone coral as needed to add depth to the flowers. Now you have some magical springtime flowers in a tea tin, and they look so good!

Cozy Stained-Glass Lamp

Stained-glass lamps are so fun to paint; there are so many options for the decorative shapes and bright colors! For this lamp, we'll be using a shape reminiscent of flower petals, complete with all the happiest colors of springtime. There's not much that's cozier than a glowing lamp on a dark evening or early in the morning while the cottage witch enjoys a cup of tea and a good book. This stained-glass lamp has so much added charm with its beautiful colors, so let's get started!

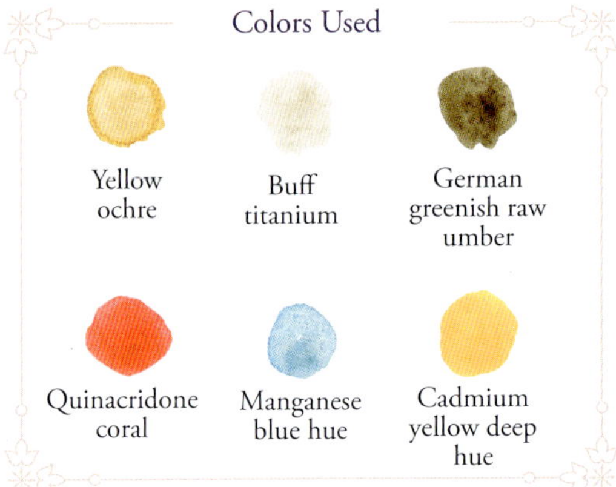

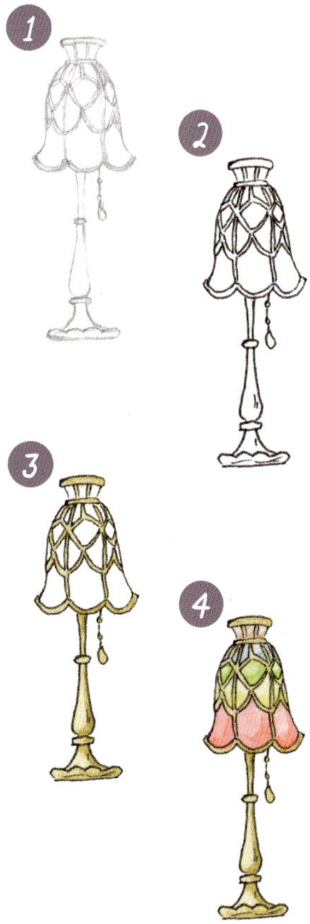

1 Start off your pencil sketch with a very light vertical line down the center, and then make small marks at the top and bottom of the lampshade. Draw the outline of the lampshade and the stand, as well as the individual pieces of stained glass.

2 Fill in the pencil outline with your waterproof pen. Once the ink is dry, gently erase the pencil layer.

3 Mix up yellow ochre and buff titanium, and use your smaller brush to fill in the welds as well as to add a single layer to the whole stand. Then use German greenish raw umber to add shadows to the stand towards the right side, building up several layers until it looks like shining gold. Make sure the welds are completely dry before you move on to the next step so the colors don't bleed!

4 Now for the best part, the stained glass! Use your smaller brush to fill in the top row of pieces with a very, very light mixture of buff titanium with the slightest, tiniest hint of quinacridone coral, and then dab a second layer towards the bottom right edges of each piece for some texture. Follow that same process with manganese blue hue combined with buff titanium for the next row, cadmium yellow deep hue combined with manganese blue hue for the row below that, buff titanium added to the tiniest bit of cadmium yellow deep hue for the next one, and buff titanium with a bit more quinacridone coral for the bottom row. Once everything is dry, you can use another layer of each color to add more texture as needed. Your lamp is ready to glow!

Pumpkin from the Witch's Garden

Fall might be one of the best seasons for cozy cottage witchery, and this pumpkin is the perfect way to incorporate some seasonal elements on the shelf! You can have lots of fun with it by adding carvings to make a jack-o'-lantern, or switch up the color to add a splash of blue or white to the shelf.

Colors Used

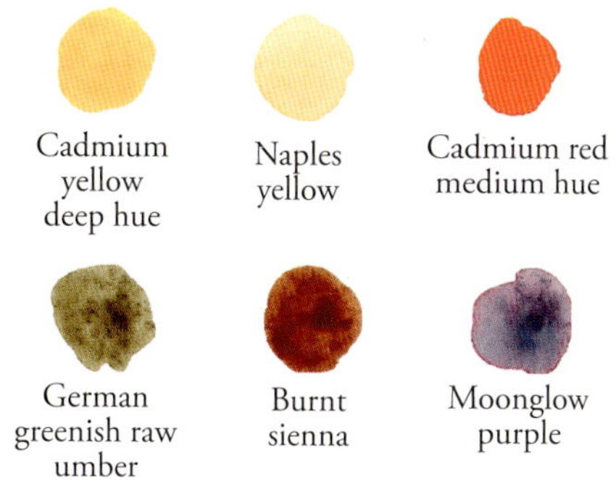

1

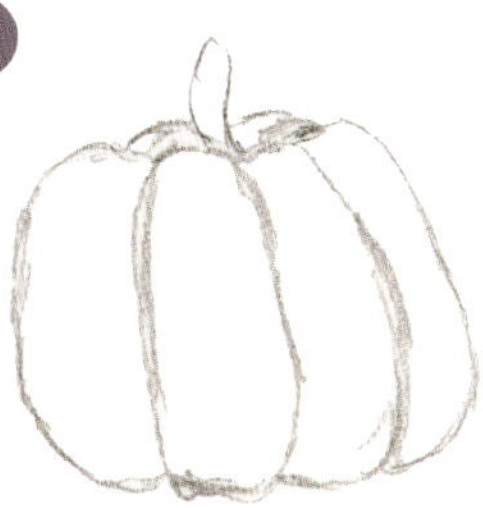

2

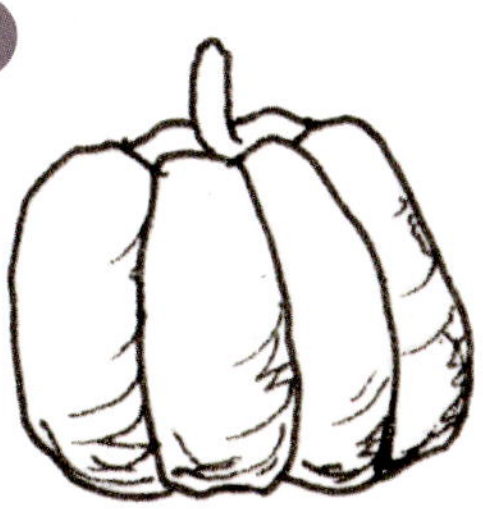

3

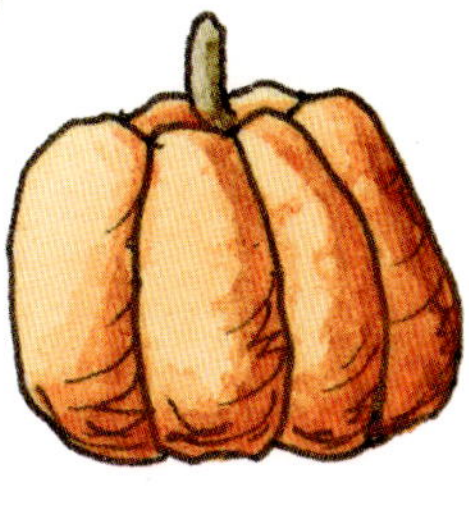

1. Sketch a light oval with your pencil, and then add curving lines for the shape of the pumpkin and a stem for the top. You can add a bit more greenery to the shelf by elongating the stem and adding some leaves if that suits your fancy!
2. Use your waterproof pen to go over the pencil outline, adding lots of nice shading towards the lower right side of each section of the pumpkin. Once the ink is dry, gently erase the pencil layer.
3. Grab your larger brush and use it to fill in the whole pumpkin with a mixture of cadmium yellow deep hue, Naples yellow, and cadmium red medium hue. Then add German greenish raw umber to the stem. Start building up shadows with burnt sienna added to your previously mixed orange, and then add the darkest shadows with a bit of moonglow purple added in, building up layers until the pumpkin looks round and shiny. Great job, it looks wonderful!

Cozy Witch's Hat

A cozy hat is a staple of any cottage witch's shelf—it can be used to keep the sun out of her eyes while traipsing through the fields during the summer or to stay warm while wandering the snowy woods in the winter. Our cottage witch's hat is dark green, reminiscent of pine trees, with floral and gold accents, since you can never have too many flowers!

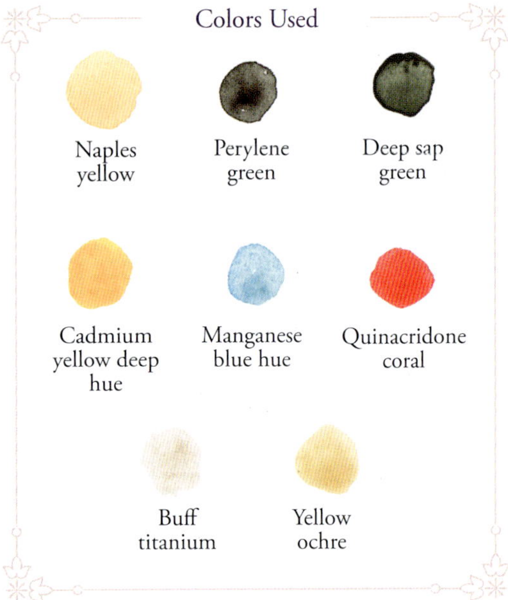

1

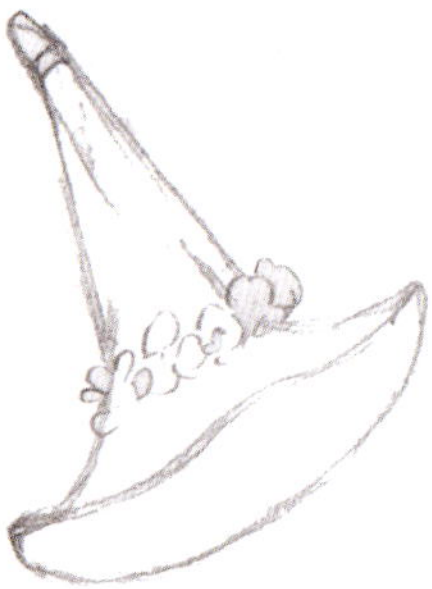

2

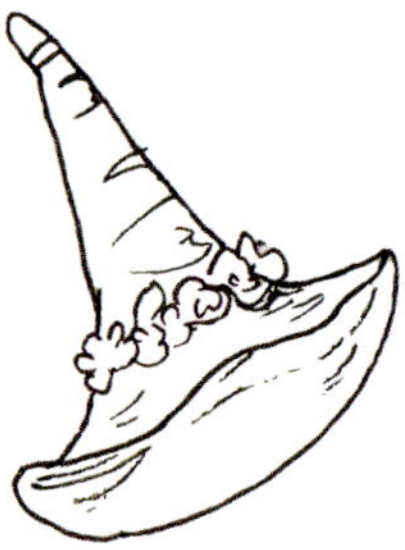

1 As always, start with the pencil sketch, beginning with an oval for the base of the hat and two swooping curves that come together in a point for the sides. Add as many floral details as you'd like, depending on how vibrant you'd like the hat to be.

2 Use your waterproof pen to go over the pencil outline from the previous step, making sure to add extra lines for shading where you'll find shadows. In this example, the light is coming from the upper left corner, so the shadows will be towards the lower right sides of the hat and flowers. Once the ink is dry, gently erase the pencil layer.

3

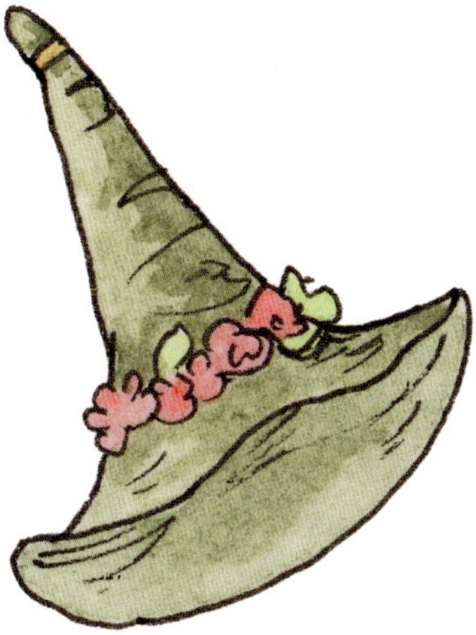

4

3 Use your larger brush to fill in the whole hat with a very light mixture of Naples yellow, perylene green, and deep sap green, building up a few layers to begin the shadows. Then add the greenery with a mixture of cadmium yellow deep hue and manganese blue hue, and add some quinacridone coral mixed with buff titanium for the first layers of the flowers. Using your smaller brush, use yellow ochre to add the gold band near the top of the hat.

4 Now for all the beautiful details where it all comes together! Use a mixture of deep sap green with perylene green to build up progressively darker shadows on the hat, including the shadows that'll be cast by the flowers and on the underside of the hat. Use the colors you mixed in the previous step to add some shadows to the greenery and depth to the flowers, using a dab of yellow ochre in the center of each flower, and you have a cozy witch's hat that's ready to wear!

Three-Tier Tower of Treats

One can never have too many desserts and snacks, so the cottage witch's shelf has a three-tier tower of treats, made from delicate glass and gold, that's filled with macarons, tiny cakes, and tea sandwiches. If you have a favorite baked good or treat, this is a great place to incorporate it, and be sure to have fun with the colors!

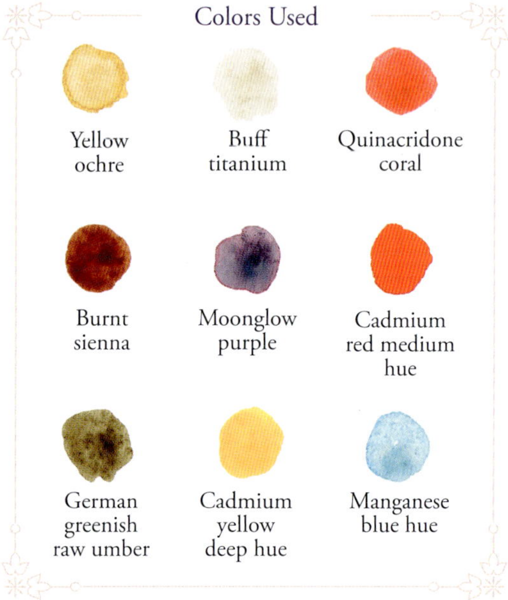

1

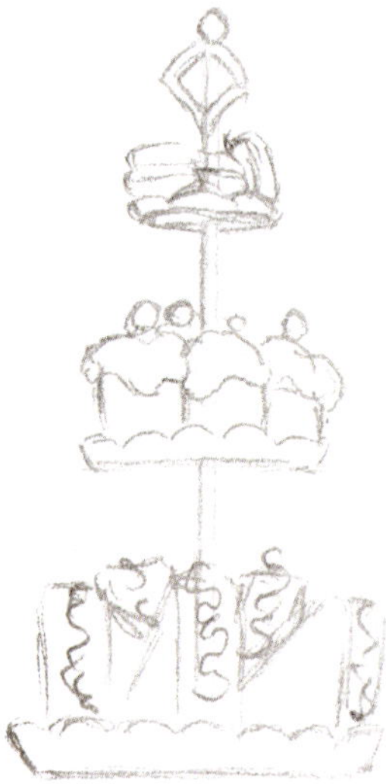

1 Begin the pencil sketch with two vertical lines to make the center bar of the tower. Then mark the height and width of each tier to make sure the whole thing looks balanced. Add a gently scalloped edge to the top of each tier, and then add the outlines of the treats. You can, of course, fill the tower with your favorite confectionary delights, or in the example here, we've got macarons (a squashed oval with two lines through the center), cupcakes (be sure to add wiggly lines for the frosting), and tea sandwiches (triangles with loose, wiggly lines to indicate lettuce in the middle).

2

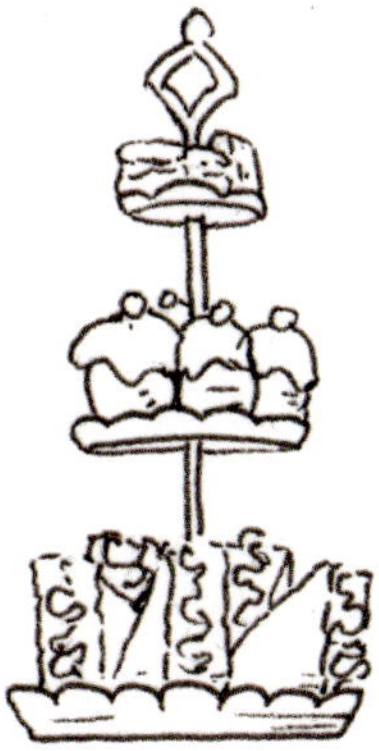

3

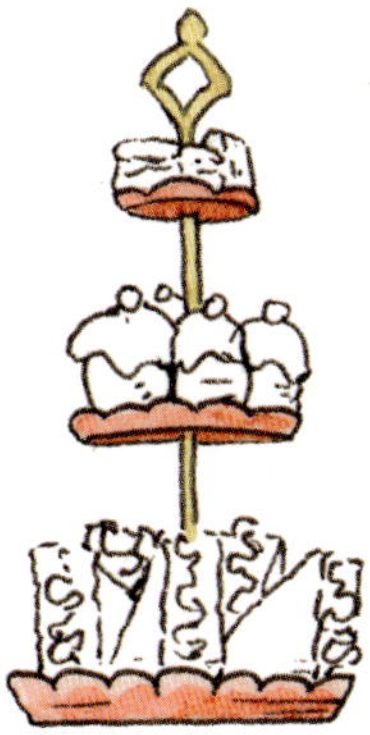

4

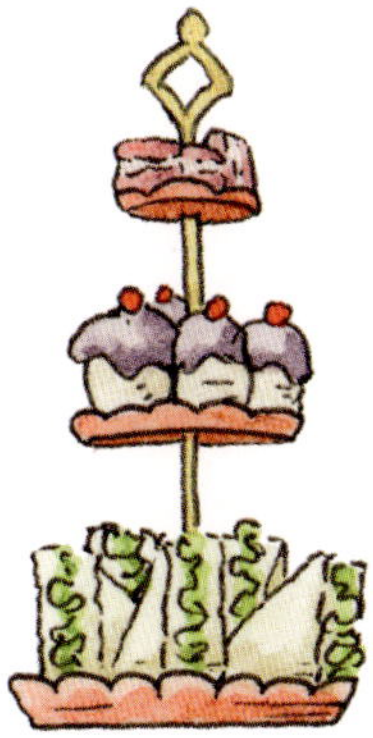

2 Since there are a lot of overlapping pieces in our tower, start off the ink drawing by outlining the individual tiers with your waterproof pen, and then ink in the desserts before finally adding the vertical bar and handle. Add some texture and shading to the desserts, erase the pencil outline once thc ink is dry, and get ready to paint!

3 Let's start off with the tower: Use your smaller brush to fill in the bar and handle with a light mixture of yellow ochre and buff titanium. Mix together quinacridone coral and burnt sienna and fill in the plates. Since you can see a bit of the underside of two of the tiers, add some additional burnt sienna to your color mixture for shadows on the right sides and undersides of the tiers.

4 Let the tower dry completely, and then it's onward to the desserts! Starting with the macarons at the top, fill in each one with a light layer of quinacridone coral mixed with a hint of moonglow purple, and then add several layers of moonglow purple on the cookie sections to build up the colors and shadows. For the cupcakes, add cadmium red medium hue for the cherries on top, moonglow purple mixed with buff titanium for the frosting, and buff titanium for the cakes themselves. Add more layers with a hint of German greenish raw umber as needed for shadows. Finally, for the tea sandwiches, use buff titanium and German greenish raw umber with a hint of yellow ochre to fill in the bread and cadmium yellow deep hue mixed with manganese blue hue to add lettuce. Then use German greenish raw umber and a stronger mixture of cadmium yellow deep hue and manganese blue hue to add shadows to the bread and lettuce respectively, and your tower of treats is ready to enjoy!

Mysterious Crystal Ball

It can be exhausting to figure out what to make for dinner every night or to come up with the perfect gift for a birthday. That's why the cottage witch has a mysterious crystal ball that somehow has all the best culinary and gifting ideas. We'll build up several layers of color to achieve the look of glass, and you can switch out the pink for any color you enjoy!

Colors Used

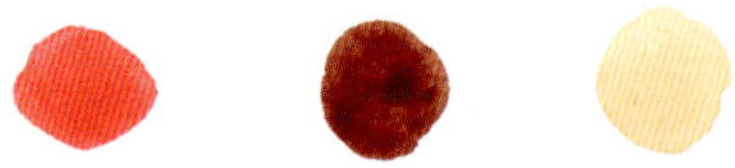

Quinacridone coral | Burnt sienna | Naples yellow

1

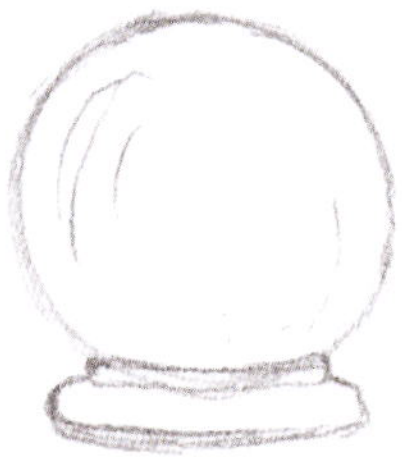

2

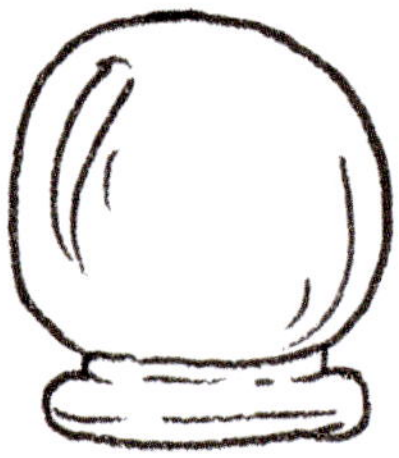

3

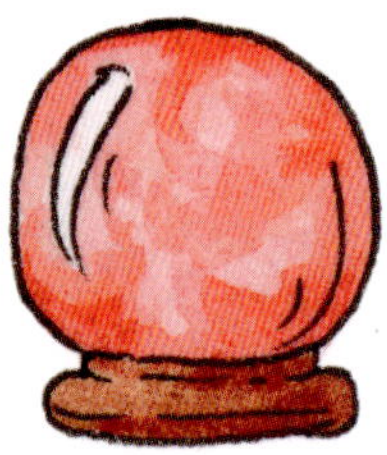

1 The pencil sketch for this one is nice and easy—just sketch a circle for the ball, and add a small rectangular base so it doesn't roll off the shelf!

2 Go over the outline with your waterproof pen, adding a bit of shading to the stand and some lines on the ball to show how the glass reflects. Once the ink is dry, gently erase your pencil layer.

3 Use your smaller brush to fill in the whole ball with a light layer of quinacridone coral mixed loosely with burnt sienna, building up three to five thin layers so the ball has an almost misty look. Then add several layers of burnt sienna mixed with Naples yellow to the base while the ball dries. Now, go back to the ball and build up details by adding very light layers of quinacridone coral and burnt sienna in various parts of the ball, allowing each layer to dry before adding the next until it looks deep and mysterious!

Wellies for Traipsing in the Garden

Every cottage will have some rainy days, and the cottage witch needs some wellies (rain boots!) for traipsing in the garden to tend to flowers and pick herbs for various potions and spells. These wellies are a bright, happy red, but you can always add a design, such as flowers or polka dots, for an extra touch of whimsy.

Colors Used

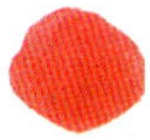
Quinacridone coral

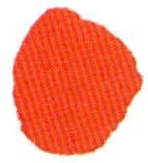
Cadmium red medium hue

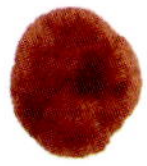
Burnt sienna

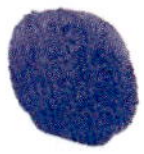
Prussian blue

1

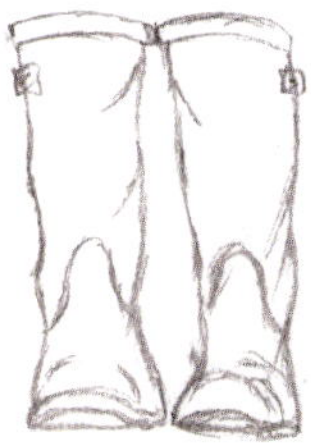

2

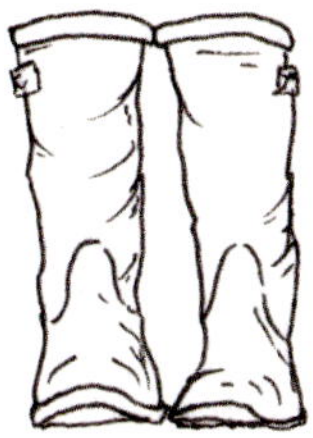

3

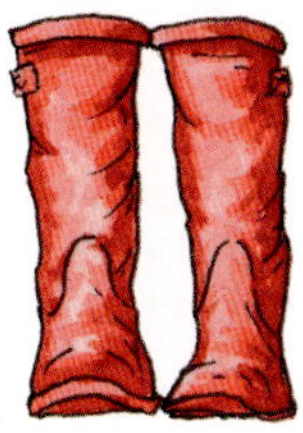

1 Start off your pencil sketch with light markings for the tops and sides of the boots to block out the general rectangular overall outline, and then fill in the details. Start off by adding some loosely wiggling lines to indicate the sides of the boots, some buckles at the top, soles at the bottom, and a curving line upwards near the ankle of each boot.

2 As always, use your waterproof pen to go over the pencil sketch, making sure to add bold lines for the shading and details for the toes of the boots and the curves at the ankles. Once the ink is dry, gently erase the pencil layer.

3 Use your larger brush to fill in the wellies with a bright mixture of quinacridone coral and cadmium red medium hue. Then build up three or four layers of that, adding in small amounts of burnt sienna and Prussian blue as you move towards the right edge of each boot, until you have beautiful contrast and shadows. I prefer to let each layer dry almost all the way before adding the next one, but if you want a smooth color gradient, you can add each successive layer while the previous one is still quite wet, and then use a clean, slightly damp brush, to ensure the edges are blended perfectly. And now you're ready to go traipsing in the garden!

Delicate China Teapot

This cute little teapot feels like something right out of a fairy tale, and it's spelled to always keep your tea at exactly the right temperature—no more forgetting you've left something to brew and coming back to cold tea! We'll slowly build up the colors and shadows here to achieve an almost luminous look, with some gold accents to add to the whimsy. Happy painting!

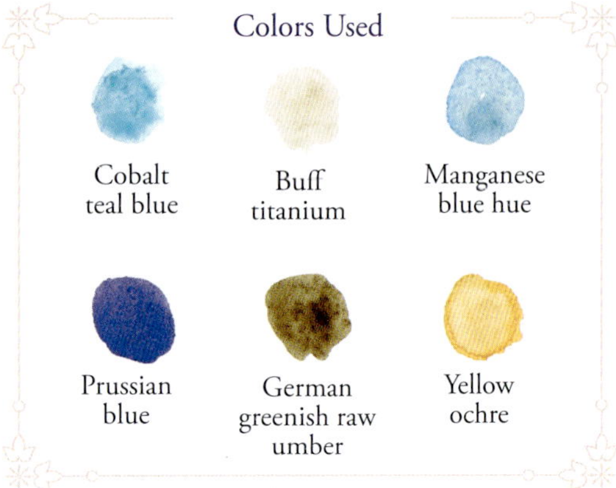

1

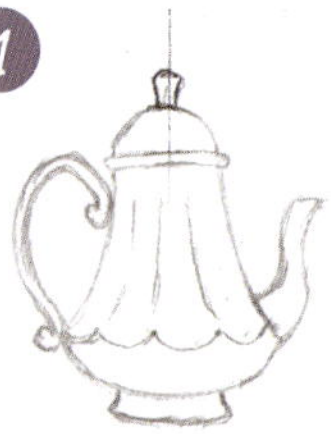

2

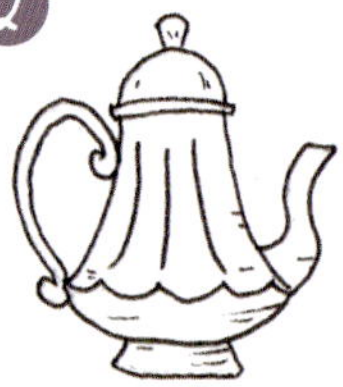

3

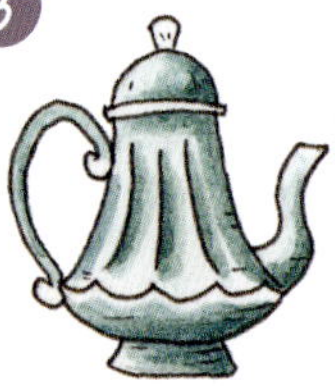

4

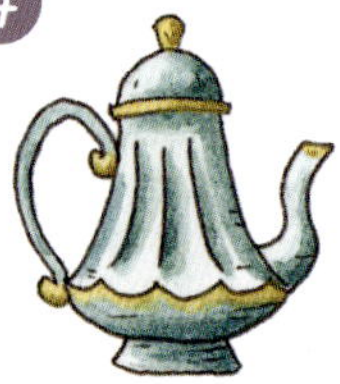

1 Sketch a very light vertical center line so you can make sure the teapot is symmetrical, and then place a mark for the top of the lid. Draw the outline of the teapot, and then add the handle and spout. Add the scalloped detail at the widest point near the base, and then add gently curving lines coming up from the tips of the scallops.

2 Use your waterproof pen to go over the pencil outline, adding shading and additional details, and then once the ink is dry, gently erase the pencil sketch.

3 Use your larger brush to fill in the whole teapot (except for the spots for the gold accents) with a very light layer of cobalt teal blue combined with buff titanium and manganese blue hue. Then combine cobalt teal blue, manganese blue hue, and a tiny hint of Prussian blue and German greenish raw umber, and slowly build up three or four layers of shadows until the teapot looks like it's glowing. Depending on how much water you're using, you may need to let the shadows dry between layers, but eventually the highlights will start to pop, so don't give up!

4 Once the blue is dry, use your smaller brush to add a layer of yellow ochre mixed with buff titanium for the gold accents, and use German greenish raw umber to add shadows on the right sides so the gold looks like it's reflecting the light. Congratulations! Now you can go make yourself a nice cup of tea!

Clever Mouse Hiding from the Cat

This adorable little mouse, cleverly hiding from the napping cat, is such a fun detail to incorporate into the cottage witch's shelf, and the best part is you can tuck little mice away in any nook or cranny that could use a little more magic. This tutorial shows a whole mouse, but mice are a delightful detail to tuck away behind objects on shelves, so feel free to adjust the tutorial to suit whatever arrangement of critters and objects you choose!

Colors Used

Buff titanium

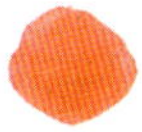

Quinacridone coral

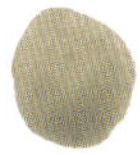

Gray titanium

1

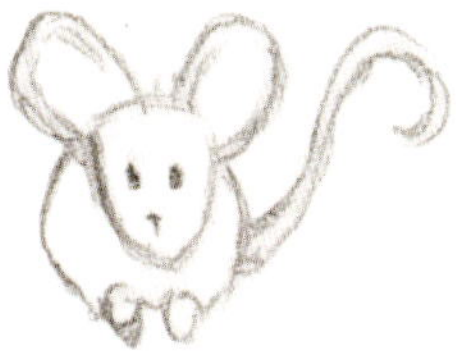

2

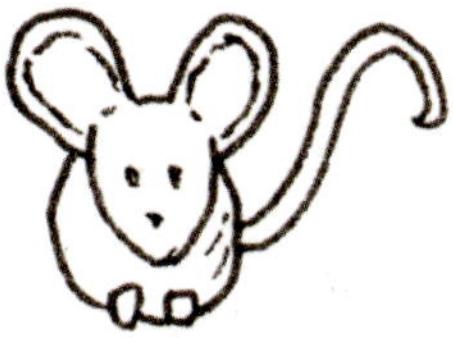

3

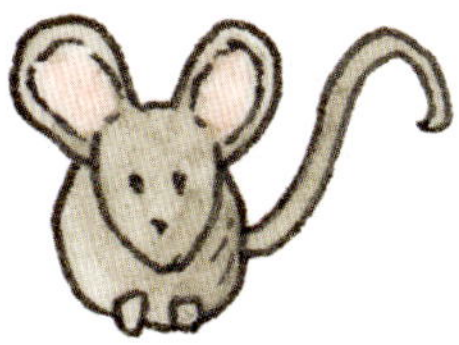

1 Use your pencil to gently sketch a pointed oval for the mouse's face, and then add some little ears and as much of the body as will be visible.

2 Since the mouse is so small, you'll need to carefully add the waterproof ink outline so as not to overwhelm the tiny details. You can add eyes and a nose either with ink now or paint later, whichever you prefer. If you run into trouble with the placement of facial features, a few layers of buff titanium (or, ideally, white gouache) will get you back to the beginning and you can try again—the waterproof pen will look slightly different on top of watercolor though, so you may want to use black or indigo watercolor to redraw the facial features if you decide to cover up the first attempt. Once the ink is dry, gently erase the pencil layer.

3 Use your smaller brush to fill in the ears with buff titanium with a hint of quinacridone coral, and then add gray titanium to the whole body of the mouse. Build up as many layers of gray titanium as needed to add shadows to the mouse, and you can add a bit of any deep blue or purple if you need a bit more contrast. Now your clever mouse is ready for all sorts of adventures!

Books of Magic Spells and Recipes

The cottage witch needs an assortment of books of magic spells and recipes, and some of them have the instructions to make the magically delicious desserts for the tower of treats! Books make great filler on shelves and work wonderfully as small horizontal surfaces upon which to arrange other items. Or you can add vertical books to fill small spaces. Really, who doesn't need more books in their life? You can modify the designs on the books to incorporate shapes and colors you enjoy, or add titles to describe the contents of each book—the options are endless!

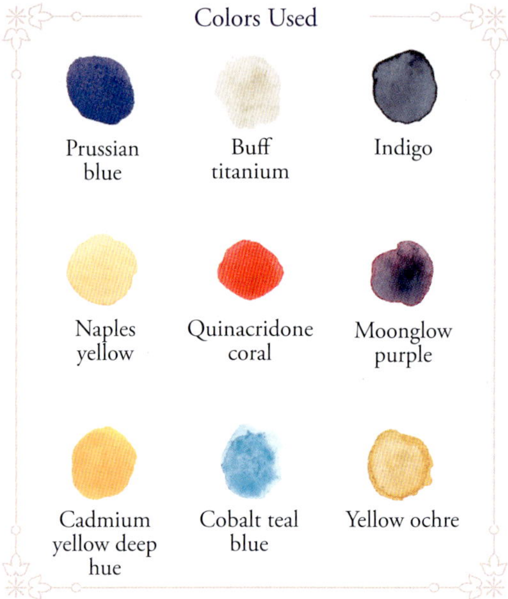

1

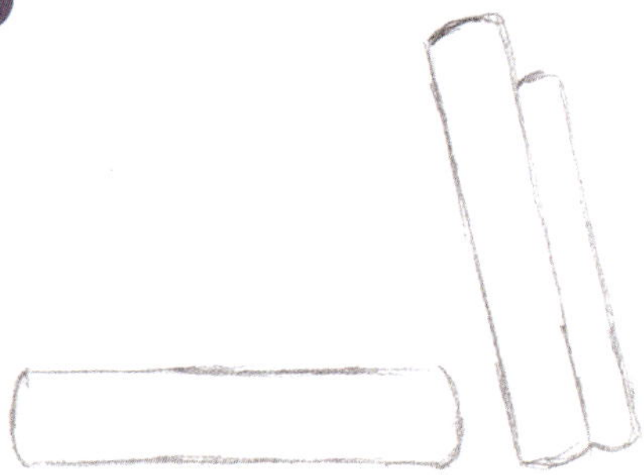

1 Begin with the pencil outlines for the books, using a ruler if you want perfectly straight lines or free drawing the edges for a more organic look.

2

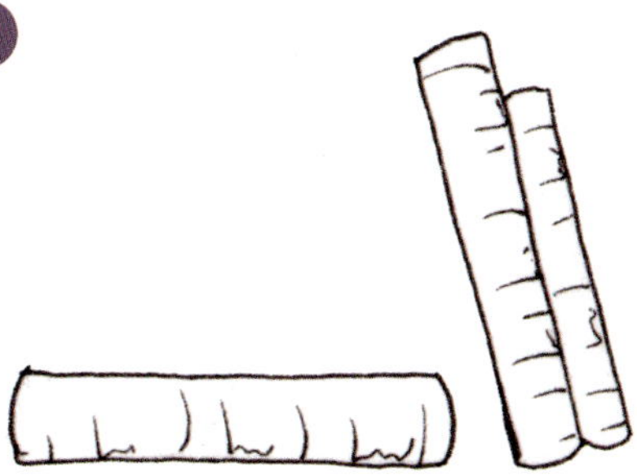

3

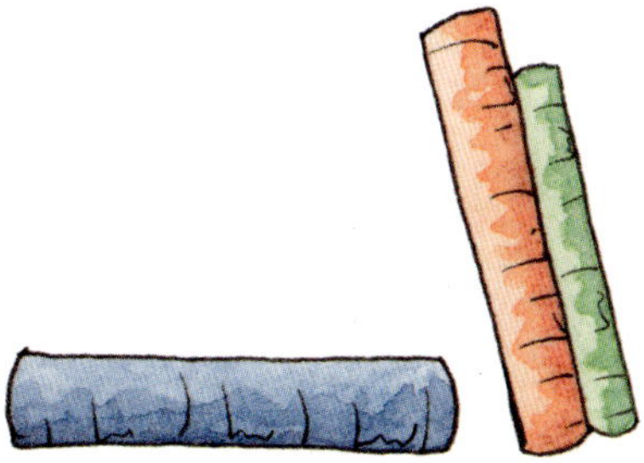

4

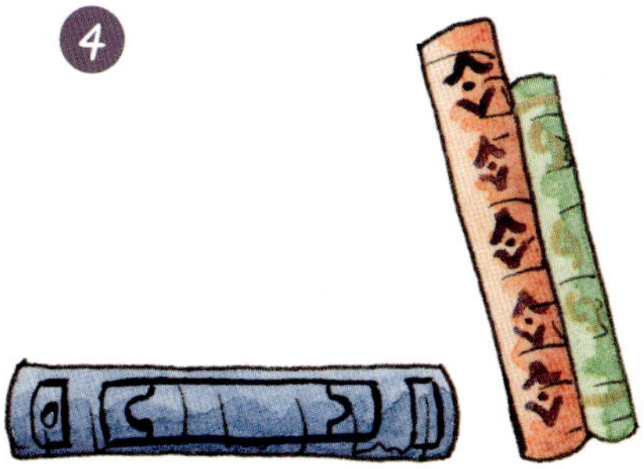

2 Use your waterproof pen to go over the outlines of the books, adding some gently curving lines to shade the base of the horizontal book and the right edges of the vertical books. Once the ink is dry, gently erase the pencil layer.

3 For the horizontal book, use your larger brush to fill in the whole book with Prussian blue, buff titanium, and a hint of indigo, and then build up three or four layers of that mixture with increasing amounts of indigo towards the base. For the vertical book to the left, fill in the whole thing with Naples yellow mixed with quinacridone coral, and then build up contrast by adding layers of that with increasing amounts of moonglow purple. Finally, use cadmium yellow deep hue, cobalt teal blue, and buff titanium to fill in the last book, adding shadows by slowly incorporating tiny (very tiny!) amounts of indigo into the layers towards the right hand side of the book. Now is the perfect time to take a quick break for a cup of tea or a different project while everything dries, since we don't want the colors to bleed when we add all the fun final touches!

4 Once the books are completely dry, it's time to add the decorative details! For the horizontal book, use a concentrated mixture of indigo and your smallest brush to add a whimsical design. Use moonglow purple mixed with a bit of buff titanium for the vertical book to the left and yellow ochre mixed with a small amount of buff titanium for the one on the right. Your books of magical spells and recipes are ready to read!

Wooden Trinket Shelf

One can never have quite enough space for trinkets and treasures, so the cottage witch has a beautifully carved wooden trinket shelf! The carvings on the top remind me of smiling faces, perhaps of the cottage witch and her sisters, and I hope they make you as happy as they make me!

Colors Used

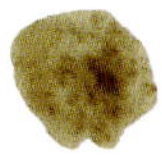

German greenish raw umber

Buff titanium

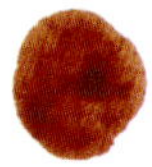

Burnt sienna

Moonglow purple

1

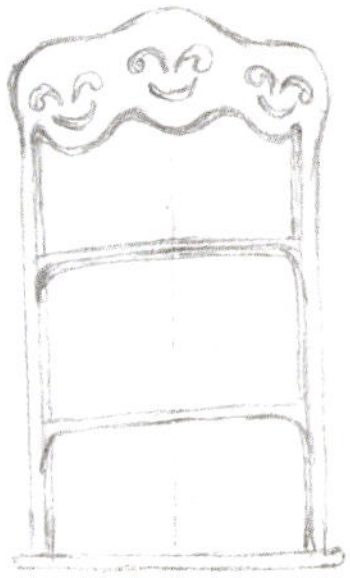

2

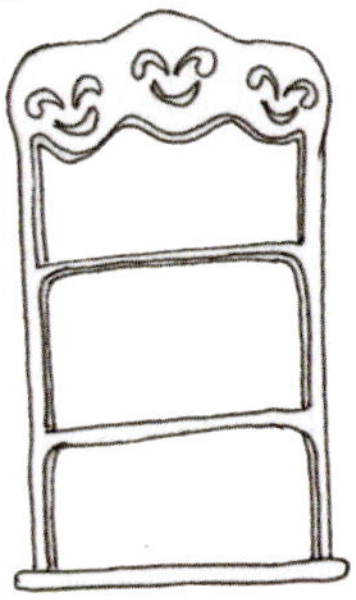

3

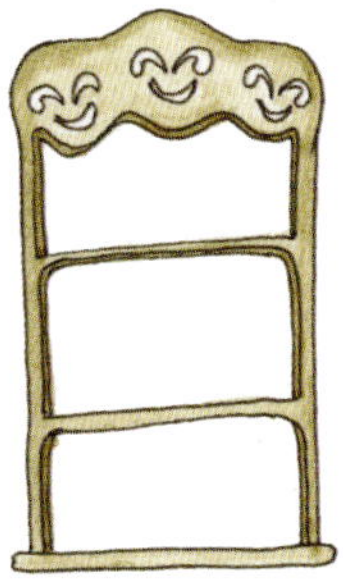

4

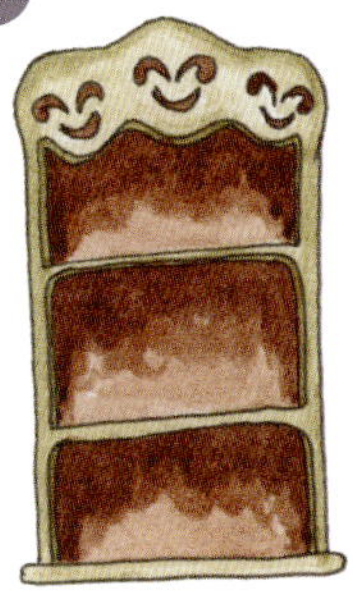

1 Use your pencil to sketch the sides, the curving top and its carvings, and the individual shelves. If you're adding trinkets and treasures to the shelf, they should be part of the pencil and ink sketches so you don't paint shadows where you want an object to be! See Assembling Your Cottage Witchery Shelf (page 84).

2 Go over your pencil outline with a waterproof pen, and, once the ink is dry, gently erase the pencil layer.

3 Let's start off with the lighter wood color, filling in the sides, top, and shelves with German greenish raw umber mixed with buff titanium. I recommend using the smaller brush here so you have the most control over where the paint ends up. (But this depends on how large you've drawn the shelf.) Add three or four light layers to build up shadows and a gentle wood texture, as well as some shadows with pure German greenish raw umber.

4 Use your larger brush and a mixture of burnt sienna and moonglow purple to add shadows to the back of the shelf and inside the carvings at the top, building up layers until you have a rich, dark brownish-purple color. Be sure to add anything you'd like on the shelves before you fill in the shadows!

Floral Teacup

The cottage witch needs a lovely teacup to go with her teapot, and this floral teacup with a matching saucer is the perfect complement, with its coordinating blue design and crisp white base. Teacups are a fabulous place to add tons of personality to your shelf—you can change up the size, shape, and pattern to give your shelf a different feel or add a few teacups to reflect your own space if you're prone to finding half-finished cups of tea and cocoa around the house!

Colors Used

Buff titanium

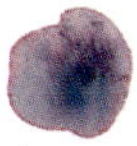
Moonglow purple

Manganese blue hue

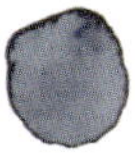
Indigo

1

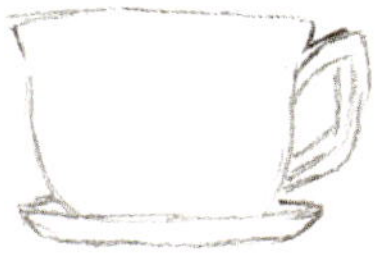

2

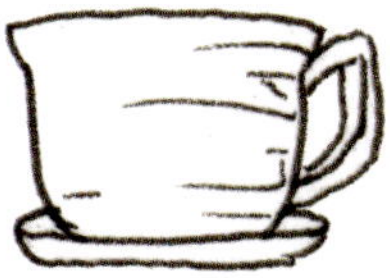

3

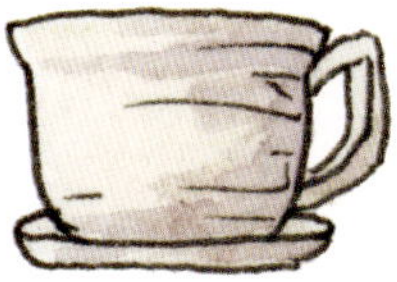

4

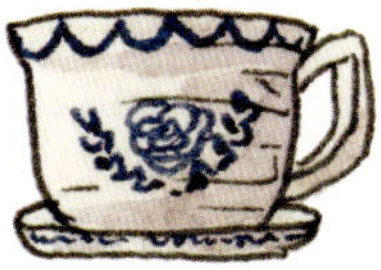

1 Draw a light pencil outline of the teacup and saucer, including a delicate, curving handle.

2 Go over the pencil outline with a waterproof pen, adding shading to the bottom right edges of the teacup and saucer, and then once the ink is dry, gently erase the pencil outline.

3 Use your smaller brush to fill in the whole teacup with a light layer of buff titanium, and then add shadows using buff titanium mixed with a hint of moonglow purple. It's important for this to dry completely before we add the floral details, so now is a great time to take a break and find a tasty snack!

4 Now let's add the beautiful, floral details! Mix up some concentrated manganese blue hue mixed with indigo, using a minimal amount of water so it's easier to control the movement of the paint. Add the scallops to the tops of the saucer and teacup, as well as the floral design on the teacup itself, and your teacup is ready to enjoy!

Magical Crystals

Any cottage witch will have a collection of beautiful rocks, tiny knickknacks, and magical crystals, so let's paint some beautiful amethyst to tuck away on a wooden trinket shelf. You can swap out amethyst for any color, shape, or type of crystal you enjoy, or perhaps a rock, acorn, or other trinket you've collected from a hike or fun adventure. It's always fun to add a personal touch to your shelf, and this is a great place to do it!

Colors Used

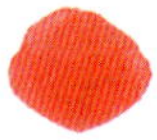

Quinacridone coral

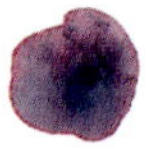

Moonglow purple

1

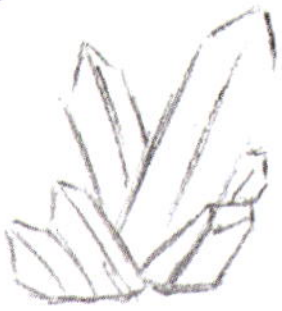

2

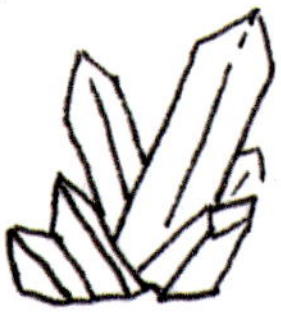

3

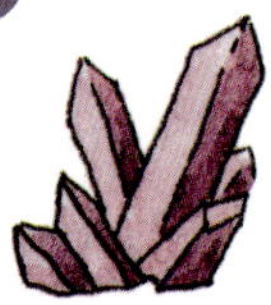

1 Sketch a series of very light lines starting from a small base area—these will help guide the placement of the crystal section. Now draw three lines that come together in a point, using the light lines as a guide for the positioning of each crystal section.

2 Starting with whichever crystal section is in the front, outline each piece using your waterproof pen. Once the ink is dry, gently erase the pencil layer.

3 Using your smaller brush and a light mixture of quinacridone coral and moonglow purple, fill in each section of the crystal. Let that dry for a bit, and then use a mixture with more moonglow purple to add shading towards the right face of each section, adding more shading near the base where all the pieces overlap. Build up the shading until your crystals look luminous, and you're done!

Tiny House for Fairy Visitors

The cottage witch will, of course, make many fairy friends on her travels, and it's important for them to have a cozy place to sleep when they visit. Let's paint a tiny house for fairy visitors, which can be tucked away on the wooden trinket shelf when it's not needed or placed in the sunniest spot on the windowsill when the fairies come. You can make the fairy house as large and complicated or as small and simple as you'd like. You could paint a fairy mansion with lots of tiny windows, and swap that out for one of the larger items on the shelf, or keep it here as a whimsical, hidden detail—whatever suits your fancy!

Colors Used

Burnt sienna
Manganese blue hue
Indigo
Cadmium yellow deep hue
Naples yellow
German greenish raw umber

1
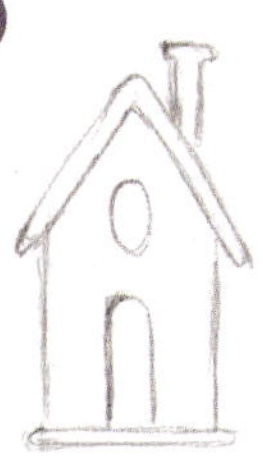

2
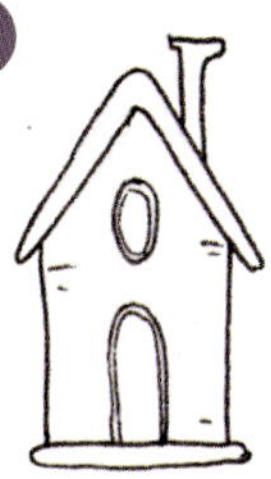

3
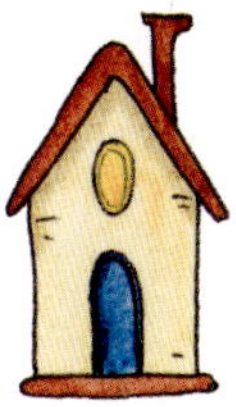

1 Lightly draw the outline of a house with a gently sloping roof, a front door, and a whimsical round window to let in some light.

2 Go over your pencil outline with a waterproof pen, adding some light shading and any additional details you'd like to see.

3 Use your smaller brush to add burnt sienna to the roof and base of the house, and then use manganese blue hue mixed with a smidge of indigo to fill in the door, adding a bit of wood-grain texture by building up the color. Pop in a bit of burnt sienna for the chimney bricks, fill in the window with cadmium yellow deep hue, and then take a minute to let everything dry before adding Naples yellow to the front of the house. While that's still wet, add a light layer of German greenish raw umber just under the roofline to make a shadow, and your fairy house is ready for visitors!

Romantic Paperback Books

After a long day traipsing through the woods or gathering flowers in the garden, the cottage witch can curl up with a romantic paperback book to read with a cup of tea. It's important to have a selection of books, since you never quite know what you'll be in the mood to read, so let's give the cottage witch an assortment of little books with lots of fun colors! If you'd like to add more itty-bitty details, you can add titles to some or all of the books—perhaps favorite books you've read or names of pets or beloved friends.

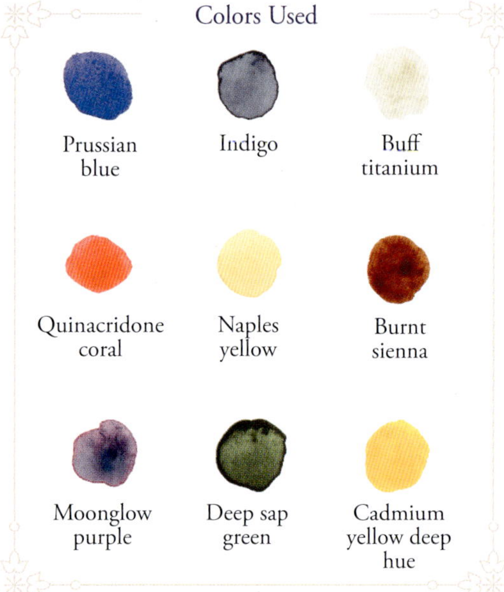

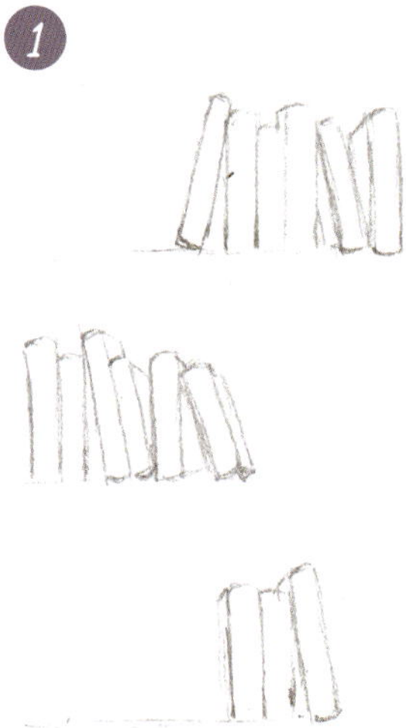

1 The first step, of course, is to decide where you'd like to place the books. For Assembling Your Cottage Witchery Shelf (page 84), they're on the wooden trinket shelf; however, they'd also look charming as a precariously towering stack or nestled between other objects on the shelf. Once you know where you'd like the books, draw a series of rectangles with rounded edges, making the arrangements as neat or as messy as you'd like.

2

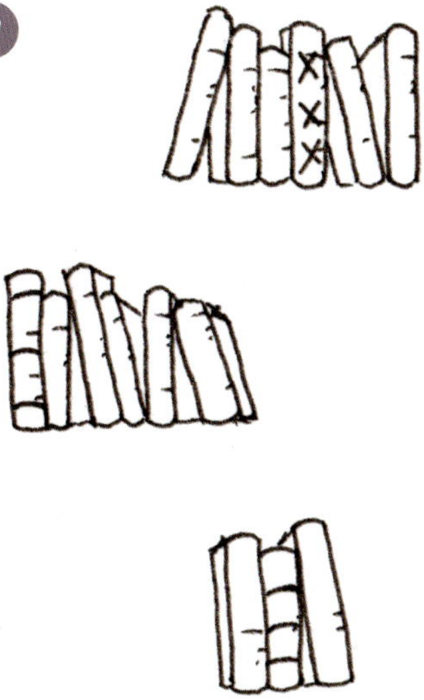

3

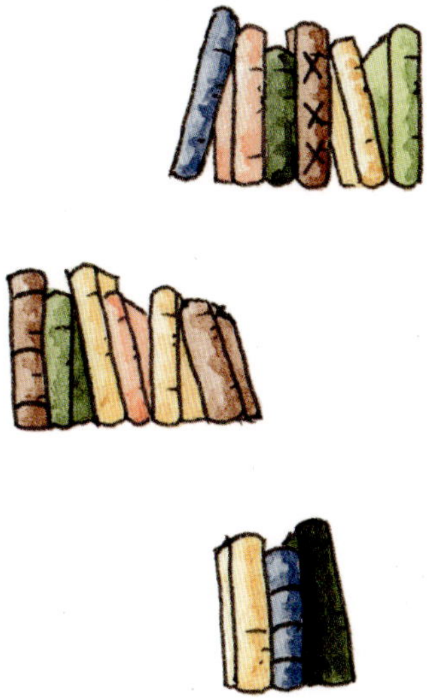

2 Using your waterproof pen, go over your pencil outline, adding some shading on the right edges of the book spines as you go. You can also add some decorations to the spines of the books in this step (as I've shown here), or you can use paint later on. Once the ink is dry, gently erase the pencil layer.

3 Let's color in the books! If you'd like the books to blend into the shelf (or whatever you've chosen to put near them), use slightly more muted colors. If you'd like them to stand out and be a focal point, you can use brighter colors with more contrast. For each book, use your smaller brush to add a single layer of color over the whole thing, and then add shadows along the right side with either a second layer of that color or a darker color made by adding a touch of Prussian blue or moonglow purple, whichever you prefer. For the blue books, mix together Prussian blue, indigo, and buff titanium. For the pink books, mix quinacridone coral, Naples yellow, and buff titanium. For the brown books, mix burnt sienna and moonglow purple with buff titanium. For the green books, use a combination of deep sap green, Naples yellow, buff titanium, and cadmium yellow deep hue to make a range of muted greens. And finally, for the yellow books, use Naples yellow mixed with a small amount of burnt sienna. Now your books are ready to be enjoyed—I wonder what stories you'll find!

The Cottage Witchery Shelf

We need a shelf to place all the beautiful items for our cottage witch, and this rustic, whimsical one is the perfect match! With its charming floral design contrasting with the darker wood color on top, it makes a nice complement to any arrangement of witchy items that suit your fancy! I love tinkering with the designs on each shelf. For example, the brackets and shelves add so much personality to the overall design that they're a wonderful place to add little details and pops of color—all of which are important to consider when deciding on the overall color balance of your painting. If you choose a dark color for a shelf, you may want to consider including some lighter-colored items on top, or if you have a very light-colored shelf, you may want some darker items resting on it for some nice contrast.

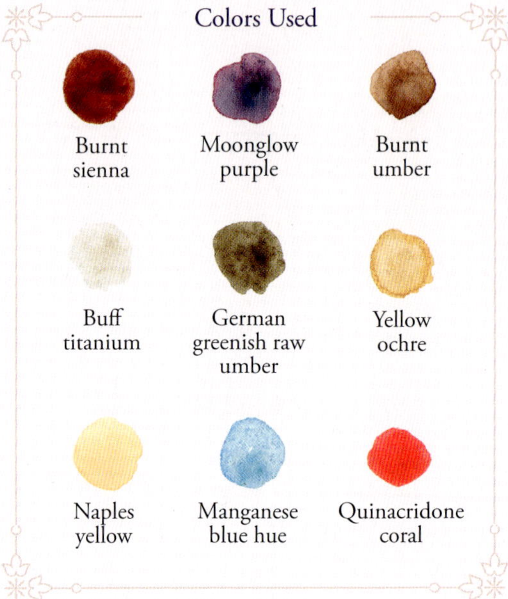

1

1 Outline the horizontal shelf, adding a rustic edge on both ends by drawing an almost stair-step shape to indicate rough wood. Then sketch in the brackets, starting with the vertical center beams, and then add the curving side pieces. Next, draw two triangles inside each bracket, with the edges curving to fit within the brackets. Then carefully draw swooping lines and circles inside those triangles, with whatever level of symmetry and detail you'd like to give the impression of a hand-painted floral design. We're now ready for the next step!

2

3

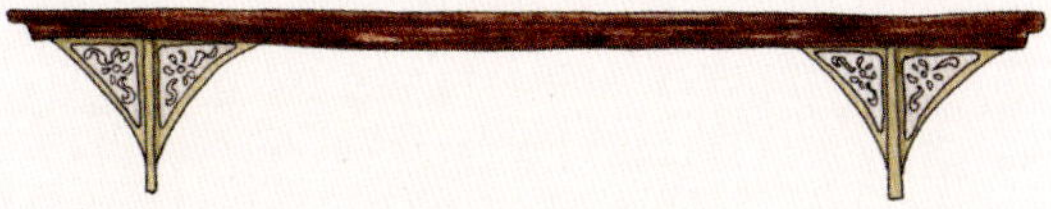

4

2 Before you add ink, it's important to draw the rest of your items, since some of them will overlap with the shelf, covering up sections of it, and you don't want the shelf to show up behind those items! Once you know which sections to leave empty, use your waterproof pen to outline the shelf. Then add the outlines of the floral designs on the shelf supports, keeping them loose and organic or detailed and symmetrical, depending on your preference. Once the ink is dry, gently erase the underlying pencil sketch, and let's start painting!

3 Using your larger brush, build up several layers of a combination of burnt sienna, moonglow purple, and burnt umber to achieve a wood-grain texture with a deep color. It'll help to let it dry between layers so you can alternate shelf layers with working on the brackets. Go over the parts of the brackets outside the triangles with buff titanium mixed with a hint of German greenish raw umber and yellow ochre, and then fill in around the floral design inside the triangles with buff titanium. Add a light layer of German greenish raw umber to make shadows on the brackets. Let this layer dry completely, and then it's time for the floral design!

4 Using your smaller brush, fill in the center circle and the petals on each bracket with Naples yellow, and then use manganese blue hue in the smaller curls. On the longer ribbons, use a mixture of quinacridone coral and burnt sienna, and add additional layers of each color as needed. Now your cottage witch's shelf is ready for all sorts of magical items!

Assembling Your Cottage Witchery Shelf

All right, let's put all our new items together and make the cottage witch's shelf come alive! As always, the exact arrangement of the items and the order in which they're painted is just a guideline—mix and match between the shelves, add items of your own, rearrange, color left to right . . . do whatever makes the most sense to you and enjoy the process!

Colors Used for the Background

Quinacridone coral

Buff titanium

1

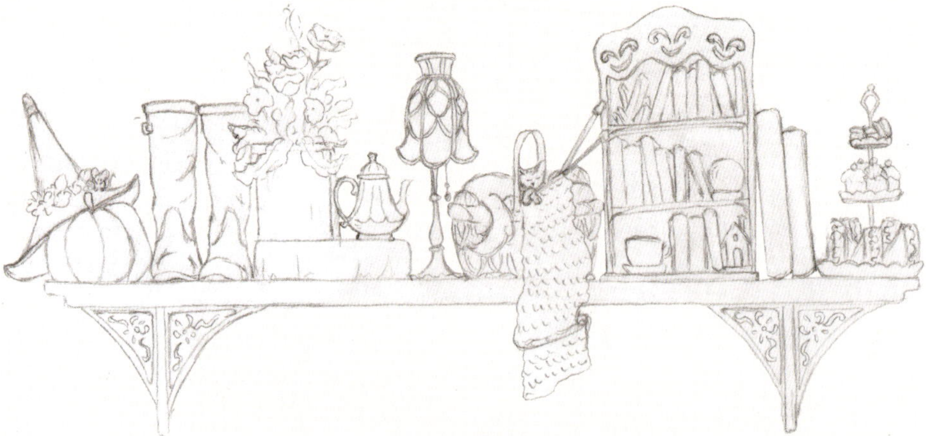

1 Start with a pencil outline for the shelf, and then gently mark the edges where you'll place each item on the shelf. I find this to be helpful, since it ensures you've allocated sufficient space for each item—you don't want half the desserts falling off the edge because another item ended up being too wide! Refer to The Cottage Witchery Shelf (page 82) for tips on sketching the shelf, and refer to each project's tutorial for details on sketching each item.

2

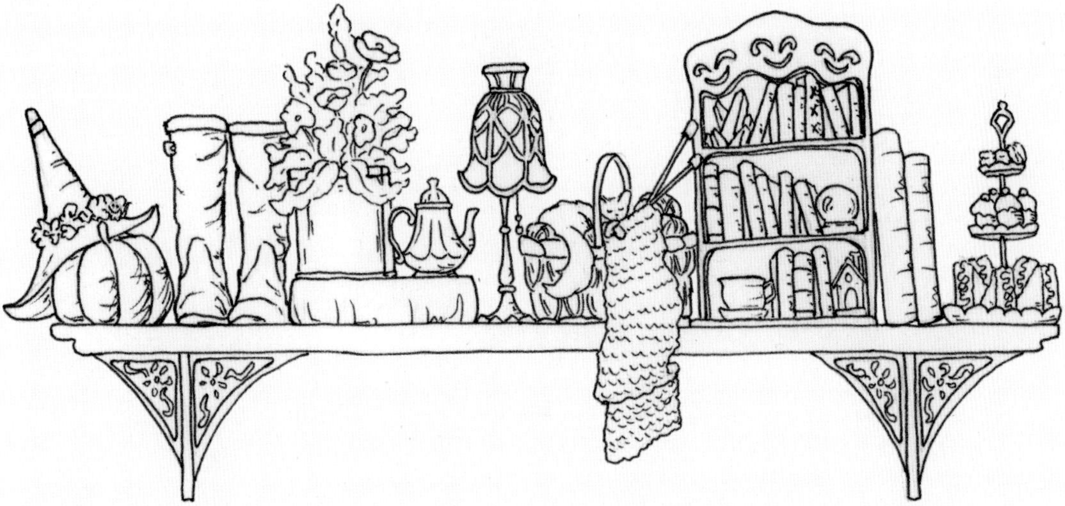

2 Now let's add the ink with your waterproof pen so we can get started painting! It's easy to add ink to an area that's actually covered by another item, and we'd like to avoid that! So let's start off with the Cozy Witch's Hat (page 66), Magical Springtime Flowers in a Tea Tin (page 62), Cat Napping with Spelled Knitting (page 60), and Wooden Trinket Shelf (page 76) first, referring to each project's instructions if you need a bit more detail. Now, carefully fill in the outline for the shelf, being very careful not to draw through the outline of the scarf that drapes over the shelf. Add ink to the brackets and the remaining items. Once the ink is dry, gently erase the pencil layer. It's time to start painting!

3

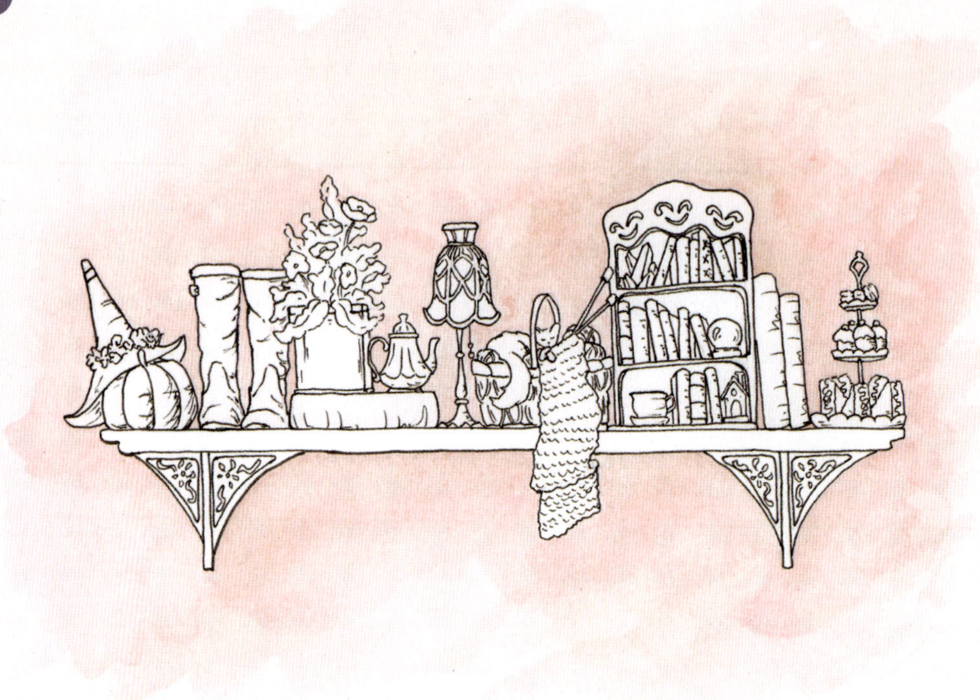

3 Before we paint all the items on the shelf, we can add a colored background, although it's totally optional—your shelf will look amazing either way! Begin by using a relatively small brush dipped in clean water to trace just outside all your ink lines—we want the colored background to go just up to, and not into, the items, so it's important to be very careful here. Next, use a larger brush, if you have one, to add some water to however large of an area you'd like to cover in the background color. Now, mix together quinacridone coral and buff titanium (if you want to match the color in the finished project example) to make a very, very light pink, and carefully build up several layers of that in the dampened area. Keep an eye on the background as it dries, since watercolor washes can sometimes end up with odd-looking edges. If you see the background drying with lines near the ink outlines, take a very slightly damp brush and gently dab the line to re-blend it with the rest of the background. Once your background color is completely dry, we can start on the shelf!

4

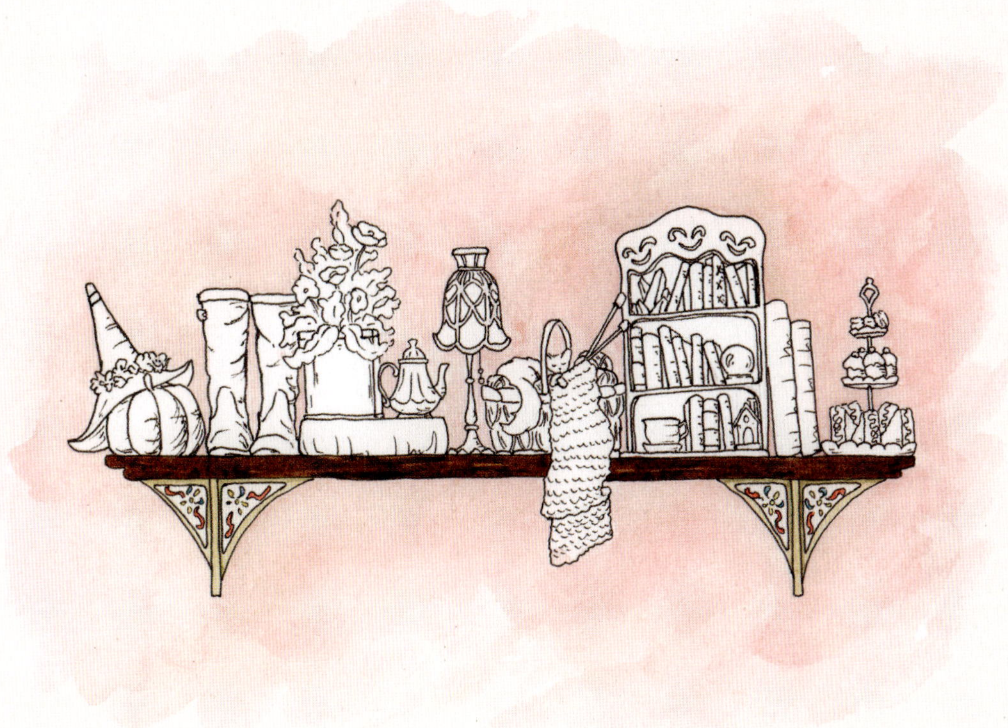

4 In general, it's a good idea to paint background to foreground, so we'll start off with the items farthest back on the shelf and finish with things closer to the front. The exception to this is the actual shelf, which is the first thing we'll paint so we can make sure all the other colors match it. Refer to The Cottage Witchery Shelf (page 82) for instructions, and add some beautiful wood and bright floral motifs to your shelf. Congratulations! It looks awesome already. Let's now move onto all the items!

5

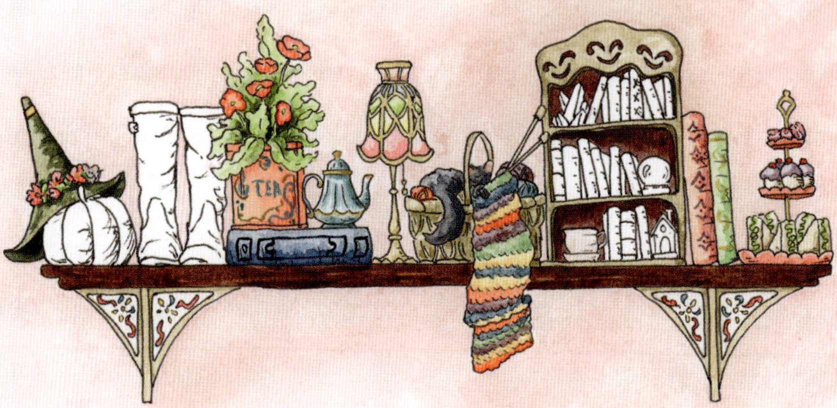

5 This step might feel like a lot, but you can swap between items as the various layers of paint dry, and you'll be done before you know it! If you're right-handed, it can be helpful to paint left-to-right to avoid smudging wet paint, or you can paint in the opposite direction if you're left-handed. Start off with the Cozy Witch's Hat (page 66), Clever Mouse Hiding from the Cat (page 73), Magical Springtime Flowers in a Tea Tin (page 62), Delicate China Teapot (page 72), Books of Magic Spells and Recipes (page 74), Cozy Stained-Glass Lamp (page 64), Cat Napping with Spelled Knitting (page 60), Wooden Trinket Shelf (page 76), and Three-Tier Tower of Treats (page 68).

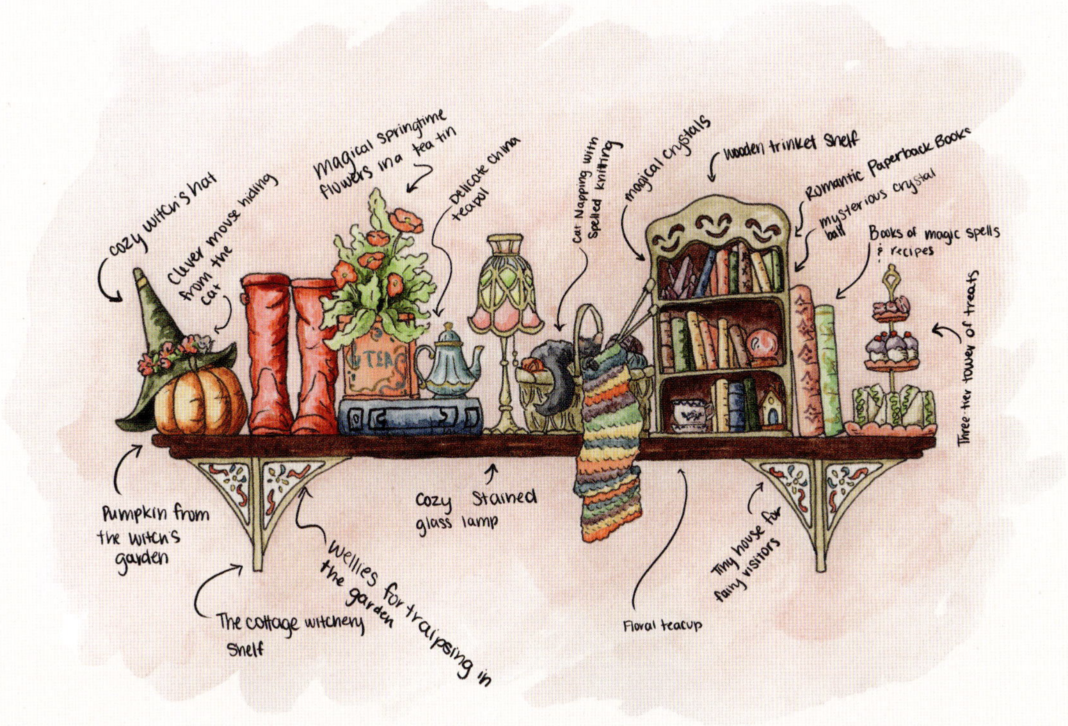

6 Almost there! Now that the items in front have dried, paint the Pumpkin from the Witch's Garden (page 65), Wellies for Traipsing in the Garden (page 71), Magical Crystals (page 78), Romantic Paperback Books (page 80), Mysterious Crystal Ball (page 70), Floral Teacup (page 77), and Tiny House for Fairy Visitors (page 79). And there you have it, a cozy cottage witch's shelf full of whimsical, magical items!

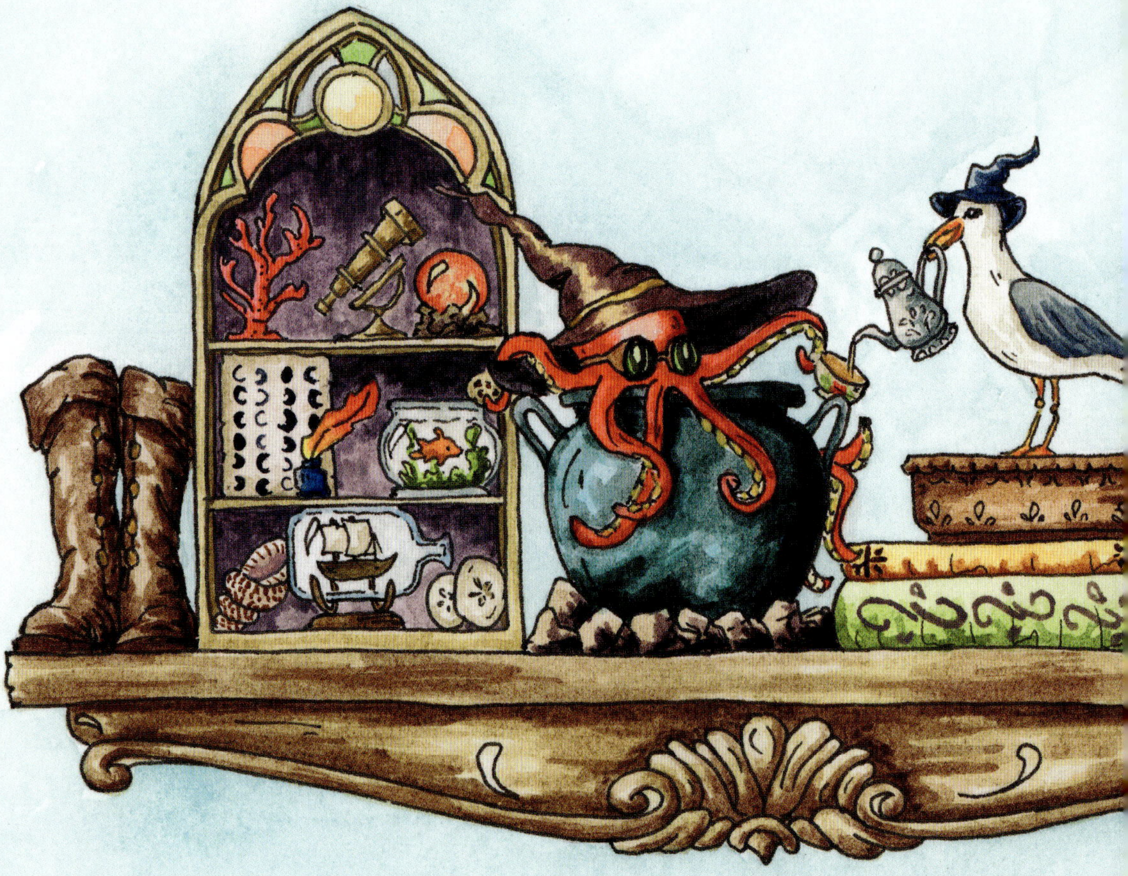

Sea Witchery

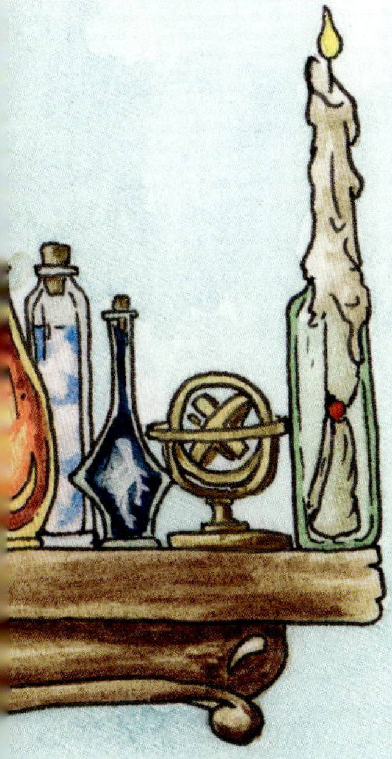

The sea witch's shelf is full of treasures and mysterious trinkets collected while exploring the charming towns dotted along the coastline and endless beaches where you can always find seashells and friendly crabs to chat with. With the bottled weather spells you'll find on this shelf, you can always go for a walk in whatever weather best suits your mood, accompanied by an octopus familiar and a distinguished seagull who can generally be found enjoying a cup of tea with cookies and gossiping about the goings-on of the local wildlife. This shelf has so many fun details and interesting items, and I'm sure you're going to love painting it!

Octopus Familiar in a Magical Cauldron

A delightfully chatty companion, this octopus familiar in a magical cauldron is so much fun to paint, and you can easily swap out the colors for your favorites. You can also add flowers or other trinkets to the hat or include things that remind you of days spent walking along the beach and watching the waves.

Colors Used

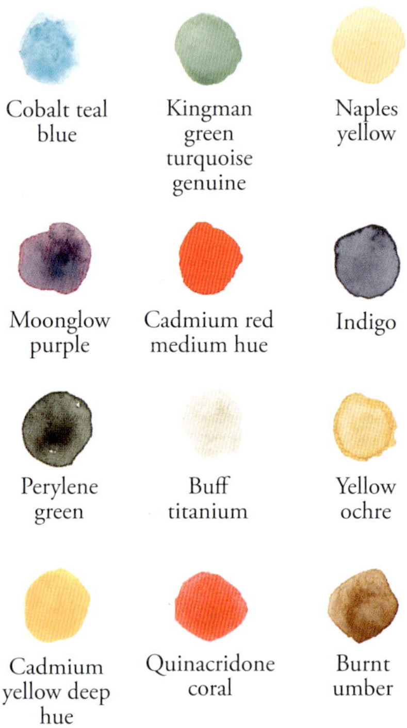

1

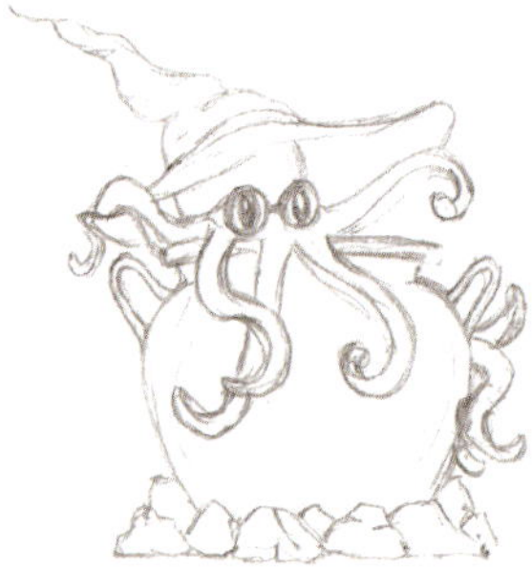

2

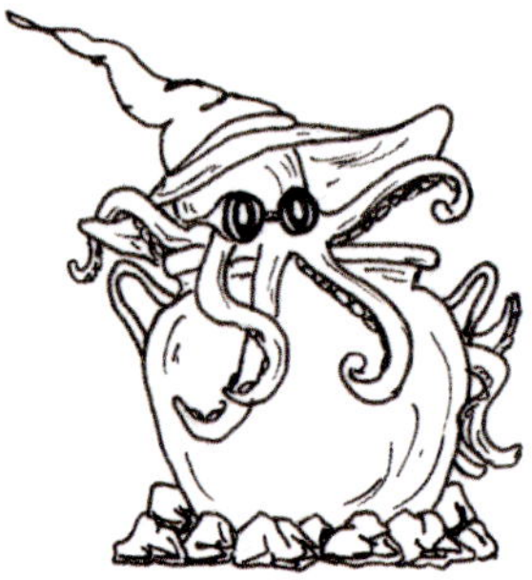

1 Sketch an oval for the cauldron, and then draw the octopus, double-checking to make sure you've got the correct number of arms. Finally, add the rocks, hat, and goggles.

2 Carefully go over your pencil sketch with a waterproof pen, adding shading to the underside of the hat and where you'll find shadows on the cauldron from the octopus's arms. Once the ink is dry, gently erase the pencil layer.

3

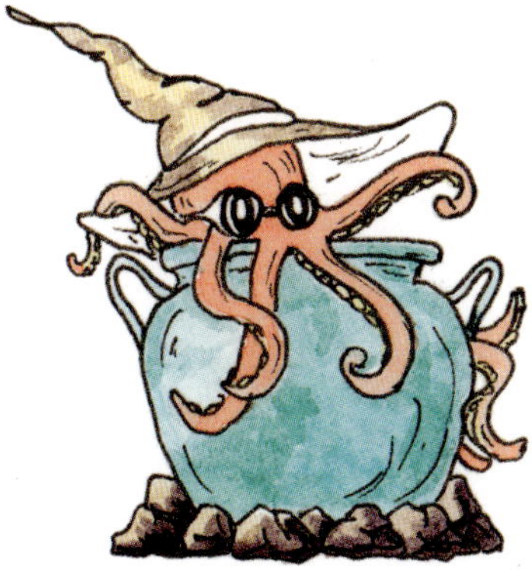

4

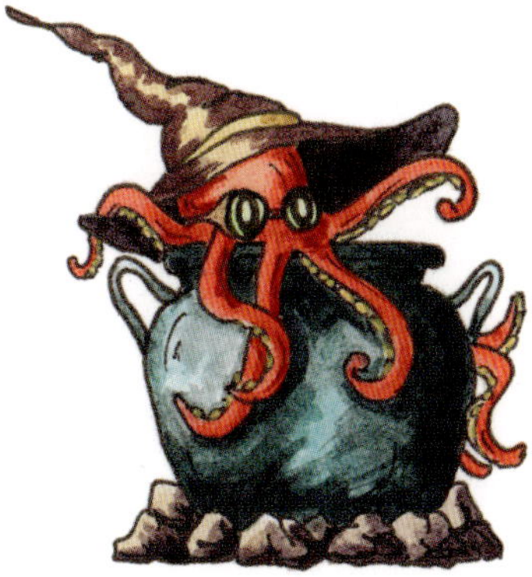

3 Using your larger brush, go over the whole cauldron with a combination of cobalt teal blue and Kingman green turquoise genuine, building up several layers to begin the shadows. Fill in the rocks with Naples yellow combined with moonglow purple, again building up shadows on the lower right side of each rock. Go over the outside of the whole hat (other than the band in the middle) with a light layer of Naples yellow. Then, leaving the middle of the hat with just that yellow, add a mixture of moonglow purple and Naples yellow to the edges of the hat to lay down the first blocks of color. Go over the whole octopus with a light layer of Naples yellow on the inside of the arms and Naples yellow mixed with cadmium red medium hue on the rest of the octopus (other than the goggles and eyes).

4 Now let's add all the shadows using the same brush and see your painting come to life! You'll build up successive layers of each shadow color until you're happy with the contrast, so let's start with cobalt teal blue and Kingman green turquoise genuine mixed with increasing amounts of indigo and perylene green for the cauldron and moonglow purple for the rocks. Then use moonglow purple mixed with cadmium red medium hue and the tiniest amount of buff titanium to add shadows to the hat and yellow ochre to fill in the band. Mix together moonglow purple and perylene green and build up a few layers of that deep shadow color on the underside of the hat's brim, making the darkest area by the octopus's face for some nice contrast. Fill in the octopus's eyes with cadmium yellow deep hue mixed with Kingman green turquoise genuine. Then add layers of cadmium red medium hue mixed with quinacridone coral to the body of the octopus. Add shadows to the arms with just a hint of indigo or moonglow purple combined with the cadmium red medium hue. Build up several layers of Naples yellow combined with cadmium yellow deep hue on the underside of the arms, adding a tiny hint of moonglow purple if you want some darker shadows. Using your smaller brush, add burnt umber mixed with Naples yellow to the goggles. Go back and add more shadows if needed, and your octopus familiar in a magical cauldron is done!

Distinguished Seagull with a Witch's Hat

While the octopus familiar is wise and steady, the seagull with a witch's hat has quite a tendency to get into trouble, generally in the pursuit of French fries and ice cream cones. The seagull does make an excellent cup of tea though and is great at grabbing items off high shelves, so you don't have to climb up to reach them. The seagull's jaunty hat adds lots of personality to the bird, but you can also add a scarf or sweater to liven things up even more!

Colors Used

- Buff titanium
- German greenish raw umber
- Prussian blue
- Indigo
- Naples yellow
- Cadmium yellow deep hue
- Cadmium red medium hue

1

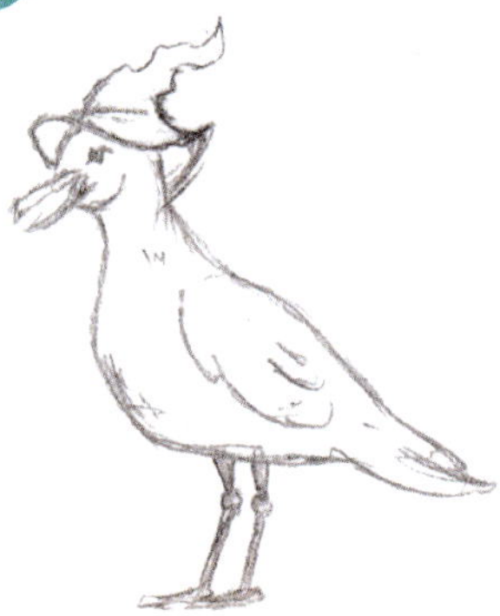

1 Sketch the shape of the seagull, beginning with the body, and then adding the head and feet. Then sketch the witch hat, adjusting the size and shape however you'd like. Should your seagull have an enormous, floppy brimmed hat with seaweed draping off the edges, or a smaller, demure hat so the seagull can see better while causing mischief?

2

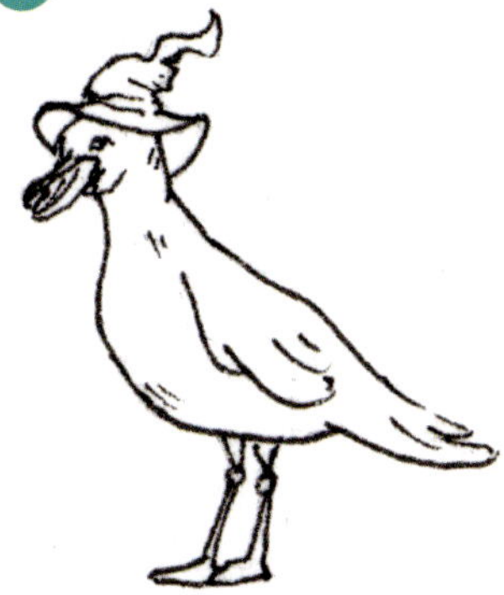

3

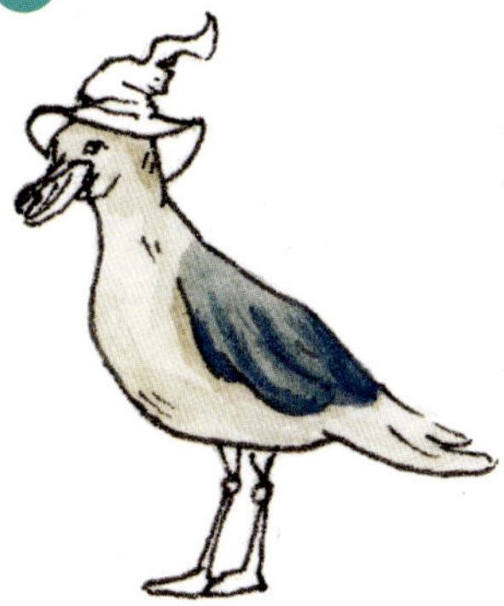

4

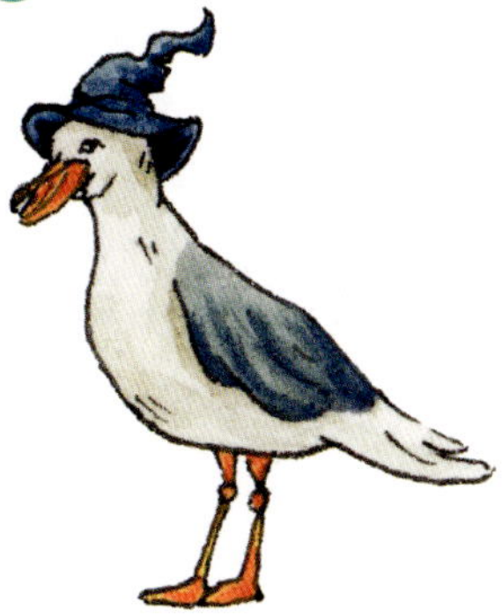

2 If you've chosen to draw the seagull holding a teapot, like the example shown at the beginning of this chapter (page 90), make note of where the teapot's handle will overlap with the seagull's beak—we don't want to add ink to those spots since they'll be covered by the handle. Go over the pencil sketch with your waterproof pen, adding some extra lines for shading and to give the impression of feathers. Once the ink is dry, gently erase the pencil layer.

3 Using your larger brush, go over the whole seagull with buff titanium, adding German greenish raw umber to make some gentle shadows on the white feathers. Use buff titanium mixed with teeny, tiny amounts of Prussian blue and indigo to fill in the wings, building up several layers to make shadows and the shapes of the feathers.

4 Use your smaller brush to fill in the beak and legs with Naples yellow combined with cadmium yellow deep hue and cadmium red medium hue. Then use Prussian blue combined with buff titanium and indigo for the hat, building up several layers with increasing quantities of indigo to make shadows, and then use a bit of pure indigo to add the darkest shadows on the hat. Your seagull looks awesome and is ready to fly around causing all sorts of mischief!

Magical Ship in a Bottle

There's definitely something magical about tiny, intricate ships in glass bottles, and the sea witch has one tucked away on her shelves so she always has a boat handy in case she wants to go sailing. We'll be drawing a pirate ship in a bottle for this tutorial, but you can easily swap out the ship for any style that you prefer, or add a tiny skull and crossbones flag!

Colors Used

Buff titanium

Manganese blue hue

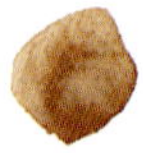

Burnt umber

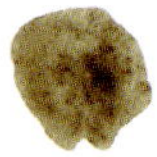

German greenish raw umber

1

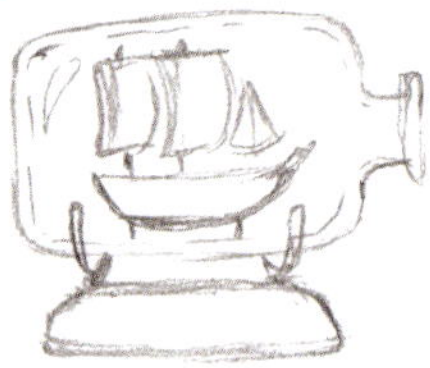

2

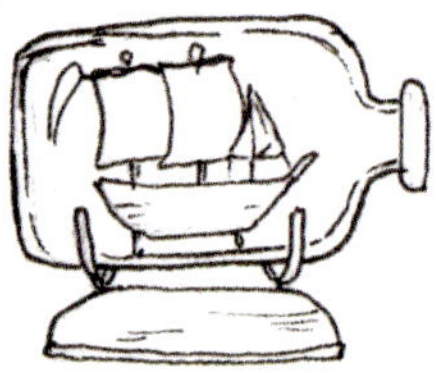

3

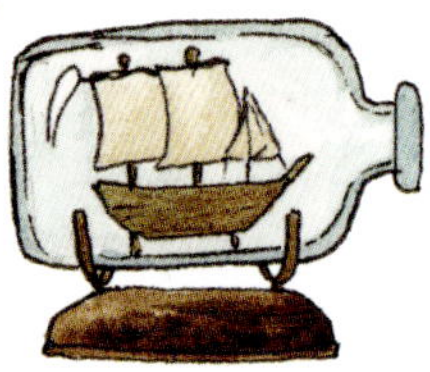

1 Begin your pencil sketch with an outline of the bottle. It can help to draw a horizontal line where you'd like the center of the bottle to be, so you can draw it symmetrically around the line. Add the stand and, of course, the ship. Start off by sketching the body of the ship, which will end up looking like a very squashed capital "D" with a pointy end, and then add two or three very light vertical lines for the masts. Sketch the sails, starting from the right and working to the left, since the sails in the front (on the right) will cover the ones in the back (towards the left).

2 Go over your pencil sketch with a waterproof pen, making sure to add some reflection lines in the glass and shading to the ship. Once the ink is dry, gently erase the pencil layer. Let's start painting!

3 Fill in the whole bottle (except for the ship), with a very light layer of buff titanium combined with manganese blue hue. While that dries, use your smaller brush to build up several layers of burnt umber combined with German greenish raw umber on the stand, painting with small strokes to make a wood-grain texture. Now that the first layer of "glass" is dry, use your smaller brush and a mixture with a bit more manganese blue hue to fill in the areas at the edges where the glass will be darker to give it a more three-dimensional look. Use buff titanium to fill in the sails and German greenish raw umber to fill the body of the ship. Add shadows to the sails with a hint of German greenish raw umber and to the ship with a bit of burnt umber, and you're ready to sail away!

Enchanted Spellbooks

The sea witch needs books not only to reference spells and tide tables, but also to read on stormy afternoons and late into the night. These colorful books are enchanted so that, when you open them, you'll be able to read any book you want. When you're done, just close the book and re-open it to see what's next! The designs on the books are always one of my favorite parts of painting a shelf, and they're a fun place to incorporate thematic elements or details. Also remember that you can add real titles from your favorite books or designs that remind you of your favorite things!

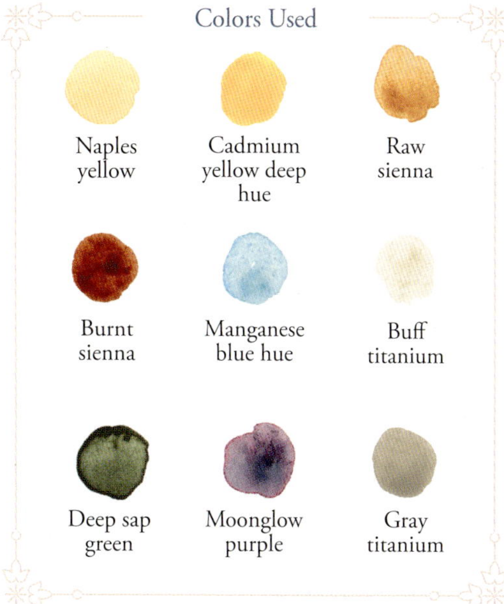

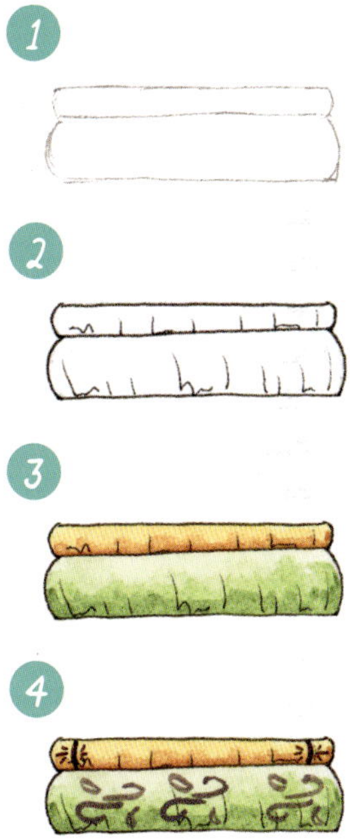

1. Lightly draw two rectangles with rounded sides. You can adjust the size, number, and placement of books to accommodate any arrangement of items on your shelf.

2. Trace your pencil outline with a waterproof pen, adding curved lines near the bottom edges to make shadows. Once the ink is dry, gently erase the pencil layer.

3. Using your larger brush, fill in the upper book with Naples yellow combined with cadmium yellow deep hue and raw sienna. Then build up several layers of raw sienna with increasing quantities of burnt sienna along the lower edge to make the shadows cast by the spine of the book. Once that's dry, fill in the lower book with cadmium yellow deep hue combined with manganese blue hue and buff titanium, and build up shadows with increasing amounts of manganese blue hue with the tiniest bit of deep sap green. Let dry completely.

4. Using concentrated moonglow purple, with your smallest brush, add a decorative design to the upper book. Mix moonglow purple with gray titanium, and decorate the lower book. Happy reading!

Sturdy Boots for Seaside Adventures

The sea witch needs a pair of sturdy boots for seaside adventures since it's important for one's feet to stay warm and dry while hiking and traipsing through the surf. These boots can be as worn or shiny as you like, and you can add some color or a fun design on the buttons!

Colors Used

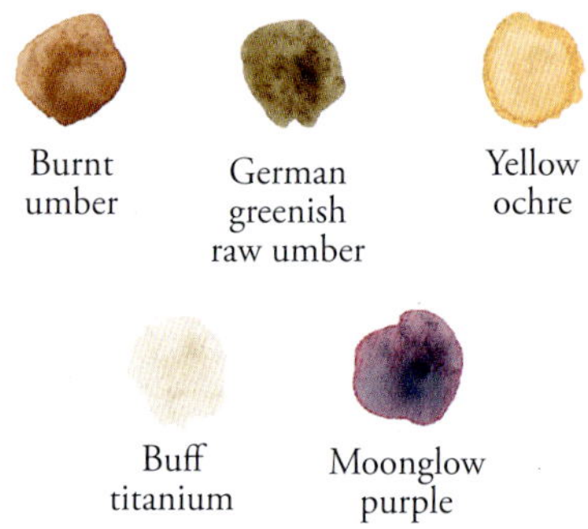

1

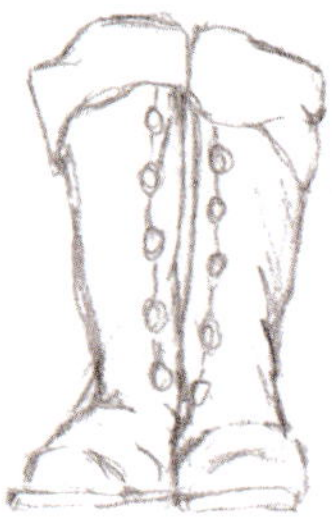

2

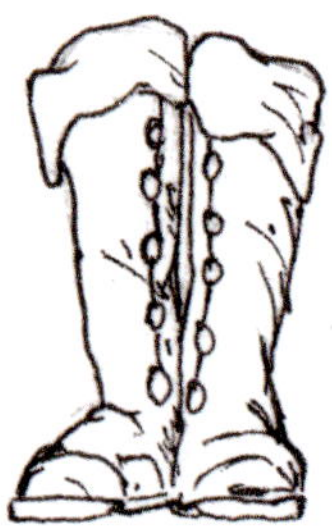

3

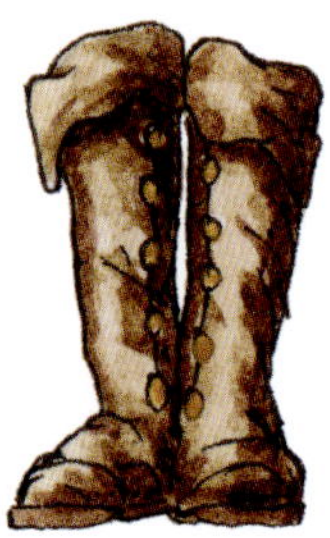

1 Use your pencil to draw the outline of the boots, adding extra wrinkles in the leather if you'd like them to look more worn. Add some oblong circles for buttons, and we're ready for the next step!

2 Use your waterproof pen to go over the pencil outline, adding shading to accentuate the folds and rounded shapes in the boots. Once the ink is dry, gently erase the pencil layer.

3 Using your larger brush, fill in the boots (except for the buttons) with a mixture of burnt umber, German greenish raw umber, yellow ochre, buff titanium, and the tiniest bit of moonglow purple. Slowly build up layers of shadows with increasing amounts of burnt umber, German greenish raw umber, and moonglow purple until you're happy with the shape and contrast. For the final detail, use yellow ochre and your smaller brush to fill in the gold buttons for a little pop of color. It can be helpful to wait a few minutes for the current layer of paint to dry before adding the next one when building up shadows, since it helps the new layer to not blend into the prior one and gives your eyes a break from staring at one project for too long. Now your boots are ready for endless seaside adventures; where will you go first?

Fishbowl with a Brightly Colored Fish

The octopus familiar and distinguished seagull need a friend, so let's paint a fishbowl with a brightly colored fish to keep them company! Depending on how you choose to arrange your shelf, you can turn the fishbowl into a larger tank full of all sorts of tropical fish, sea monsters, or whatever suits your fancy! (Check out vintage fish tank designs for inspiration—there are some spectacular ones!)

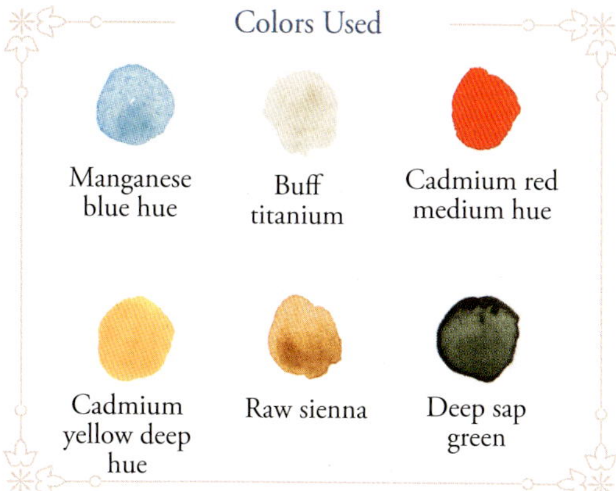

1

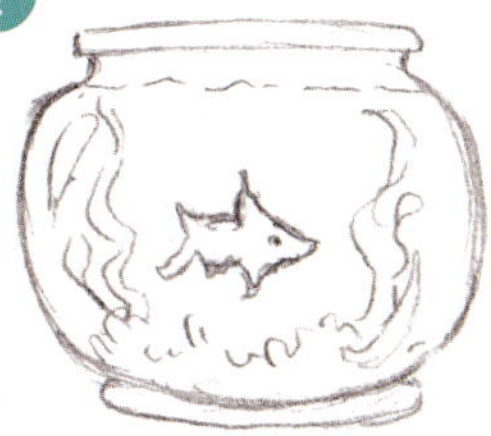

2

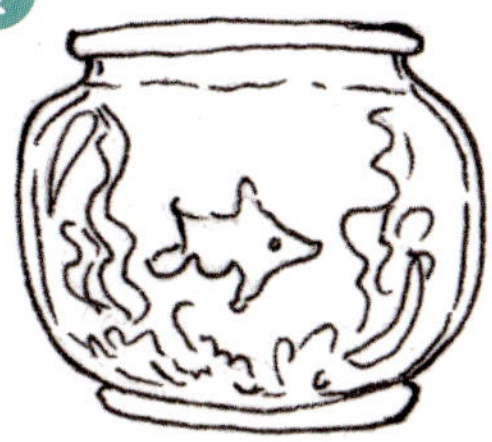

3

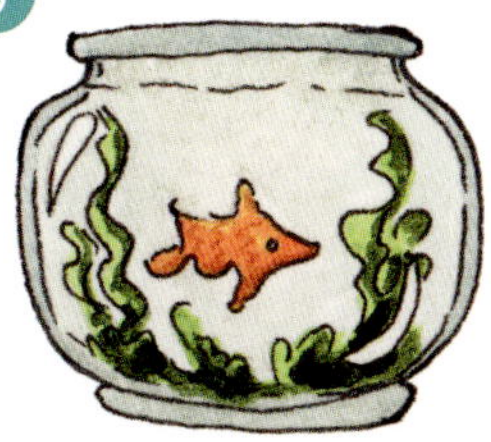

1 Gently sketch a pencil outline for your fishbowl, and then add some foliage and a happy little fish.

2 Go over your pencil outline with your waterproof pen, adding a gently curving line near the top to be the waterline in the fishbowl, teardrop shapes or lines for light reflecting on the glass, and texture on the fish and foliage. Once the ink is dry, gently erase the pencil layer.

3 Using your larger brush, fill in the glass for the fishbowl with manganese blue hue mixed with buff titanium. Then add additional buff titanium to that mixture for the water, avoiding the fish, foliage, and reflections. Let that dry, and then switch to your smaller brush and fill in the fish with cadmium red medium hue combined with cadmium yellow deep hue, adding shadows and scales with raw sienna. Then mix manganese blue hue and cadmium yellow deep hue and fill in the foliage, making shadows with deep sap green, so your fish can swim happily amongst the greenery!

Bottled Weather Spells

You never know when your afternoon plans might call for a colorful sunset, billowing clouds in a blue sky, or a ferocious thunderstorm, but with potion bottles full of weather spells, you'll always be prepared! These bottles are definitely an exercise in patience—you'll want to work slowly and keep your brush fairly dry to keep the details from blending together. The bottles may look a bit odd right up until you add the darkest layers at the end of each one, but I promise that the payoff is worth it!

Colors Used

- German greenish raw umber
- Naples yellow
- Cadmium yellow deep hue
- Manganese blue hue
- Buff titanium
- Cobalt teal blue
- Quinacridone coral
- Titanium white
- Moonglow purple
- Prussian blue
- Indigo

1

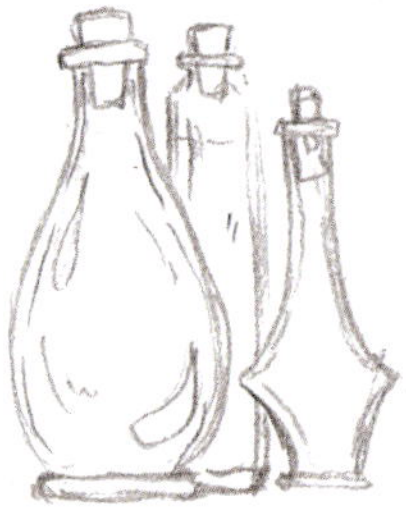

2

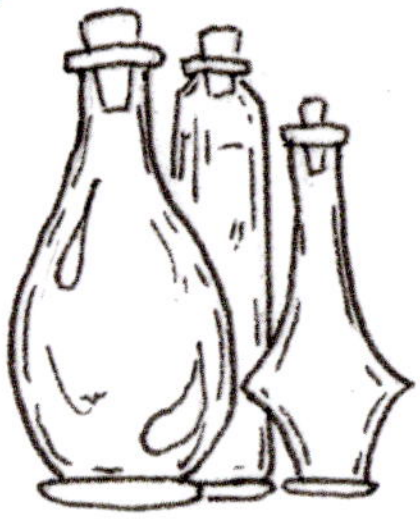

1 Using a pencil, lightly sketch the outlines of your potion bottles, varying the sizes and shapes to suit your taste.

2 Go over your pencil outlines with a waterproof pen, adding reflections in the glass and shading near the edges of the bottles. Once the ink is dry, gently erase the pencil layer.

3

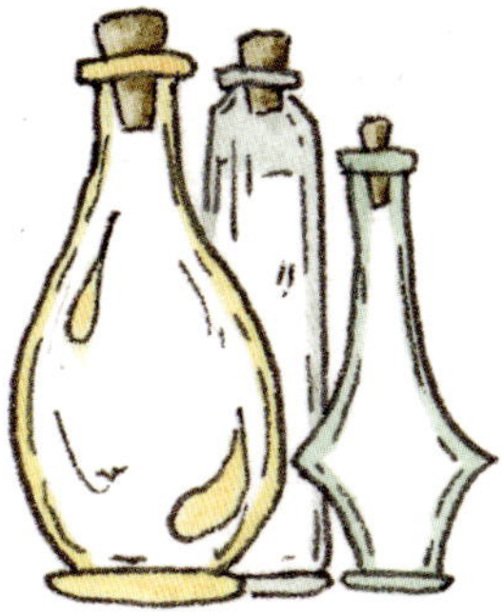

4

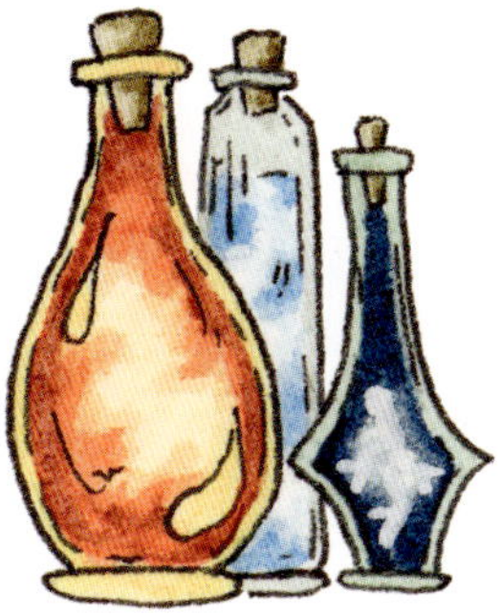

3 With your smaller brush, fill in all three corks with German greenish raw umber, building up several layers towards the right sides to make shadows. We'll paint a sunset potion in the left bottle, so let's fill in the glass bottle outline and the two teardrop-shaped reflections on the glass with Naples yellow combined with cadmium yellow deep hue. Fill in the outline and top portion of the center bottle with manganese blue hue mixed with buff titanium, and fill in the whole right bottle with a very (very) light layer of cobalt teal blue mixed with buff titanium and a teensy bit of cadmium yellow deep hue.

4 Let the bottles dry, and then we'll start off with the sunset potion. Fill in the whole interior of the bottle with a very light layer of Naples yellow mixed with cadmium yellow deep hue. Then, leaving a section of that light yellow untouched in the center, gently dab a circle of quinacridone coral, followed by quinacridone coral mixed with manganese blue hue near the edges to create the effect of a sunset coming from the center of the bottle. Use a slightly damp brush to blend the edges together, and add more cadmium yellow deep hue as needed to bring out the highlight in the center once it's dry.

For the blue sky potion, go over the whole interior of the bottle with a very small amount of water to avoid making any harsh edges, and then gently dab manganese blue hue to make the sky around some cloud shapes, leaving the white base color of the paper to form the clouds. Use titanium white (or white gouache) to add highlights to the clouds as needed, and gradually build up the manganese blue hue layers.

Finally, for the thunderstorm bottle, use some very watered-down cobalt teal blue mixed with a hint of cadmium yellow deep hue to fill in the whole bottle. Then build up layers of cobalt teal blue mixed with varying amounts of moonglow purple and Prussian blue going away from the center, finally including a smidge of indigo near the edges to make the darkest bits of the thunderstorm. Let that dry all the way, and then use some titanium white or white gouache to draw a lightning bolt in the center. If you don't have white paint, you can use your smallest brush and watered-down cobalt teal blue to very lightly outline the shape of a lightning bolt, and then fill in the area around the lightning with alternating sections of cobalt teal blue and cobalt teal blue mixed with a smidge of moonglow purple and Prussian blue. Then transition to using moonglow purple and Prussian blue mixed with indigo to fill in the rest of the bottle, blending the edges so there's a smooth transition from the lighter to darker clouds. Now you're ready for whatever weather you need!

Shelf with Stained-Glass Details

It's impossible to spend much time at the seaside without collecting an assortment of treasures, so our sea witch needs a shelf to display knickknacks and useful items. This shelf has stained-glass details with colors of a summer day at the beach, which will filter the light and make beautiful patterns on the objects on the shelf.

Colors Used

- Yellow ochre
- Buff titanium
- German greenish raw umber
- Moonglow purple
- Cadmium yellow deep hue
- Naples yellow
- Quinacridone coral
- Manganese blue hue

1

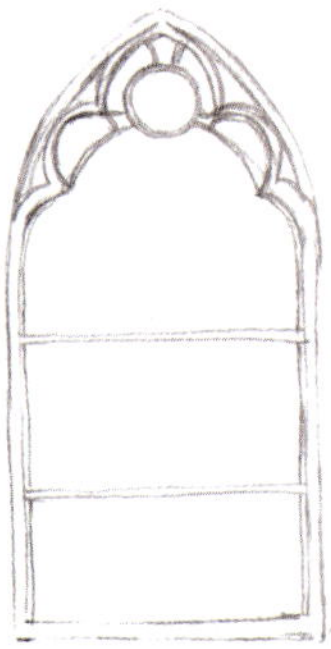

2

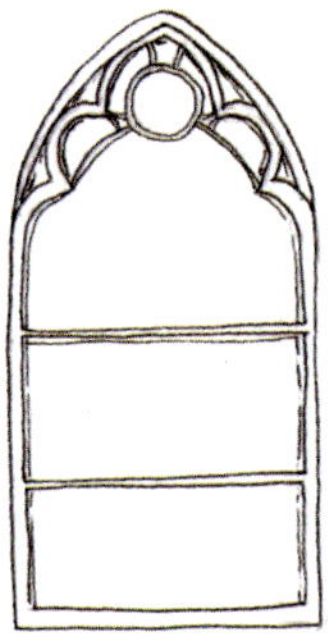

1. Sketch the pencil outline for your shelf, using a ruler if you want perfectly straight lines, and then add the details for the stained-glass shapes. It can be helpful to draw a center line and work out from that if you want the shelf to be symmetrical, but you should use whatever technique works best for you. Now is the time to decide on the placement of items on your shelf, especially if they're going to overlap with the structure of the shelf. You don't want to add ink or watercolor to the areas where you want to place items!
2. Go over your pencil outline with a waterproof pen. Be mindful of where the items on the shelf will be placed—don't add pen lines to those areas! Once the ink is dry, gently erase the pencil layer.

3

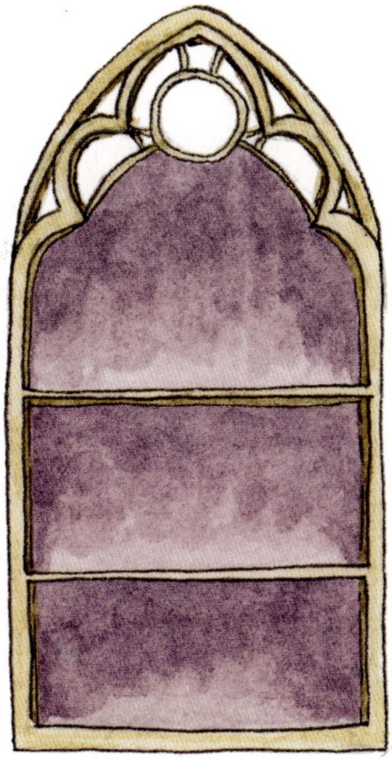

4

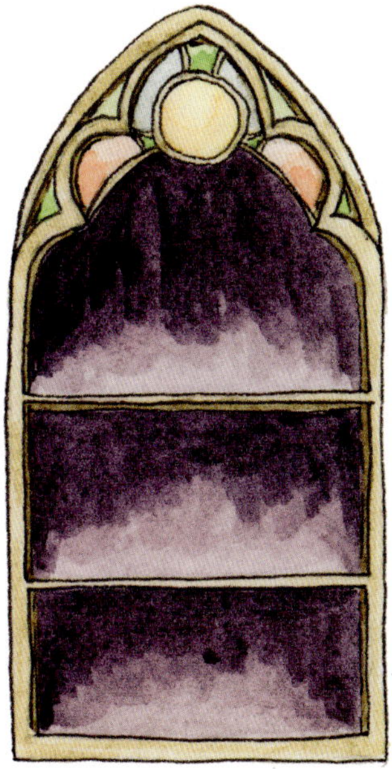

3 Using your smaller brush, fill in the wood portions of the shelf with a light mixture of yellow ochre, buff titanium, and German greenish raw umber, building up several layers to create shadows and a subtle wood grain. Make sure that layer is completely and totally dry, and then go over the interior sections of the shelf with a combination of moonglow purple and buff titanium, avoiding the areas where items will go, and build up the beginnings of shadows using additional moonglow purple.

4 Let's paint some stained glass! Fill in the center circle with cadmium yellow deep hue mixed with Naples yellow. Fill the semicircles with quinacridone coral mixed with Naples yellow. Paint the small arches on either side of the circle with manganese blue hue mixed with buff titanium. Paint the upper pair of arched triangles with manganese blue hue combined with cadmium yellow deep hue and buff titanium. Finally, paint the remaining five spaces with manganese blue hue and cadmium yellow deep hue. Using those same colors, add a second layer towards the lower right edge of each section to create shadows and texture on the glass. Now that the first layer on the interior of the shelf has dried, build up several more layers of moonglow purple as needed to achieve the level of shadow and contrast you'd like. Congratulations! Your shelf looks awesome!

Stargazing Telescope

A stargazing telescope is a staple of any sea witch's shelf, and this intricate, golden telescope is so fun to paint! If you'd like it to be a larger focus of the shelf, you can easily adjust its size, and you could even add a tripod stand. For a more lived-in look, you could add some seaweed draped around the telescope with a few seashells scattered about. If you enjoy bird-watching, you can add a tiny bird perched atop the telescope. There are so many options to incorporate things you love, so grab your art supplies and let's get started!

Colors Used

Yellow ochre | Buff titanium | German greenish raw umber

1

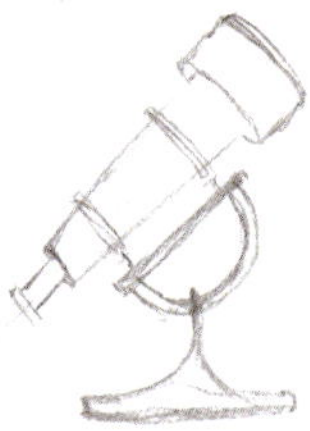

2

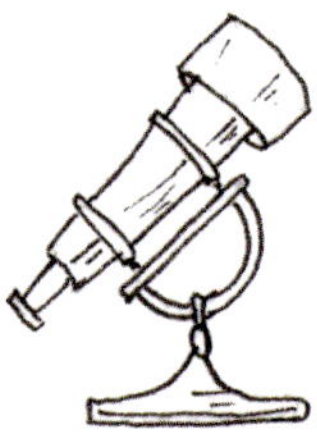

3

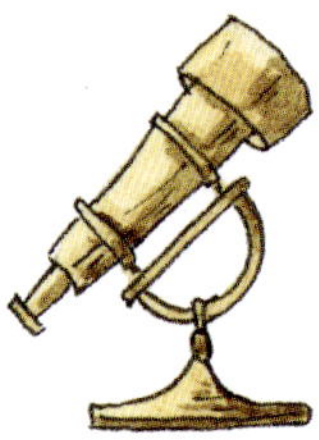

1. Start off your pencil sketch with a lightly drawn center line through the middle of the telescope, and then draw the telescope around that line. Add the stand and however much detail you'd like—you can make the stand and telescope as simple or as complicated as you'd like!
2. Trace your pencil outline with a waterproof pen, and then once the ink is dry, gently erase the underlying pencil.
3. You can use either brush for this, depending on how large your telescope is, but I'd recommend using your larger brush for the main part of the telescope and the smaller brush for the stand and tiniest details. Fill in the whole telescope with yellow ochre combined with a bit of buff titanium and German greenish raw umber, and then build up successive layers of German greenish raw umber and yellow ochre to create shadows and highlights until the telescope gleams. And that's it—you're ready to stargaze!

Warm and Gooey Chocolate Chip Cookie

There's nothing quite like a day at the beach to work up an appetite, especially an appetite for sweets! Let's paint a warm and gooey chocolate chip cookie that the octopus familiar can share with the brightly colored fish.

Colors Used

Yellow ochre

Buff titanium

German greenish raw umber

Burnt umber

1

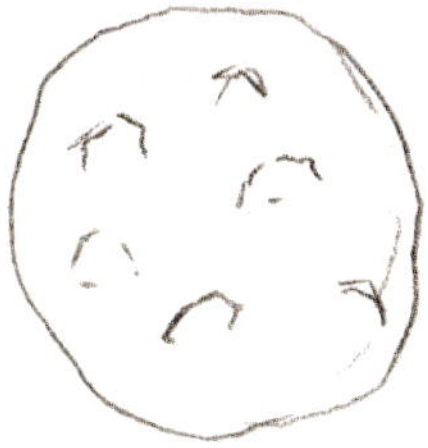

2

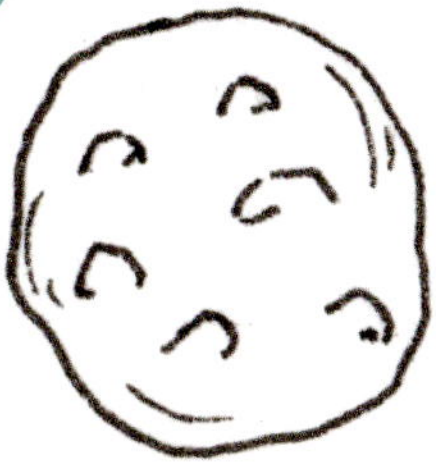

3

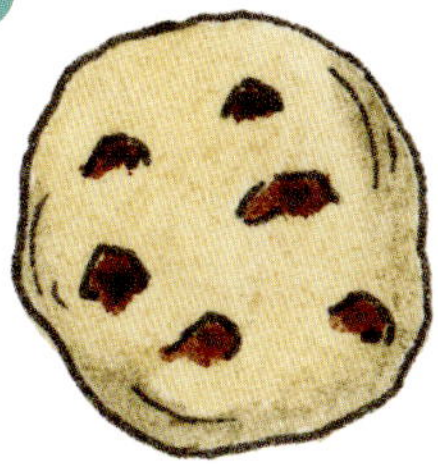

1 This one is nice and simple—use your pencil to draw a circle to make the outline of your cookie, and add some angles near the edges to indicate the gooey chocolate pieces.

2 Trace your pencil outline with a waterproof pen, and then once the ink is dry, gently erase the pencil.

3 Using your smaller brush, fill in the whole cookie with a light mixture of yellow ochre, buff titanium, and German greenish raw umber, building up shadows with additional German greenish raw umber. Give that a few minutes to dry, and then add burnt umber to the chocolate chips. Nice work! This cookie looks good enough to eat!

Enchanted Always-Warm Teacup

Our sea witch has a set of enchanted, always-warm teacups to take on long walks and to sip slowly from while reading books on the porch. It's always unfortunate to find a forgotten cup of cold tea, but with these beautiful teacups, you'll never have to worry about that!

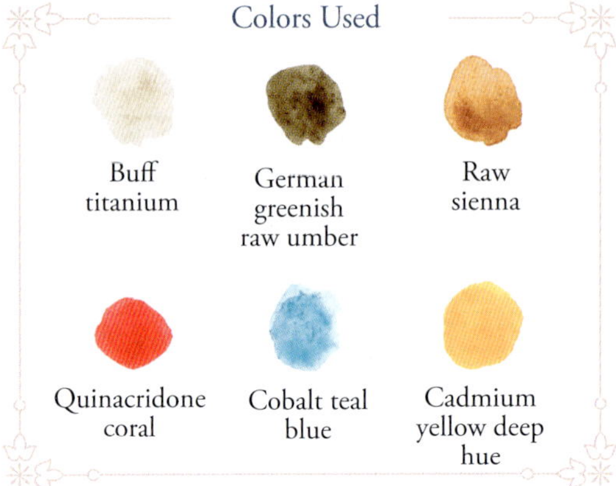

1

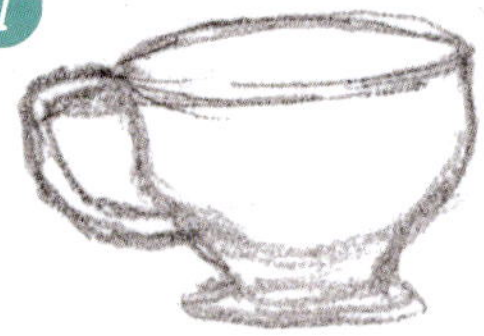

2

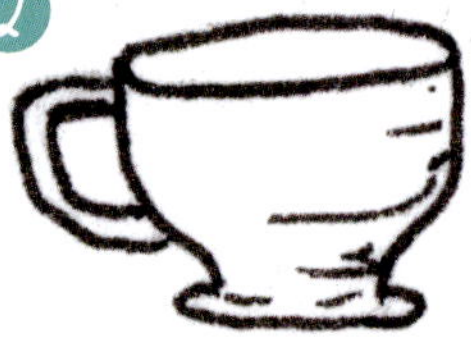

3

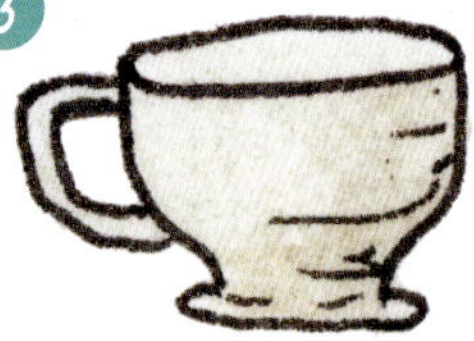

4

1 Draw a light pencil outline of your teacup, including the handle and a delicate base.

2 Go over that outline with your waterproof pen, adding lines for shading along the lower right edge to make shadows. Once the ink is dry, gently erase the pencil layer.

3 Use your smaller brush to fill in the whole teacup with a light layer of buff titanium, building up several layers of buff titanium and German greenish raw umber to make shadows. Let that dry completely before moving to the next step so the details don't bleed into the base color. Keep in mind that if you have white gouache, titanium white watercolor, or regular gouache paint, you have the option to make a dark-colored teacup with a light-colored design on top. You can mix watercolors with white gouache or titanium white watercolor to make any color you'd like, so the world of color is at your fingertips!

4 Once the cup is dry, add some tea with raw sienna and your smaller brush. Now for the best part: the floral design! Mix up some concentrated quinacridone coral with your smallest brush, and then add a delicate floral design (or any colorful design that you enjoy), including a few leaves made from a combination of cobalt teal blue and cadmium yellow deep hue, and your cup is ready to use!

Silver Filagree Teapot

Discovered while exploring a mysterious shipwreck, this silver filagree teapot makes the very best tea. The sea witch finds so many interesting items on her adventures, but this teapot may be one of the prettiest (and most useful)! Depending on the size you choose to draw your teapot, you may want to simplify some of the linework, especially in the filagree.

Colors Used

Buff titanium

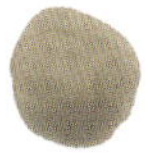

Gray titanium

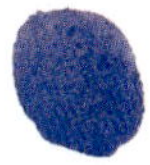

Prussian blue

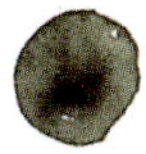

Perylene green

1

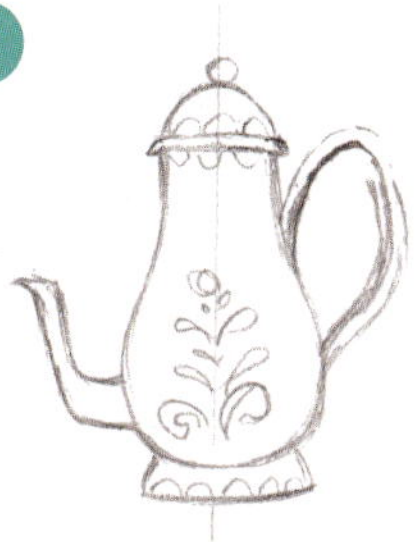

2

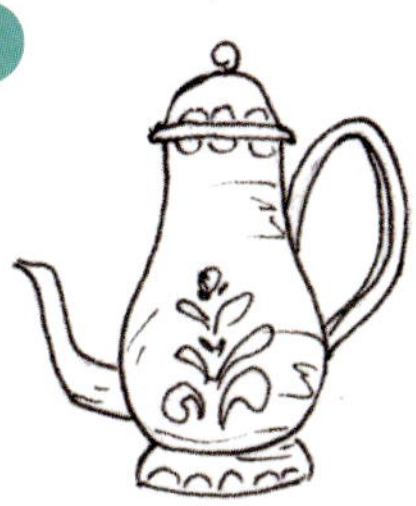

3

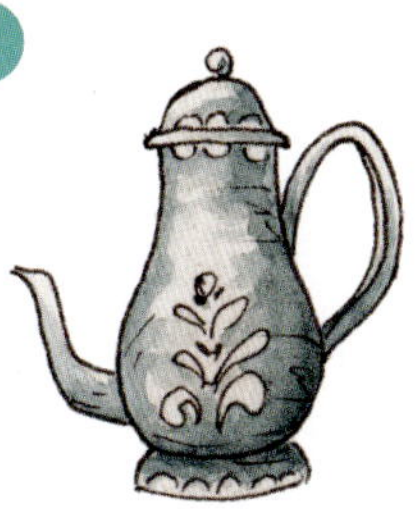

1 Using your pencil, draw a light center line and mark the top and bottom of your teapot, and then draw the body, spout, and handle. For the filagree design, we're not looking to perfectly outline every detail, but more to give the impression of a detailed, swooping design. To achieve this, draw a series of swoopy teardrop shapes near the center of the teapot, and add scalloped edges to the base and near the lid for additional whimsy.

2 Carefully trace your pencil outline with a waterproof pen, adding lines for shading and filagree. Once the ink is dry, gently erase the pencil layer.

3 Use your larger brush to fill in the whole teapot with a light layer of buff titanium mixed with gray titanium. This will peek through as highlights when we're done. Build up successive layers of shadows by slowly adding Prussian blue and perylene green, adding details for the filagree and shadow until your teapot looks shiny and delicate. And you're done!

Candle for Late-Night Reading

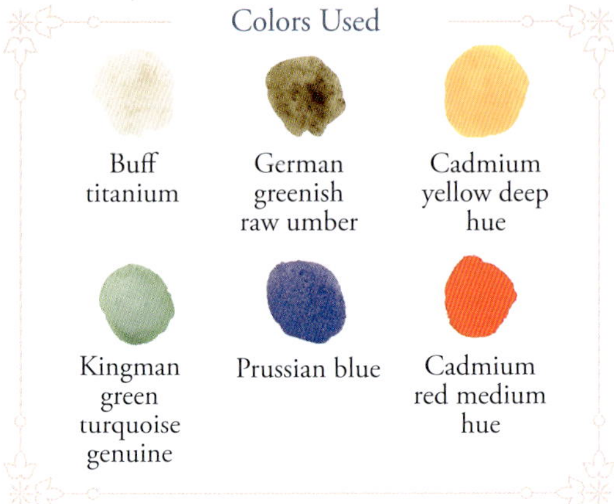

There's nothing quite like the ambiance of reading by candlelight, so let's make a candle in a bottle for late-night reading for the sea witch. As a fun added detail, let's put a rolled-up message in the bottle. What do you think it says?

1

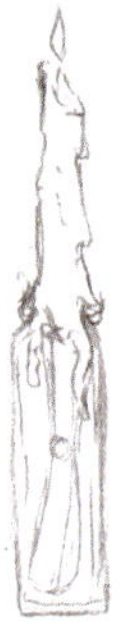

2

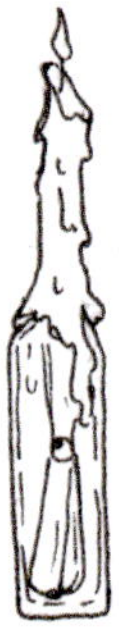

3

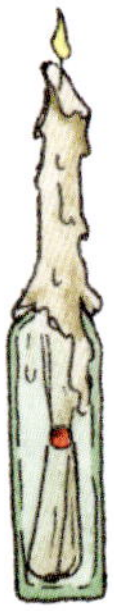

1 Using a pencil, lightly draw the outline of a bottle, and then add a melting candle and a mysterious message.

2 Go over the pencil outline with your waterproof pen, adding shading to the candle and scroll as well as lines for light reflecting on the bottle. Once the ink is dry, gently erase the pencil layer.

3 Using your smaller brush, go over the whole candle and scroll with buff titanium, and then use German greenish raw umber to add shadows. Then add cadmium yellow deep hue for the candle flame, or if you prefer a dark and mysterious look for your shelf, you could use cobalt teal blue or Prussian blue for a deep blue flame. Once those layers are completely dry, go over the whole bottle, including the scroll, with a super light mixture of buff titanium, cadmium yellow deep hue, Kingman green turquoise genuine, and Prussian blue. Allow that to dry completely before adding a second layer outside the area where the scroll is, since we don't want to cover up the parchment color too much.

Finally, mix a very slightly darker, more seaweedy green with those same colors, and use it to fill in where the glass is thicker near the edges. Once your whole bottle is dry again, use your smaller brush and some cadmium red medium hue for the wax seal on the scroll. (Cadmium red medium hue is highly pigmented, and we don't want it to bleed into the other colors, which is why we add it at the end.) And now you're ready to read!

Weathered Moon Phases Chart

The sea witch keeps careful track of the moon, since it's important for spells and tides—so let's add a weathered moon phases chart to her shelf. You may notice that the chart isn't exactly what one might, even with the most generous terms, describe as accurate, but that's okay—we're going for the general impression of a moon chart here. If, however, you'd like to make a chart that includes your birth month or some other special time in your life, you can swap out the design here for something more accurate!

Colors Used

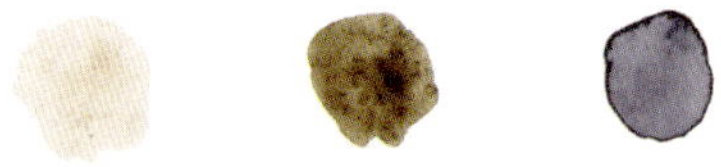

Buff titanium | German greenish raw umber | Indigo

1

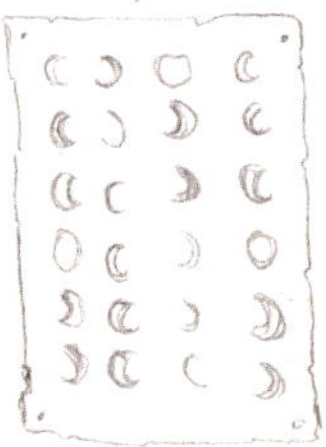

2

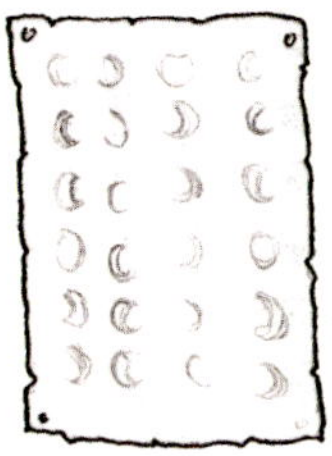

3

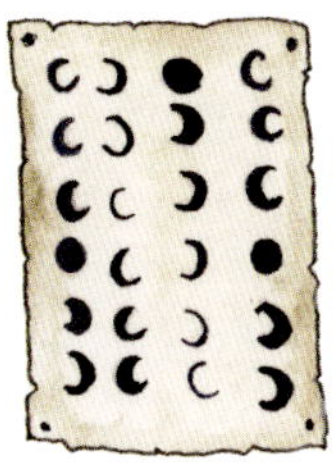

1 Draw a pencil outline for the chart, making the edges as neat or as ragged as you'd like. Sketch in a series of moon shapes as they wax and wane (it can help to think of drawing a bunch of forward- and backward-facing "C" shapes), keeping in mind that, due to the size of the chart, it won't be totally accurate.

2 Now, use your waterproof pen to trace that outline, adding a bit of shading and texture to the paper. Because the moons are so small, and the indigo we'll use to paint them in the next step is so opaque and would cover up the ink, we don't need to add ink to the moons. The parchment color isn't very opaque, so you'll still be able to see the pencil lines underneath it to guide you when painting the moons. Once the ink is dry, gently erase the the pencil outline, but not the moons.

3 Using your larger brush, fill the whole chart with buff titanium, and then add texture using German greenish raw umber, especially near the edges. Let that dry completely (this is a great time to make a cup of tea), and then use your smaller brush and some concentrated indigo to fill in the moon phases. Indigo, in particular, is easy to use for fine detail painting. Some paint colors are difficult to use for tiny details because of the texture they make when mixed with water, and it's something you may want to test on scrap paper to see what works best for you. If you'd prefer a slightly warmer look, you can use concentrated burnt umber, which also mixes with water to a nice consistency for painting details, or you could use a bright color like quinacridone coral—so many options!

Inkwell with Phoenix Feather Quill

The seagull loves to fly and visit friends, so the sea witch writes lots of letters using an inkwell with a phoenix feather quill, which has magical spellchecker abilities. The colors on the feather are so fun to paint, and you can make any color combination you want if you prefer something other than the flame theme in this tutorial. A peacock feather would also be beautiful here, and you can simply swap out the colors and draw a rounded end on the feather to make that adjustment if you'd like.

Colors Used

- Buff titanium
- Prussian blue
- Cadmium yellow deep hue
- Quinacridone coral
- Cadmium red medium hue

1

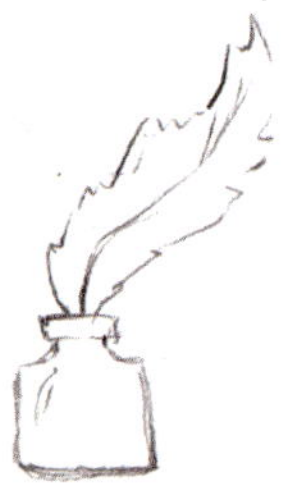

2

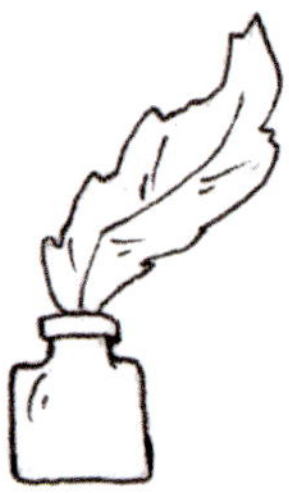

3

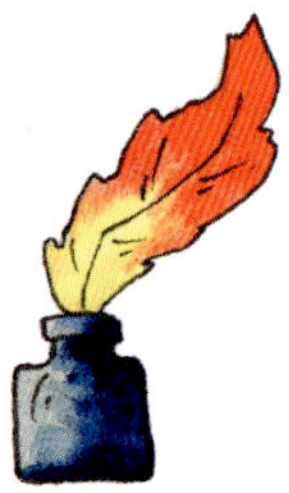

1. Using your pencil, gently sketch the outline for your inkwell and feather, keeping in mind that you can vary the shape of the feather to affect the overall feel of the shelf. A jagged, angular feather will look a bit darker and more gothic, while a gently curving, fluffy feather will look friendlier and more inviting.

2. Go over the pencil outline with your waterproof pen, adding shading and texture to the feather and inkwell, and then once the ink is dry, erase the pencil layer.

3. Grab your smaller brush, and fill in the inkwell with buff titanium mixed with Prussian blue, adding pure Prussian blue near the right edge to make a shadow. Let that dry, and then go over the whole feather with a very light layer of cadmium yellow deep hue, following that up by dabbing pure cadmium yellow deep hue near the base, quinacridone coral near the center, and cadmium red medium hue at the top. Blend the edges very slightly with a damp brush, and you're ready to write!

Armillary Stargazing Sphere

Our sea witch uses this armillary sphere in conjunction with the moon chart and telescope to keep an eye on the stars and distant planets (you never know where they might wander off to). As an added bonus, it makes a great fidget toy to keep the seagull out of trouble.

Colors Used

Yellow ochre

Buff titanium

German greenish raw umber

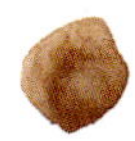

Burnt umber

1

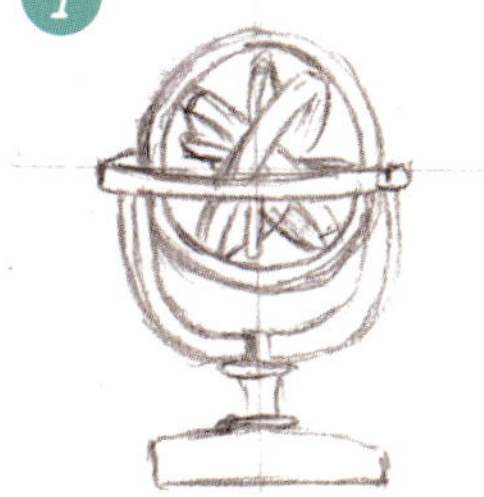

2

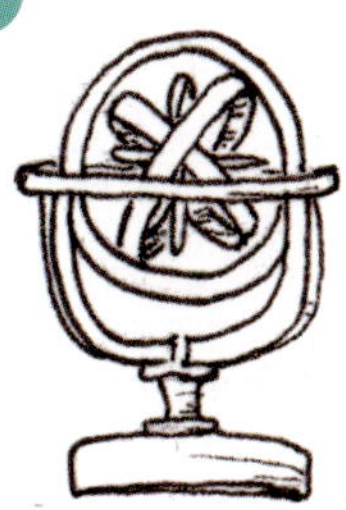

3

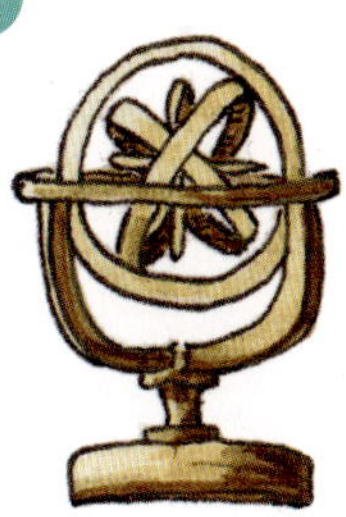

1 The shape of the sphere may look overwhelming at first, so let's draw it bit by bit. Start off with a vertical center line, and then a horizontal line where the center of the sphere will be. Now, draw the base, the middle horizontal section, and the connection between the base and that section. Finally, add the interior pieces, working from the outside in.

2 Carefully go over your pencil outline with a waterproof pen, paying close attention to what sections of the sphere overlap with others, and then once the ink is dry, gently erase the underlying pencil.

3 Using your smaller brush, fill in all the sections with yellow ochre combined with buff titanium and a hint of German greenish raw umber. Then slowly build up layers of German greenish raw umber mixed with burnt umber to make shadows so the metal looks shiny. You're ready to stargaze!

Bright Red Coral

The sea witch's shelf is full of interesting items collected on her adventures, but this bright red coral might be one of my favorites! You can have so much fun with this one by varying the size, shape, and color to suit any shelf. So draw whatever feels right to you! Coral comes in all sorts of interesting colors, so don't feel confined to the pink and red colors shown in the tutorial—this is a great place to add your favorite colors to your shelf!

Colors Used

Quinacridone coral

Cadmium red medium hue

1

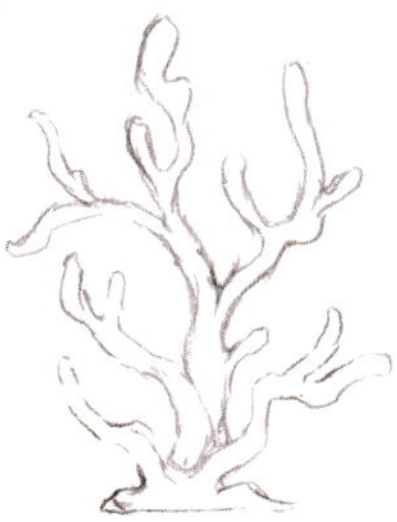

2

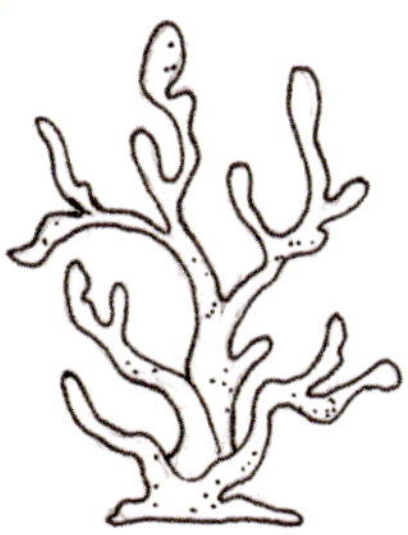

3

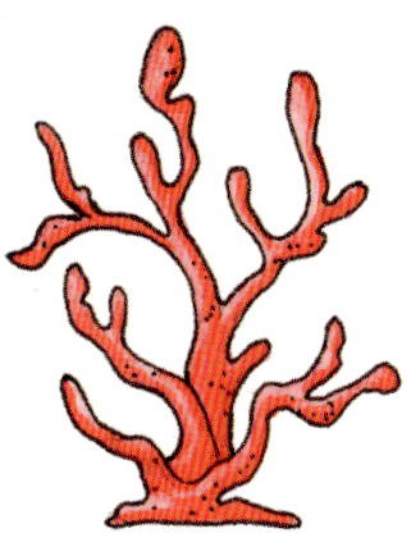

1 Using your pencil, sketch the outline for your coral, using pictures of coral or sprawling tree branches for inspiration on the shape.

2 Carefully trace your pencil outline with a waterproof pen, adding small lines or dots for shading, and then once the ink is dry, erase the pencil outline.

3 Using your smaller brush, fill in the whole coral with a light layer of quinacridone coral, building up successive layers with increasing quantities of cadmium red medium hue to make shadows, and then you're done! If you'd like to make a green-colored coral, I'd recommend using Kingman green turquoise genuine mixed with indigo for a more muted look, or with Prussian blue for a more vibrant appearance. If you'd like bright pink instead of bright red, use cadmium yellow deep hue or Naples yellow with quinacridone coral and a hint of moonglow purple for the deepest shadows. The possibilities are endless, but remember that if you want your coral to match the rest of the shelf, I'd recommend using colors you've incorporated elsewhere in your shelf. And now your beautiful coral is ready to be displayed on the shelf!

Beautiful Seashells

There's so much variety when it comes to seashells; I'm sure the sea witch has a wide collection! We'll cover two types here, but you can switch them out for any kinds that you enjoy or that are found near you.

Colors Used

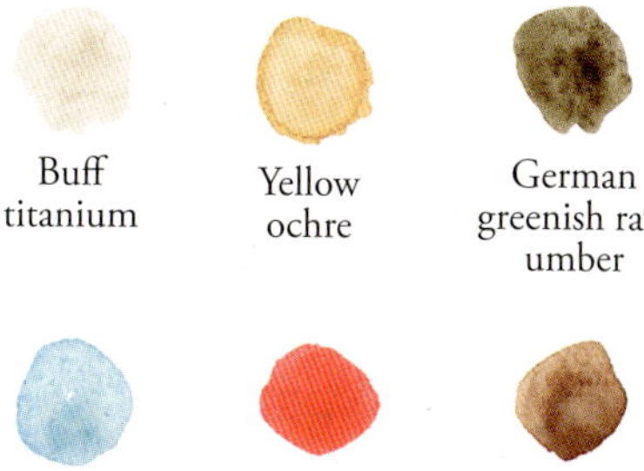

Buff titanium | Yellow ochre | German greenish raw umber

Manganese blue hue | Quinacridone coral | Burnt umber

1

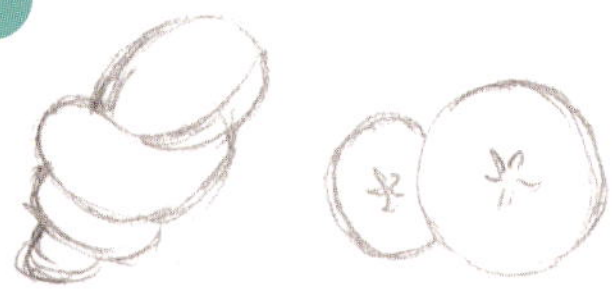

2

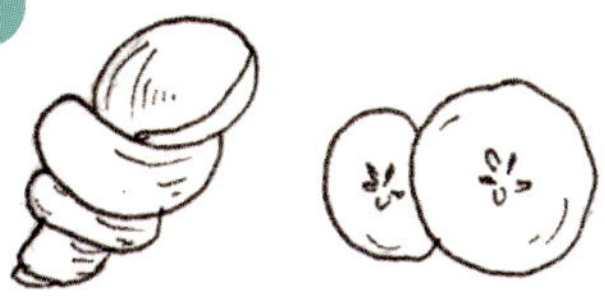

3

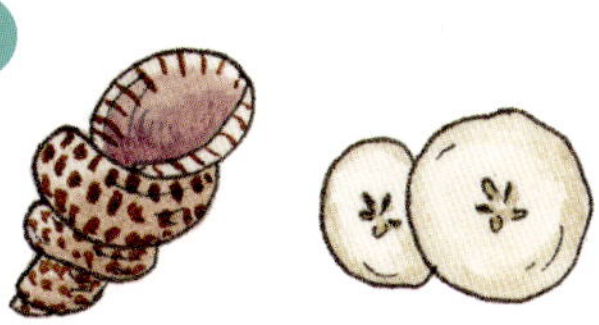

1 Grab your favorite pencil and sketch two (or more) overlapping circles for the sand dollars, and then a series of squishy ovals for the outline of the patterned shell.

2 Use your waterproof pen to go over the pencil sketch, adding lines to create shading on the shells and to make the patterns in the centers of the sand dollars. Once the ink is dry, carefully erase the pencil layer.

3 Go over all the shells with a light layer of buff titanium mixed with a hint of yellow ochre, and then use German greenish raw umber to build up shadows. Use German greenish raw umber to accentuate the patterns in the sand dollars. Then use your smaller brush to add buff titanium combined with manganese blue hue and quinacridone coral (to make a moody-but-light purple) to the opening of the patterned shell. Build up more shadows on the large shell, mixing your purple color with some German greenish raw umber and a hint of burnt umber. Once the underlying layers of shadow are completely dry, use burnt umber and your smallest brush to paint a checkered pattern on the patterned seashell, and then admire your beautiful work!

Crystal Ball with a Driftwood Stand

Crystal balls are quite handy to have around; you never know what useful information they'll convey, and they're quite pretty. The sea witch, in particular, likes to use her crystal ball to check the weather before going for long walks—it's always nice to know ahead of time whether or not you'll need a raincoat! Let's paint a lovely crystal ball with a driftwood stand for our sea witch to use.

Colors Used

Naples yellow

Cadmium yellow deep hue

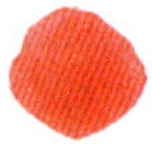

Quinacridone coral

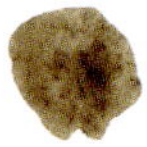

German greenish raw umber

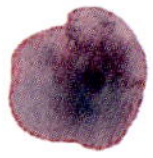

Moonglow purple

1

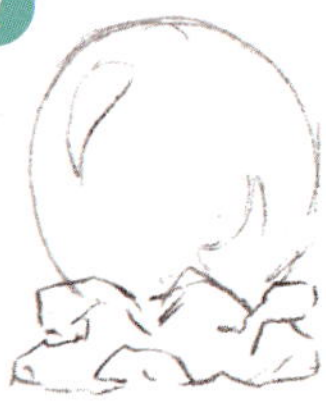

2

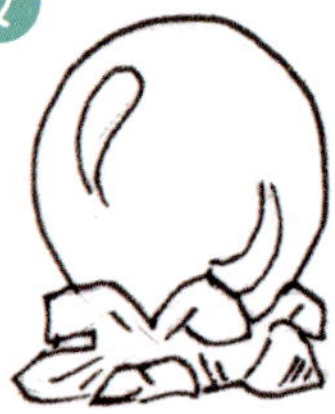

3

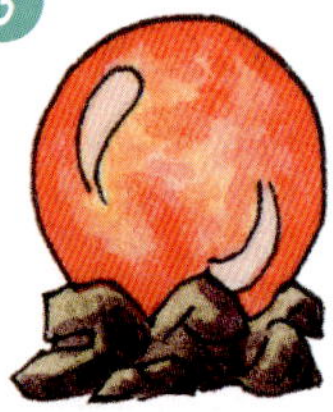

1 Start off your pencil sketch by drawing a circle for the ball, and then add the driftwood stand, making it as simple or intricate as you'd like.

2 Using your waterproof pen, trace the pencil outline, starting with the driftwood stand, followed by the outline of the crystal ball and then shapes for the reflection of light in the ball. Once the ink is dry, gently erase the pencil layer.

3 Use your smaller brush to fill in the whole ball with a light layer of Naples yellow combined with cadmium yellow deep hue. Then add quinacridone coral near the edges so the ball appears to be glowing, building up layers of both your yellow and pink until the ball has swirling and mysterious depth. Use German greenish raw umber to paint the driftwood stand, adding moonglow purple to make some lovely shadows, and then peer into your crystal ball and see what it has to say! Since this is a great place to play around with different pops of color on your shelf, you could also try a deep and mysterious ball made up of cobalt teal blue, buff titanium, and indigo, or a sunny ball made with Naples yellow, cadmium yellow deep hue, and raw sienna. Try out different mixtures on some scrap paper and see what you love the most!

Mysterious Treasure Box

Some trinkets are suitable to display on a bookshelf, but others might need to be kept in a mysterious treasure box to keep them out of the hands (or arms or beak) of inquisitive friends. Let's paint a lovely, wooden treasure box for our sea witch to store mysterious items and really good snacks.

Colors Used

Burnt umber | Naples yellow | Moonglow purple

1

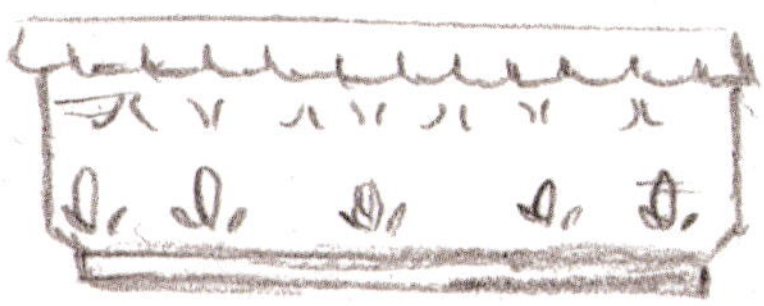

2

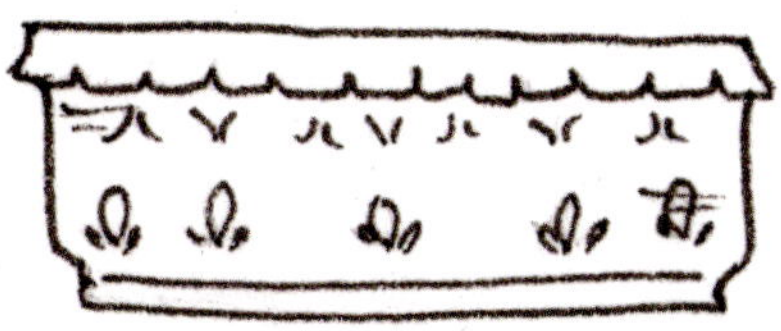

3

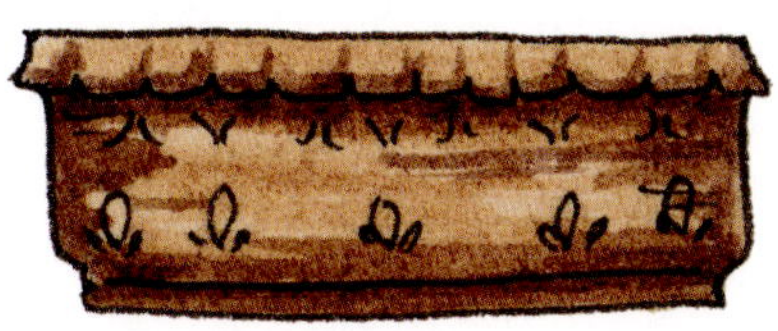

1 Once you've decided how big to make your box, draw the pencil outline and then fill in the details, adding carvings on the wood or maybe a lock.

2 Use your waterproof pen to go over your pencil outline, adding extra lines for shading and to give the impression of wood grain, and then once the ink is dry, gently erase the underlying pencil drawing.

3 Using your larger brush, go over the whole box with burnt umber mixed with Naples yellow, and then use moonglow purple mixed with burnt umber to build up successive layers of shadow and wood grain until the box looks ready to hold mysterious treasures!

The Sea Witchery Shelf

We need a shelf to arrange all the interesting items we've collected for the sea witch, so here's a beautiful, wooden shelf, reminiscent of the decorative wood carvings on old pirate ships and the gently curving lines of waves and seashells.

Colors Used

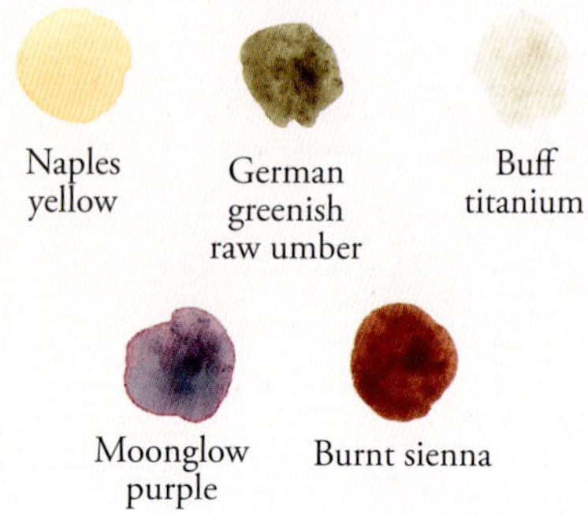

1

1 As always, let's start off with a pencil drawing. You can use a ruler if you want straight lines, or freehand the lines for a more organic look. First, draw the upper portion of the shelf, and then mark the middle point. Draw the curving, decorative base centered around that middle portion, adding or omitting detail to suit your taste.

2

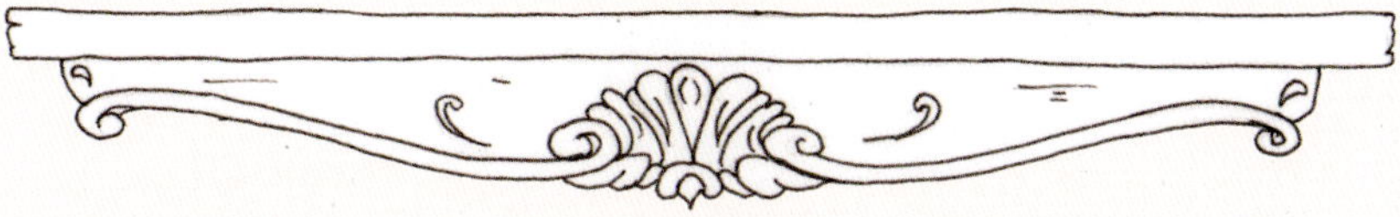

2 Before you add ink and watercolor, plan out how you'd like the items on the shelf to be arranged—do any of them overlap with the shelf? If so, you'll want to paint (or at least outline) those first! Once that's done, go over the outline of the shelf with your waterproof pen, adding shading and texture until it looks ready to paint. Once the ink is dry, gently erase your pencil sketch.

3

3 Using your larger brush, fill in the whole shelf with a mixture of Naples yellow and German greenish raw umber with a smidge of buff titanium. Then add increasing amounts of moonglow purple and burnt sienna to your mixture, and build up layers to make wood grain and shadows. It's important to really take your time and go slowly with this step—you'll end up adding between fifteen and twenty thin layers to build up depth, but I promise it's worth it in the end! Now your shelf is finished, and we can add all sorts of beautiful items to it!

Assembling Your Sea Witchery Shelf

Now that we've talked about how to paint each of the sea witchery items, it's time to arrange them and paint our shelf! Of course, you can rearrange and mix and match items however you'd like, and use the following steps as a guideline however they're useful in your process.

Colors Used for the Background

Cobalt teal blue

Kingman green turquoise genuine

1

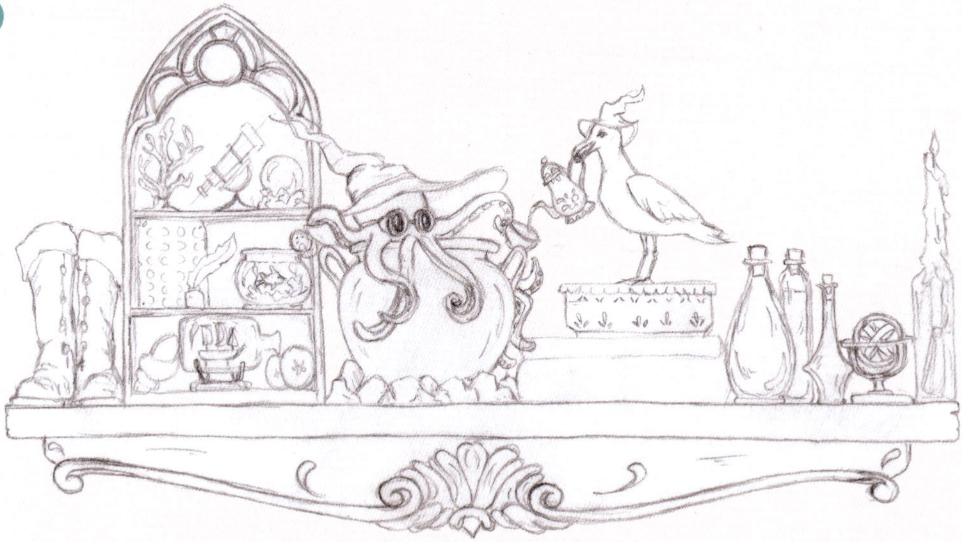

1 Begin by sketching the shelf, and then mark the edges of each item on the shelf to ensure that they're spaced in a way that's visually pleasing and nothing is left hanging off the edge. Refer to The Sea Witchery Shelf (page 116) for more guidance on sketching the shelf, and please refer back to each project's tutorial as needed for the sketches of the individual items.

2

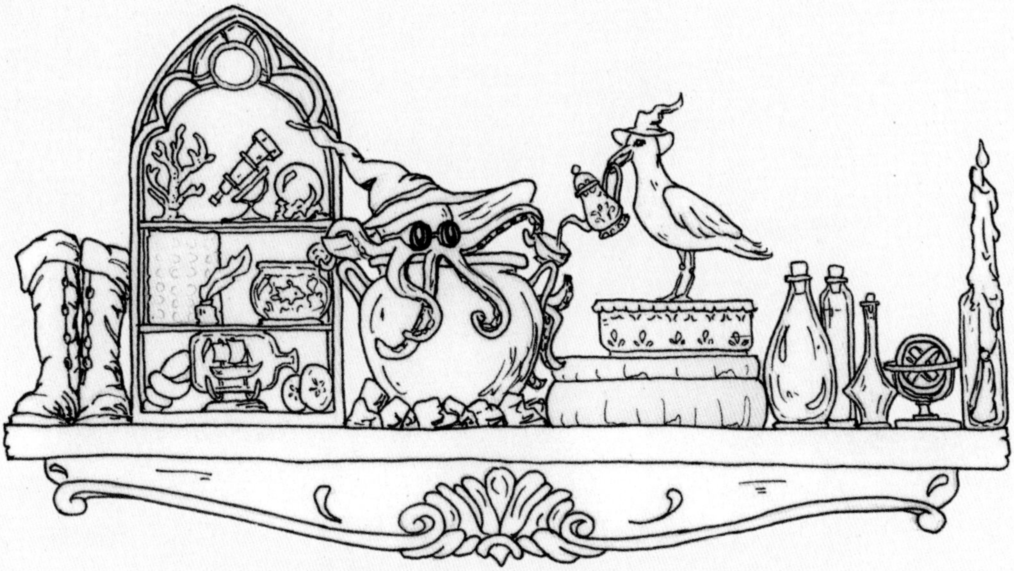

2 Start off by adding waterproof ink to the octopus familiar, since it overlaps with other objects on the shelf. Then draw the outline of the shelf with stained-glass details, and fill in the remaining items and the shelf itself in any order that makes sense to you, referring to the individual instructions for any item that you'd like more details for. Once the ink is dry, gently erase the pencil layer, other than the outlines of the moons.

3

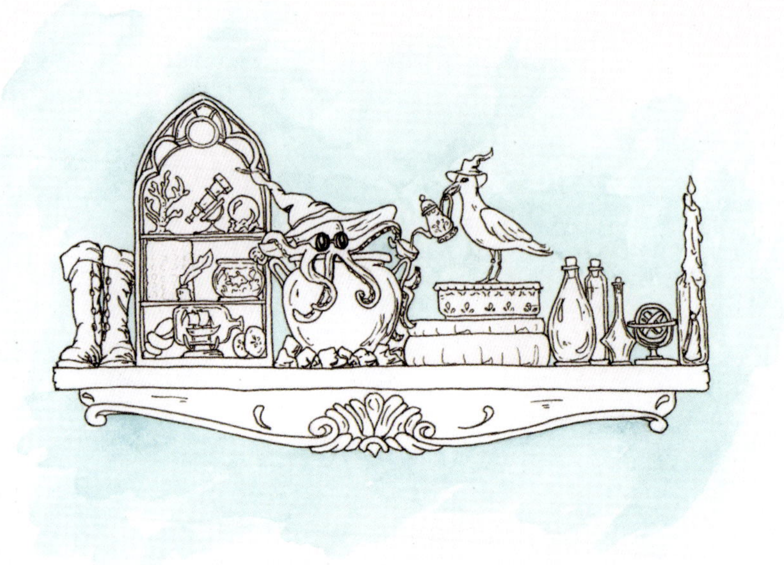

3 If you'd like to add a colored background like the one shown in the example, we'll do that in this step. If you prefer to skip the colored background, move ahead to step 4. If you have a really large brush (perhaps a filbert in size 6 to 10, but really anything will do), use that to add a thin layer of water around the whole shelf and the items on it, making sure you don't get water on the shelf itself or the items. You can use any size brush that works for you to gently add water to the small nooks and crannies between the items; just make sure you're not making puddles of water anywhere. Then while the paper is still damp, use a very, very light mixture of watered-down cobalt teal blue mixed with Kingman green turquoise genuine to go around the shelf along with all the items and creatures, taking care to not get paint inside the lines. Build up another layer or two of that color (or more, if you'd like a darker background), and then wait and let everything dry completely before moving on to the next step.

4

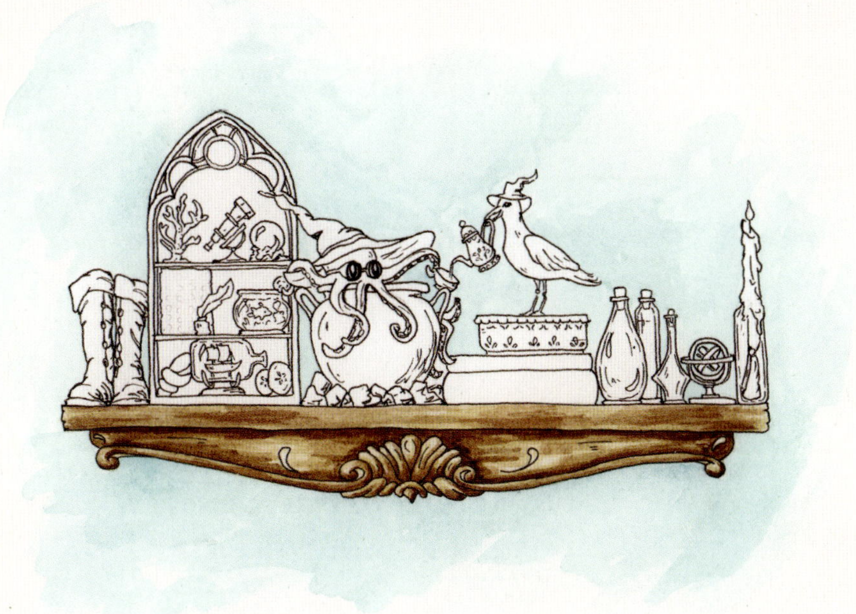

4 I always like to start off with painting the shelf first, so I can make sure everything else matches that color, so let's start there. Refer to The Sea Witchery Shelf (page 116) for more detail as needed, and paint yourself a beautiful shelf!

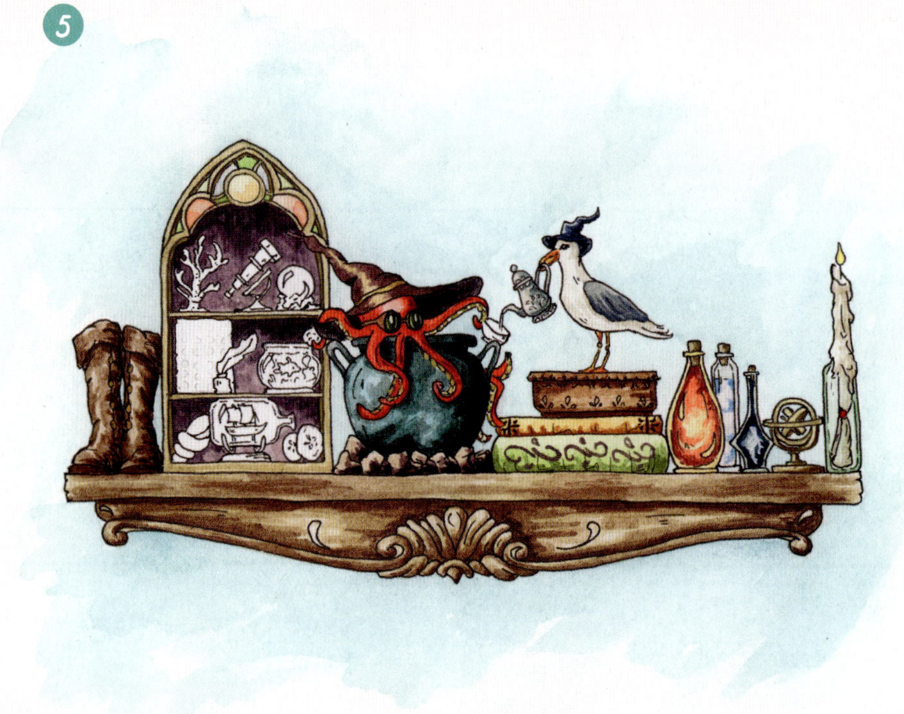

5 Now it's time to paint the sea witchery items! Ultimately, you can paint the items in any order you'd like, but I'd recommend splitting it up into two sections. Start off with the Sturdy Boots for Seaside Adventures (page 98), followed by the Shelf with Stained-Glass Details (page 102), and all the large items to the right of the shelf. That includes the Octopus Familiar in a Magical Cauldron (page 92), Silver Filagree Teapot (page 107), Distinguished Seagull with a Witch's Hat (page 94), Mysterious Treasure Box (page 115), Enchanted Spellbooks (page 97), Bottled Weather Spells (page 100), Armillary Stargazing Sphere (page 111), and Candle for Late-Night Reading (page 108). You're almost there!

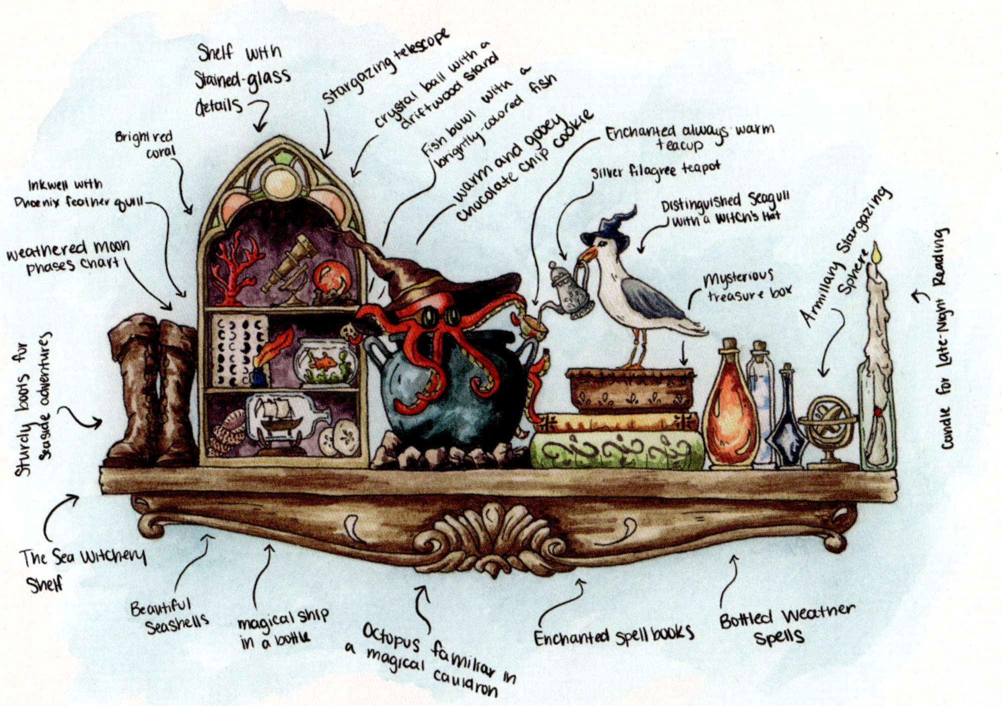

6 Okay, now let's finish up with the items on the shelf with stained-glass details! In any order you'd like, paint the Bright Red Coral (page 112), Stargazing Telescope (page 104), Crystal Ball with a Driftwood Stand (page 114), Weathered Moon Phases Chart (page 109), Inkwell with Phoenix Feather Quill (page 110), Fishbowl with a Brightly Colored Fish (page 99), Beautiful Seashells (page 113), Magical Ship in a Bottle (page 96), Warm and Gooey Chocolate Chip Cookie (page 105), and Enchanted Always-Warm Teacup (page 106). Your beautiful sea witch's shelf is finished, and it looks amazing!

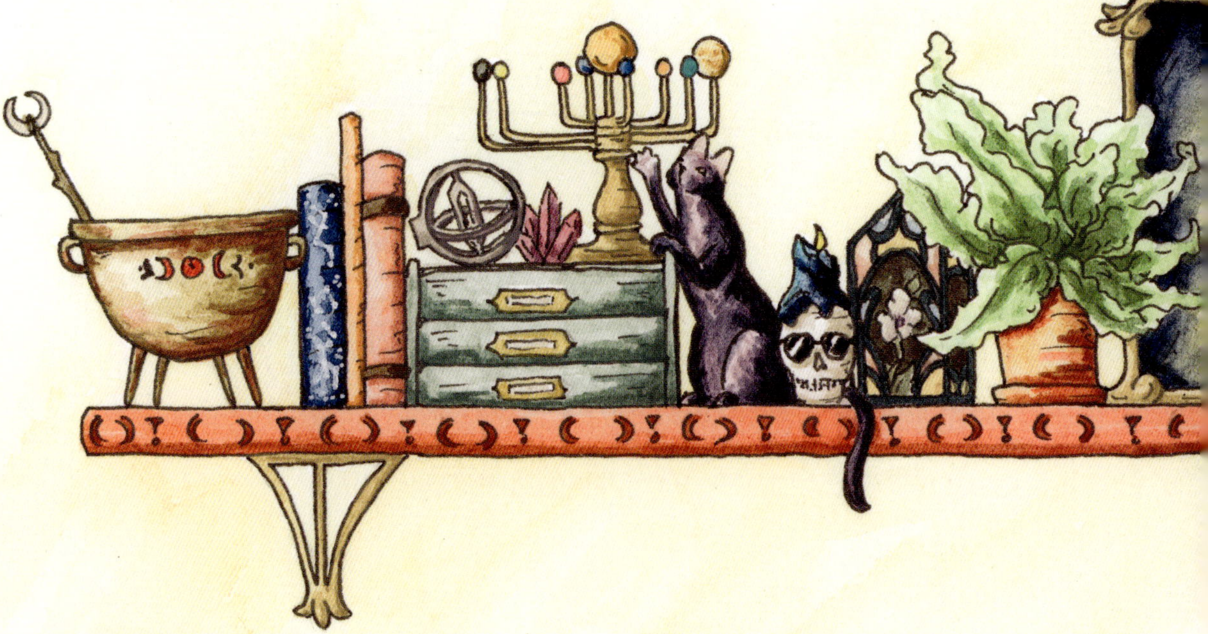

Celestial Witchery

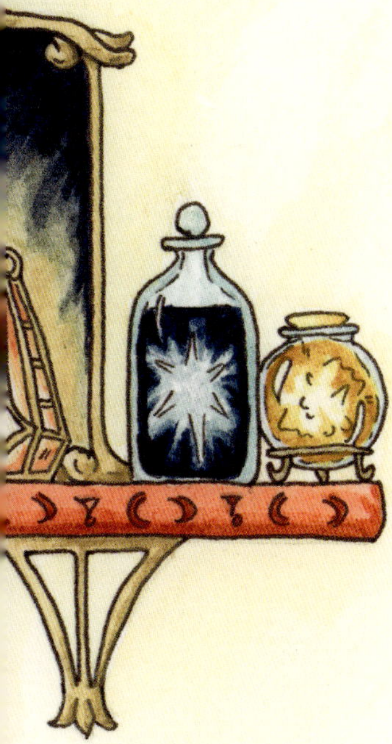

The celestial witch is very friendly and probably a bit eccentric, and their shelf is full of interesting astronomical trinkets and enchanted items. Have you ever wanted a chatty, haunted skull to provide commentary on your day and questionably helpful advice? Or perhaps a jar of liquid sunshine for those particularly gloomy winter days? With a subtle, crescent-moon design on the shelf and lots of lovely, whimsical details hidden throughout, the celestial witch's shelf is a delight to paint, and I hope you enjoy it!

Cauldron Full of Moonlight

Every witch needs a cauldron—they're useful both for storing fruit on the counter and brewing up all sorts of potions and spells. This particular cauldron is full of moonlight, which is an essential ingredient in many of the celestial witch's spells.

Colors Used

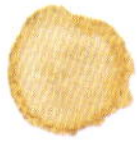
Yellow ochre

Naples yellow

Buff titanium

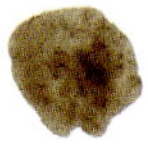
German greenish raw umber

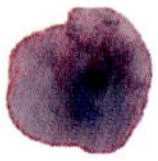
Moonglow purple

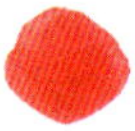
Quinacridone coral

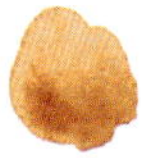
Raw sienna

1

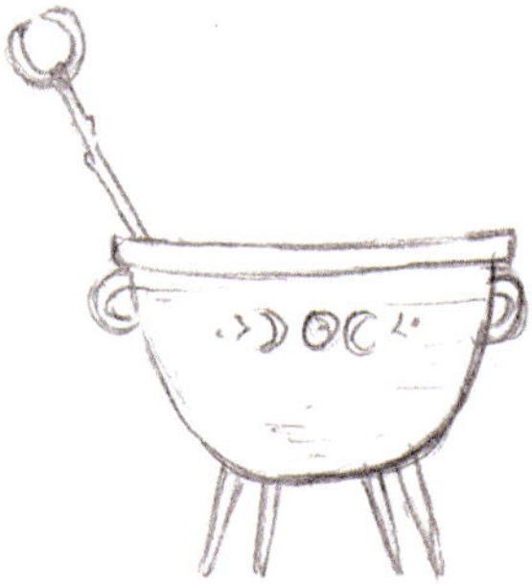

2

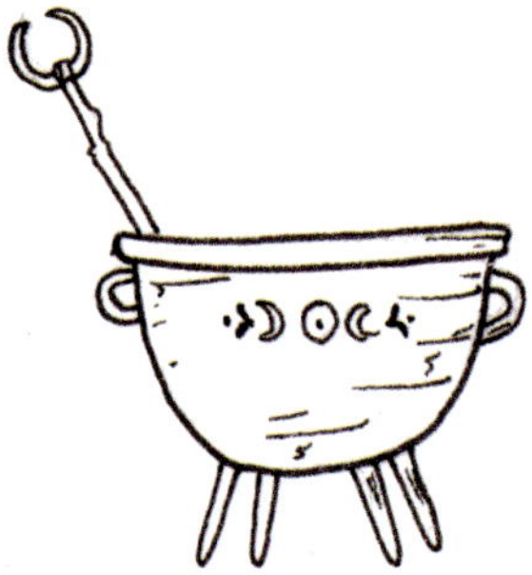

1 Start off with a light pencil sketch for the overall cauldron shape, adding legs and a stirring stick with a crescent moon handle. If you want it to be perfectly symmetrical, it can help to draw a vertical center line, and then build the rest of the cauldron from there. Add the decorative design on the front by drawing a small circle in the center of the cauldron, two crescent moons facing opposite directions on either side of the circle, and a small leaf motif on the outside of each moon.

2 Using your waterproof pen, go over the pencil outline, adding shading and texture, and then once the ink is dry, gently erase the pencil.

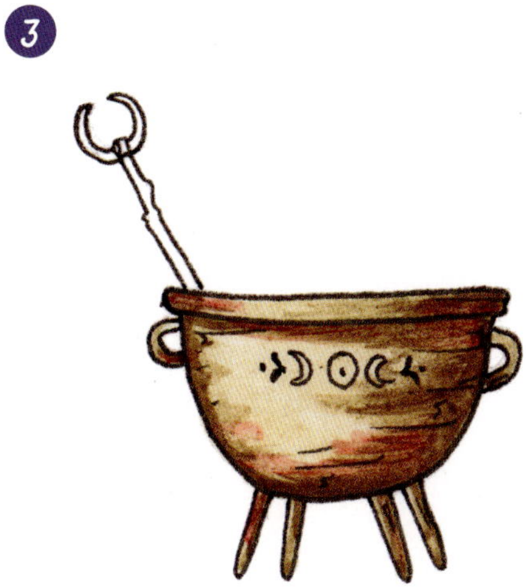

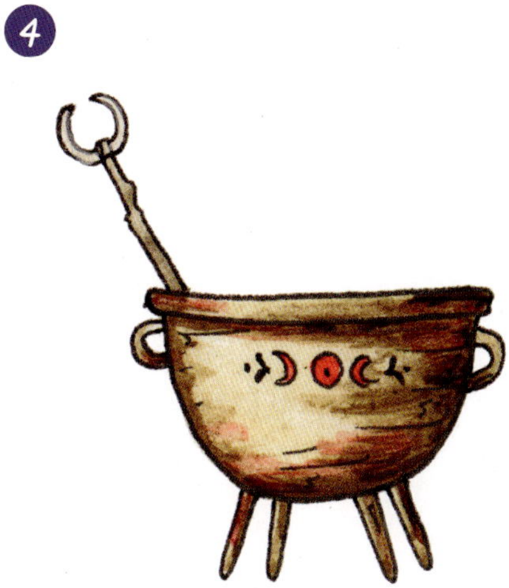

3 We'll build up the color in layers to achieve a luminous appearance here. Use your larger brush to paint a light layer of yellow ochre mixed with Naples yellow and buff titanium on the whole cauldron. While that's still wet, build up a few more gentle layers, adding some German greenish raw umber and moonglow purple each time, avoiding adding more color to the moon design on the front. While your last layer on the cauldron is still damp, add some little highlights with quinacridone coral to bring in a pop of color.

4 Now let's add the darkest shadows and the colorful highlights! Mix up some moonglow purple, German greenish raw umber, quinacridone coral, and raw sienna, and add the very darkest shadows towards the lower right side of the cauldron and just under the lip at the top, building it up until you're happy with the contrast. Then fill in the crescent moon design on the front of the cauldron with some watered-down quinacridone coral, adding as much or as little as you'd like depending on how saturated you want the color to be. Fill in the stirring stick with German greenish raw umber, adding a small amount of moonglow purple to your second layer to make shadows. With the smaller brush, add some buff titanium to the crescent moon handle. Now to brew up some mysterious spells!

Haunted Skull with Sunglasses

You may have heard of talking skulls, but have you ever come across a very chatty, sunglasses-wearing haunted skull with a candle on top? Look no further—it's your lucky day! What do you think you'd chat about? If you'd like to change up the personality of the skull, you can swap out the glasses and instead create a pair of round spectacles or some old-school, brightly colored glasses with pointy corners. So many options!

Colors Used

Buff titanium	German greenish raw umber	Cobalt teal blue
Prussian blue	Indigo	Cadmium yellow deep hue

1

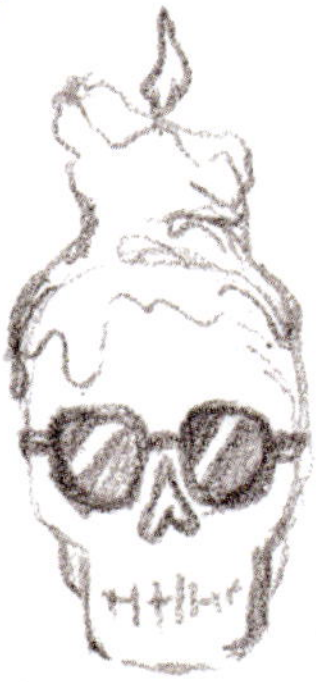

2

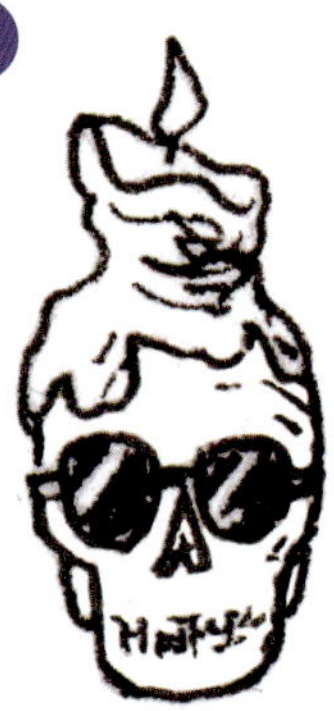

1 First, lightly sketch the outline of the skull, starting with a rounded oval and adding the jaw, sunglasses, and nose. Sketch the candle on top, starting off by lightly sketching a cylinder, then adding all the droopy melting wax so it flows away from the flame and down onto the top of the skull.

2 Go over your pencil sketch with a waterproof pen, making sure to leave highlights on the sunglasses. Add shading and just enough detail to suggest teeth without outlining every single tooth, and then once the ink is dry, erase the pencil and get out your paints!

3

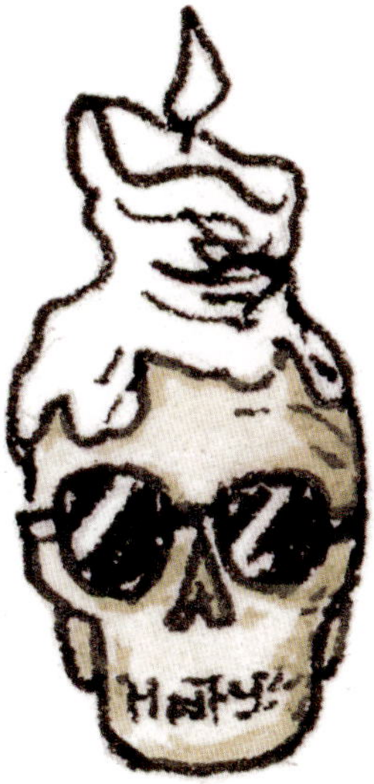

3 Using your smaller brush, fill in the whole skull with a light layer of buff titanium, and then use increasing amounts of German greenish raw umber to gradually build up shadows, making the skull as shiny white or as worn and discolored as you'd like. If you'd like to give your skull a slightly warmer and friendlier appearance, you can include a touch of yellow ochre in the shading. Now is a great time to take a quick break—you don't want to paint the candle until your skull is totally dry, or the colors will bleed together!

4

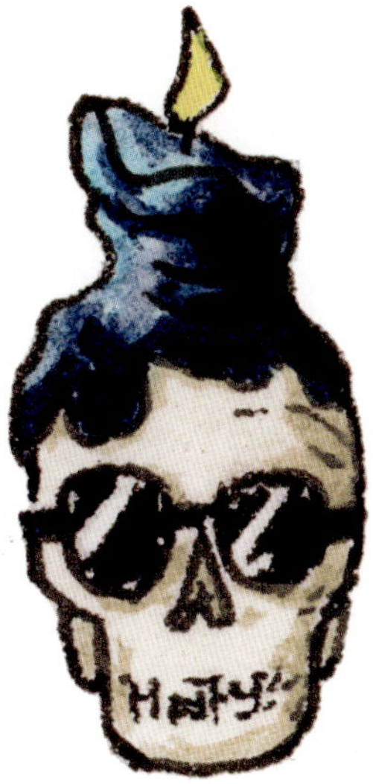

4 Now let's paint the dark candle, starting off with a light layer of cobalt teal blue. Then build up gradually darker layers of Prussian blue mixed with indigo, making sure to keep some of the cobalt teal blue peeking through for highlights. Build up the layers until your candle looks glowing. Use a bit of cadmium yellow deep hue to add the flame at the top (or some cobalt teal blue for a spookier look), fill in any gaps in the sunglasses that you don't want to be reflecting (i.e., the bridge, sides, and any parts of the lenses that aren't currently white) with a bit of indigo, and you're finished!

Enchanted Pocket Sundial

One never knows when one might suddenly have an urgent need for a sundial, so the perpetually prepared celestial witch keeps an enchanted pocket sundial on hand at all times. Couldn't one use a watch to tell time? Perhaps, but this is more interesting, and the celestial witch is astronomically interesting.

Colors Used

Gray titanium | Buff titanium | Moonglow purple

1

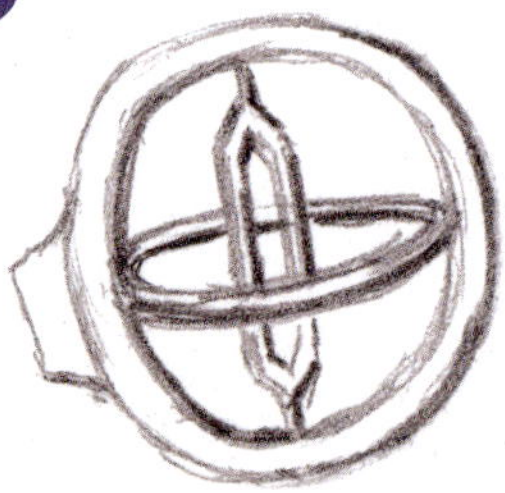

2

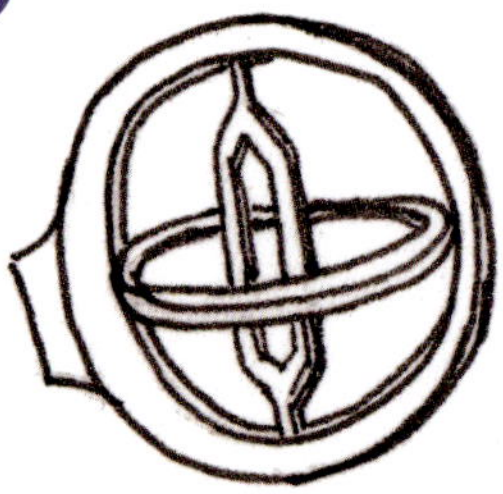

3

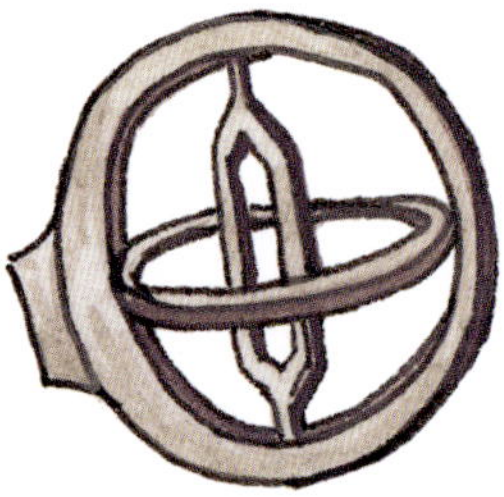

1 The pencil sketch for this is the hardest part, so let's do it in stages. First, draw the two concentric circles for the outside. Then sketch the bar in the middle, and finally, the inner circles, adding a little handle on the outside so it's easy to hold.

2 Now for the easy part. Go over the whole sketch with your waterproof pen, and then once that dries, erase the pencil layer.

3 Using your smaller brush, fill in the whole sundial with a light layer of gray titanium mixed with buff titanium, and then use gray titanium mixed with a bit of moonglow purple to add shadows. You're now ready to figure out what time it is!

Ever-Glowing Lantern

Since the celestial witch does lots of magic at night, it's handy to have an ever-glowing lantern nearby to keep them from tripping on the piles of books and odds and ends that can be found throughout the cottage. The geometric design isn't strictly necessary for the lantern to glow, but it sure is fun to paint—so let's begin!

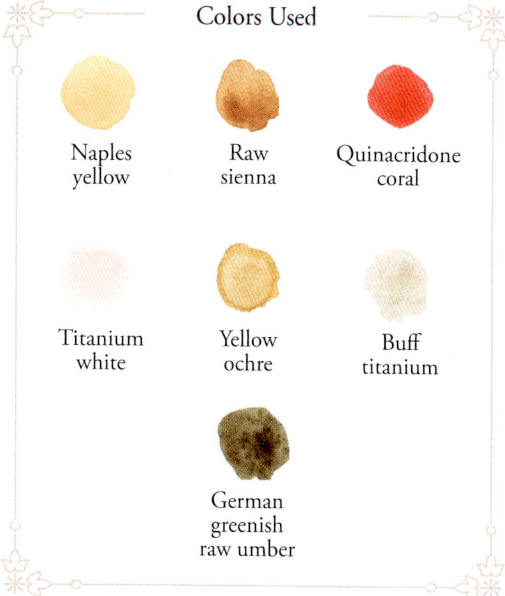

1

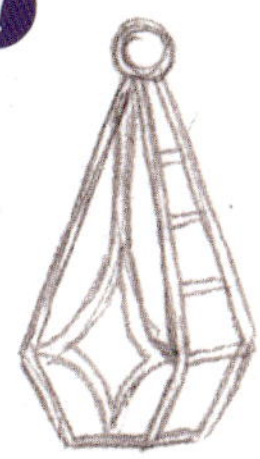

2

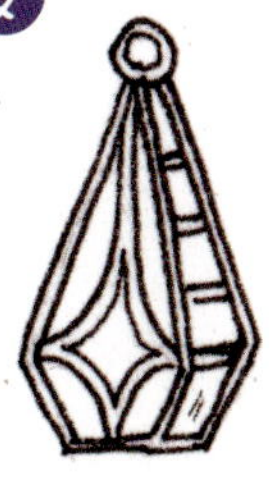

3

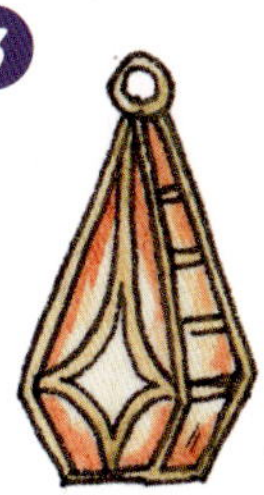

1 Begin the pencil sketch by drawing the outline of the front of the lantern (a diamond shape with the bottom corner cut off), and then add the rest of the details, making the overall lantern as swoopy or as angular as you'd like.

2 Carefully go over your pencil outline with a waterproof pen, making sure the lines are spaced far enough apart to let the light gold color show through when we start painting. Gently erase the pencil layer.

3 Use your smaller brush to fill in each of the glass sections with a light layer of Naples yellow. Then build up successive layers of Naples yellow combined with the tiniest hints of raw sienna and quinacridone coral towards the outside of the glass, keeping the area in the center light so it looks like it's glowing. If you end up with a center that's too dark (or if you just want some brighter highlights), you can go back in with titanium white watercolor or gouache to add highlights near the center of the lantern where the glow will be brightest. Once that's dry, fill in all the metal sections of the lantern with yellow ochre combined with buff titanium and Naples yellow, building up a few shadows with German greenish raw umber . . . and you're finished!

Ancient Spell Mirror

An ancient spell mirror sits on the celestial witch's shelf, and it can be full of any magic that suits your fancy. Is it a talking mirror to keep the haunted skull company? Or perhaps it can be used to communicate with other witches who possess their own enchanted mirrors? You can contemplate the many possibilities while we get started painting! In this tutorial, we'll have fun painting glowing yellow light reflecting on the mirror from an adjacent lantern, but keep in mind that your magical lantern can be glowing any color. You can easily include pink light, green light, or any other color that appeals to you!

Colors Used

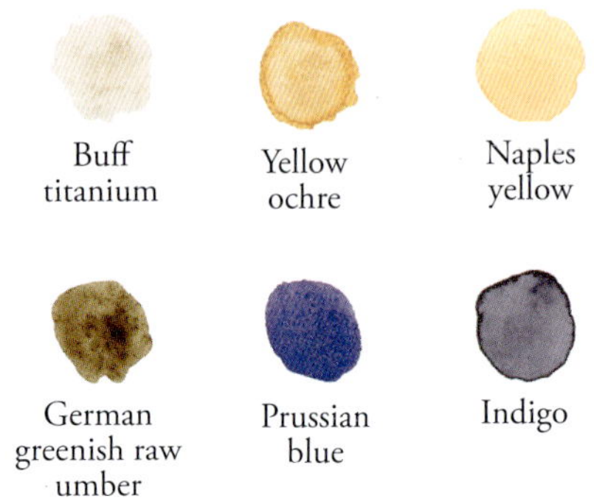

1

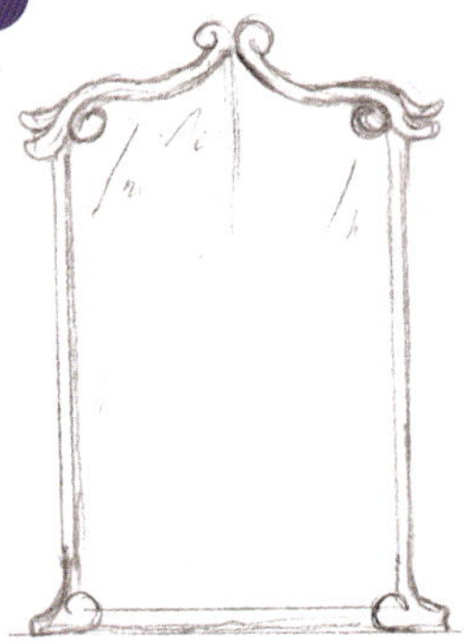

2

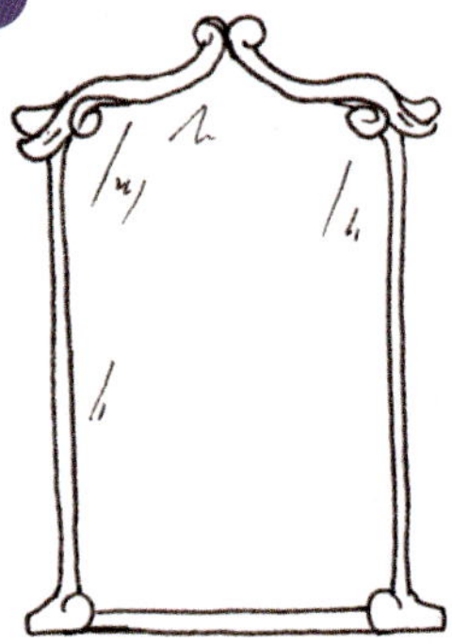

1 Start off by sketching a very light rectangle, and then fill in the rest of the details for the mirror. You can make the frame as simple or as detailed as you'd like. My favorite way to give the impression of a complicated filagree design is random, swooping squiggles, so don't feel like you have to make something perfectly symmetrical—go wild and see what kind of magic you end up with!

2 Use your waterproof pen to trace the pencil outline, adding some subtle lines for shading wherever you feel like your mirror needs it. Once the ink is dry, gently erase the pencil layer.

3

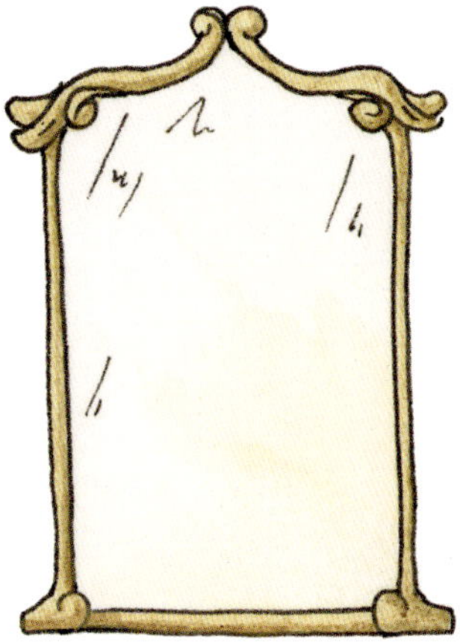

4

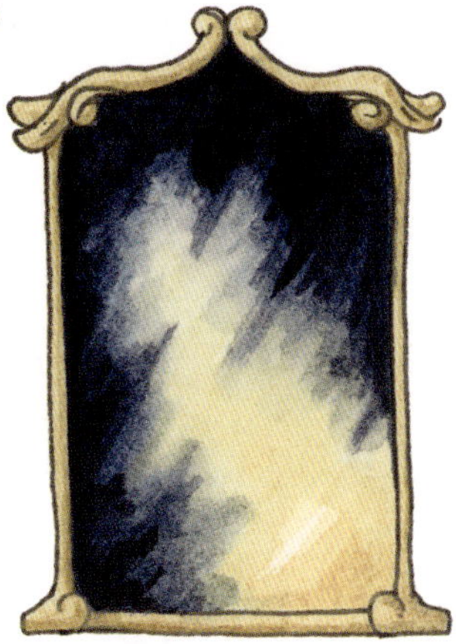

3 Use your larger brush to fill in the whole frame of the mirror with buff titanium mixed with a hint of yellow ochre and Naples yellow. Build up three to five layers of this while adding progressively more German greenish raw umber to the mixture to create shadows. Take a quick break to let your beautiful, golden frame dry completely so the edges don't blend with the mirror color. Add buff titanium mixed with a little bit of Naples yellow to the bottom right third of the mirror. Blend out the edges until you have the thinnest layer of yellow all over the mirror, with a more concentrated glow surrounding your lantern light. You'll add more yellow in the next step; we're just setting up a base layer here.

4 Once that layer is dry, go over the whole reflective portion of the mirror with a very, very light layer of water so we can make sure all the edges blend nicely together. Why are we letting it dry just to add more water? This helps build up a deeper color for the reflections, and while it seems weird, I promise it's worth it! Gently dab a mixture of Prussian blue, indigo, and buff titanium around the edges of the mirror that aren't directly adjacent to the lantern (7 o'clock to 3 o'clock—if the mirror was a clock). Add a bit more Naples yellow to the glowing yellow area, and then blend those edges together with a small amount of water. Keep adding more of each color in stages until the mirror looks like it's glowing. The two most important tips here are to go slowly and to keep an eye on the edges of any areas that are drying. Sometimes those areas can make harsh lines, so you can gently dab the area with a clean, damp brush if it looks like the paint is drying in a harsh line that'll take away from the reflective appearance of the mirror.

Once you've made a nice transition between the light and dark parts of the mirror, mix up some Prussian blue and indigo, and add a bit around the edges farthest from the lantern to add a last bit of contrast that'll really make the lantern pop. Then blend the edges out, leaving a bit of a streaky appearance to give the impression of reflected light. Your mirror looks amazing—nice work!

Essence of Starlight

You never know when you might need some essence of starlight for a spell, so it's a good idea to bottle it up on the very brightest nights. This bottle is so fun to paint because the layers of paint will start off looking like some sort of amorphous blob, only to suddenly turn into a glowing star when we add the last layers. You can use any colors you'd like—perhaps you'd prefer your starlight to glow pink or green? You'll get the most pop by choosing two colors with a lot of contrast (one really light, one very dark), so feel free to play around and find what looks best on your shelf!

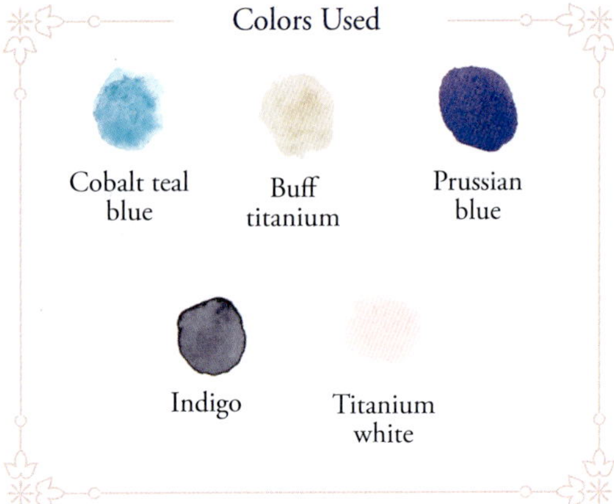

1

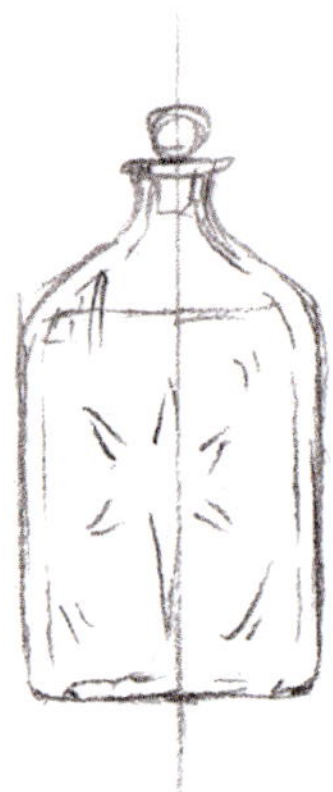

2

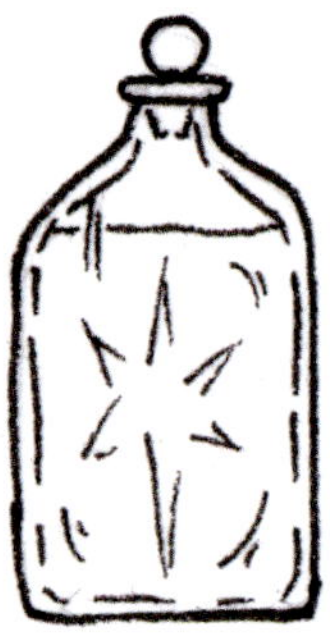

1 Sketch the outline of the bottle in pencil, beginning with a light rectangle for the overall shape, and then add the rest of the bottle, the lines where you'll place the highlights, and lines inside the bottle in a vague star shape. We'll ink them in the next step, and it's nice to be able to adjust the pencil outlines until you're happy with the shape.

2 Using your waterproof pen, trace your pencil sketch, and then once the ink is dry, gently erase the pencil layer.

3

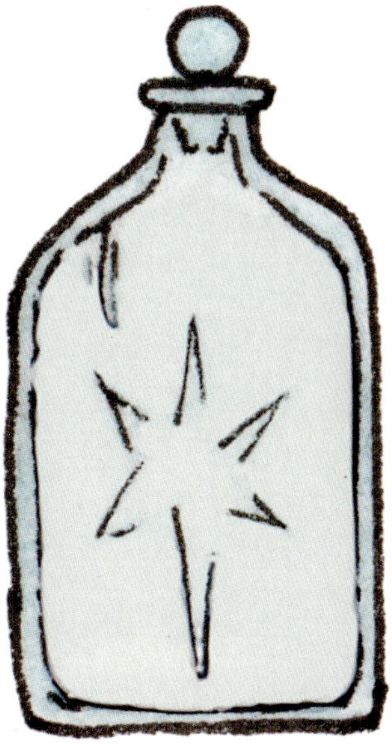

4

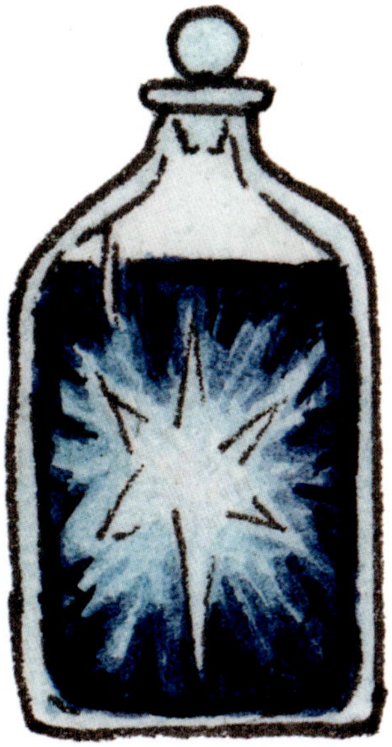

3 Using your larger brush, fill in the whole bottle, including the glass stopper, with a light layer of extremely watered-down cobalt teal blue mixed with a hint of buff titanium, adding a second layer with additional cobalt teal blue on the edges of the glass and in the stopper with your smaller brush. Allow this layer to dry completely before moving on—we don't want the next layer to bleed into this one!

4 The current light blue color is going to be the highlight of the very center of the star, so be sure to leave that unpainted while we work on adding the dark colors here. Grab your smaller brush, and starting off directly around that super light blue, add a slightly darker layer of cobalt teal blue, extending it all the way out to the edges of the bottle. Then start each layer gradually farther away from the center, building up five to ten layers of increasingly dark blue by adding more and more Prussian blue and indigo with each layer until your starlight is positively glowing! Then add a last bit of pure Prussian blue and indigo at the very outer edges of the bottle, followed by a dab of titanium white in the center of the star to bring back the brightest highlight, and your starlight is ready!

Liquid Sunshine

Have you ever longed for some warm sunshine in the middle of a rainy, dreary, winter day? This jar of liquid sunshine is exactly what you need when you're feeling gloomy, and it's a delight to paint! The celestial witch collects jars of liquid sunshine throughout the year, so there's always a supply of that crisp winter sunshine; sleepy summer sunshine; and warm and golden spring sunbeams—whatever you might fancy!

Colors Used

- Cobalt teal blue
- Buff titanium
- German greenish raw umber
- Cadmium yellow deep hue
- Naples yellow
- Raw sienna
- Titanium white

1

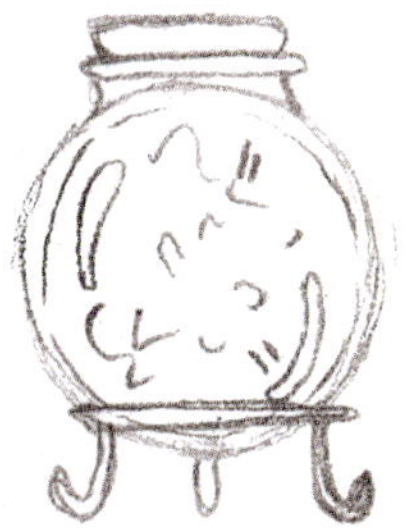

2

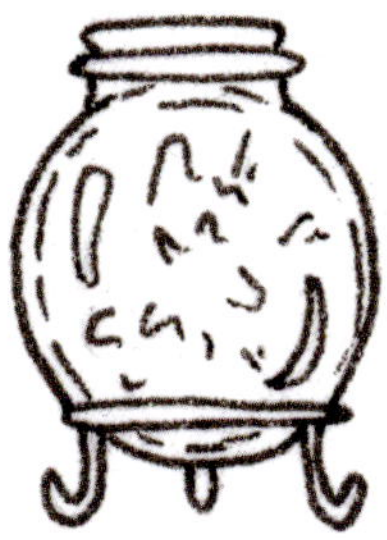

1 Start off your pencil sketch with a circle, and then build the rest of the bottle and its stand from there. Add some wiggly lines in the center to indicate the glow of the sunshine. We'll ink them in the next step, so it's nice to double-check that we're happy with the placement here while it can still be changed.

2 You know the drill—grab your waterproof pen and go over the pencil outline, making sure to start with the stand so you don't cover it with lines for the bottle. Once the ink is dry, gently erase the pencil layer.

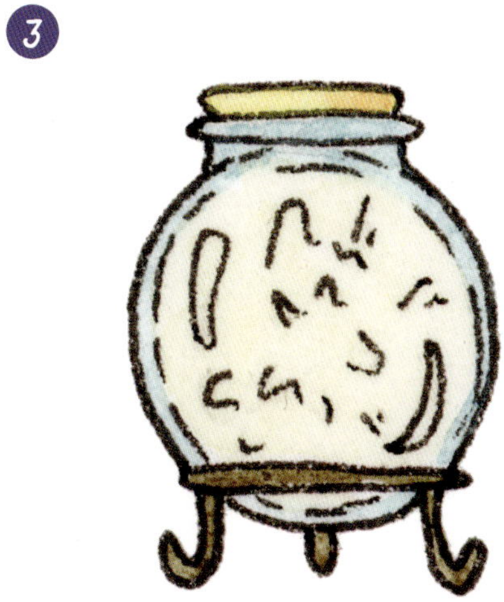

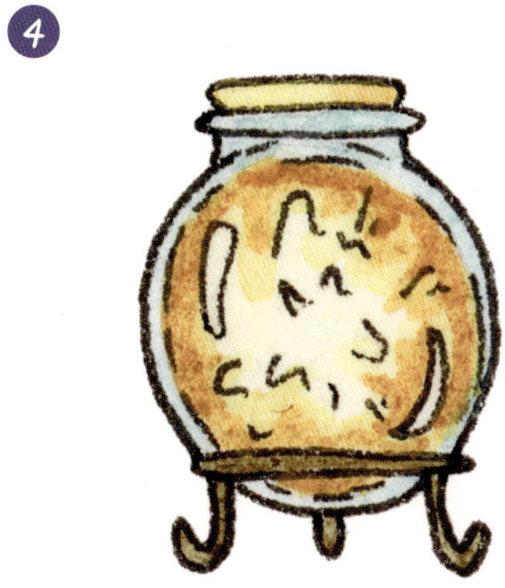

3 Using your smaller brush, fill in the glass portions of the bottle with a very light mixture of cobalt teal blue and buff titanium, and then fill in the stand with German greenish raw umber. Once the glass color is dry, fill in the lid with cadmium yellow deep hue mixed with Naples yellow, adding a hint of raw sienna towards the right side to give the barest impression of a shadow. Let that dry for a few minutes, and then fill in the whole interior of the bottle with the very lightest layer of Naples yellow—so light that it's nearly white. Let this dry completely before moving on.

4 We'll be leaving the very center of the bottle untouched from the last step—that layer of whitish yellow will be the center of our ball of sunshine. So, working out from that circle, build up layers of Naples yellow combined with cadmium yellow deep hue and buff titanium, adding more of the yellows to the mixture as needed, followed by adding a bit of raw sienna. Build up the layers slowly (you'll end up with five to ten, depending on how concentrated your paint is), making sure you're not getting the paper too waterlogged to accept new paint. Once you reach the outer edge of your sunshine, dab a bit of pure raw sienna to bring out the darkest parts of the potion, which will make the highlights pop. Take a tiny bit of titanium white, and pop it in the center of your sunshine if you'd like a bit of extra contrast, so the center looks like it's glowing. Your sunshine is bottled and ready to use!

Midnight-Colored Familiar

A notoriously nocturnal, midnight-colored familiar is the perfect companion for the celestial witch, and this deeply colored cat is a delightfully fun addition to their shelf. This inquisitive feline is exploring the delicate orrery solar system in the example, but there are endless opportunities for a cat to cause mischief however you'd like to set up your shelf. Of course, the cat doesn't have to be midnight-colored, or even this particular shape. If you'd prefer to include a napping cat, you can adapt the cats from the previous tutorials. Or if you'd like to include your own cat, you can adjust the shape and coloring to match, since it's always fun to include personal details in paintings.

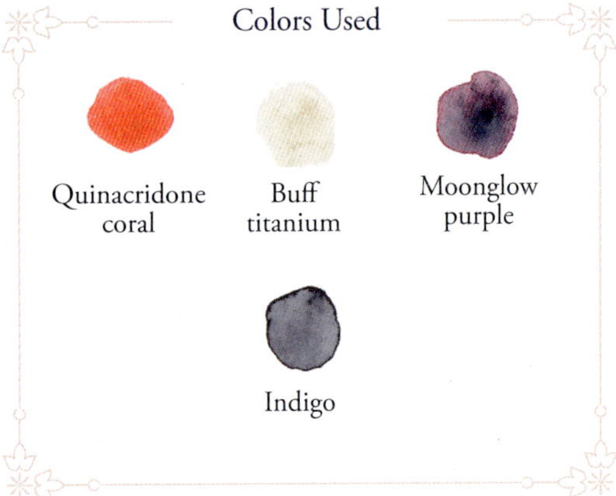

1

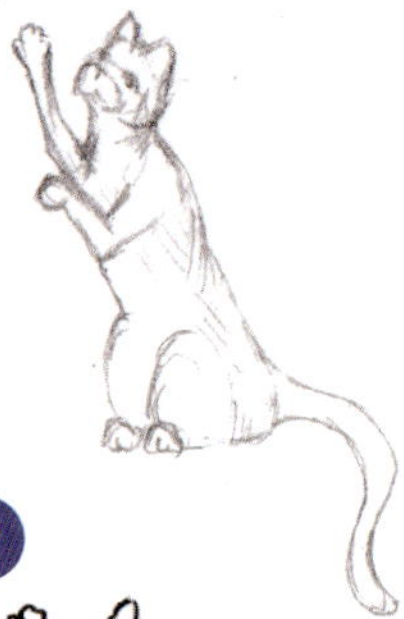

2

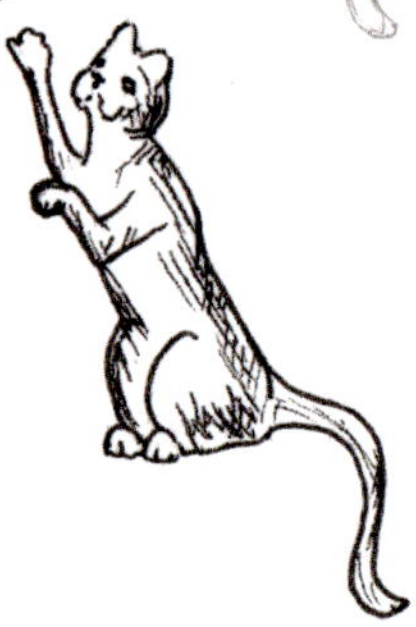

1 Use your pencil to sketch a long, skinny, very light oval for the cat's body, a small square for its head, and lines for the general position of the arms, legs, and tail. Do the overall proportions make sense when you step back and squint at the sketch? If so, build up the details. I like to start with the head, since that's the most complicated part, and then, working my way down, I add the legs, paws, and finally, the tail.

2 Go over your pencil outline with a waterproof pen, adding a bit of shading for the fur. Once the ink is dry, gently erase the pencil layer.

3

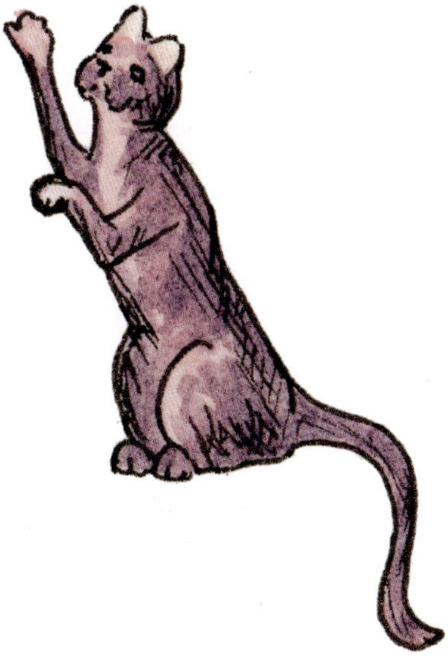

4

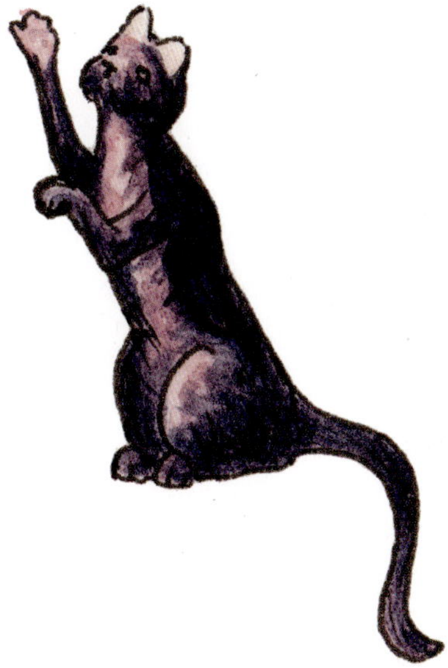

3 We'll build up the colors in two steps to really get a deep midnight color in the end. Begin by using your larger brush to fill in the whole cat—except for the ears—with a light layer of quinacridone coral, buff titanium, and moonglow purple. Use your smaller brush to fill in the ears with buff titanium mixed with a tiny hint of quinacridone coral. While that's still wet, build up a few layers of indigo mixed with your purply base color to begin the shadows and coloring on the fur.

4 Once that's at least somewhat dry, continue to build up layers of successively darker purply blue by adding a bit more indigo to each layer, being careful to leave some of your lighter highlights, including on the paws. You can use either size brush for this step, depending on how small you'd like the fur details to be. Experiment with both and see what you prefer! And just like that, your midnight-colored familiar is ready to get up to all sorts of trouble!

Delicate Orrery Solar System

Since the celestial witch often needs to know the exact positions of the planets in relation to one another, a delicate orrery solar system is an indispensable addition to their shelf. It's also a great opportunity to practice your delicate ink line work, with all the small wires holding up the planets! It's important to keep a close eye on any feline familiars though, as all the shiny planets are an utterly tempting toy, and you may often return to find your planets have mysteriously been rearranged (or a few may have disappeared entirely).

Colors Used

- Yellow ochre
- Naples yellow
- Buff titanium
- German greenish raw umber
- Perylene green
- Cadmium yellow deep hue
- Quinacridone coral
- Prussian blue
- Raw sienna
- Cobalt teal blue

1

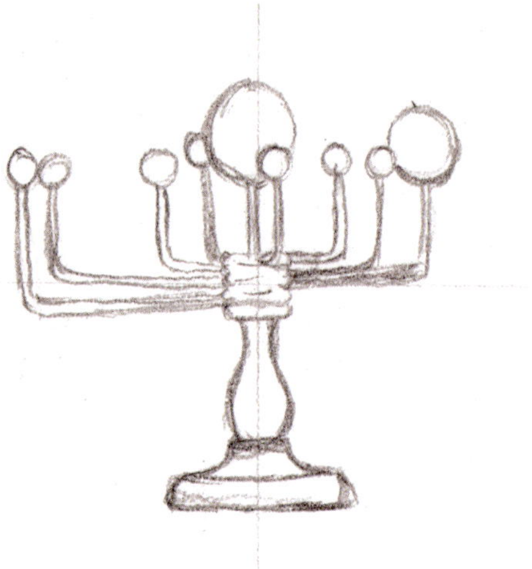

1 Before starting on the actual shape, use your pencil to draw a very light plus-sign shape, with the center being where the planets will spin around. Draw the base and sun, and then add the remaining planets, making sure to vary the lengths of the supporting arms so the planets don't bump into each other when they're repositioned.

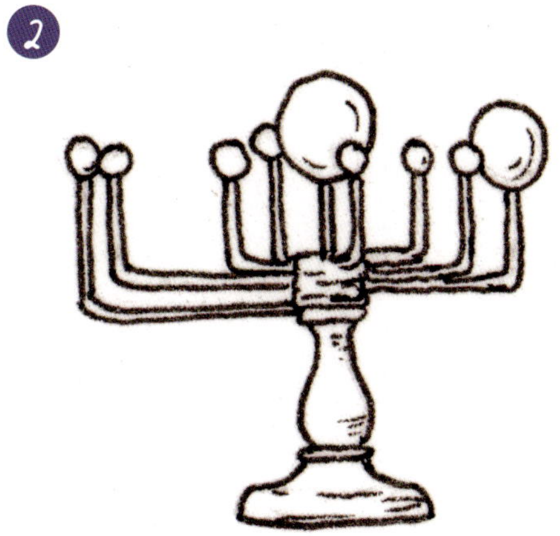

2 Carefully go over your pencil outline with your waterproof pen, making sure to add some shadows and texture on the stand and larger planets. Once the ink is dry, gently erase the pencil layer. Let's start painting!

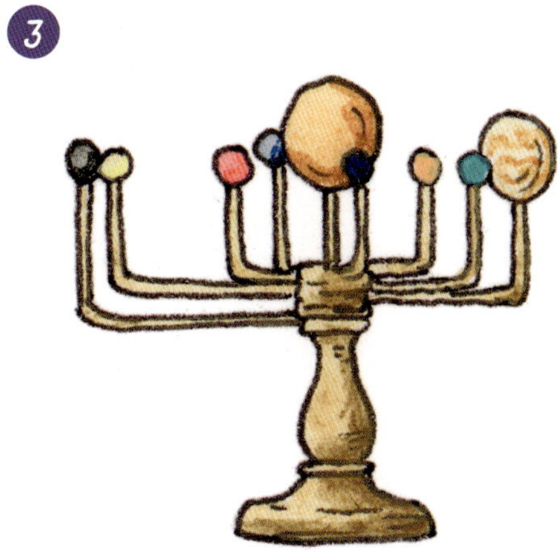

3 Using your smaller brush, fill in the base and arms with yellow ochre combined with Naples yellow and buff titanium, building up some German greenish raw umber to make shadows on the base. Going left to right, fill in the planets with pure perylene green, cadmium yellow deep hue with buff titanium, quinacridone coral with buff titanium, Prussian blue mixed with buff titanium, Naples yellow combined with a hint of raw sienna, pure Prussian blue, pure Naples yellow, pure cobalt teal blue, and Naples yellow combined with buff titanium. Add at least a second layer of each color to make shadows. For the planet on the farthest right, go back and add some swirls of raw sienna to make storm clouds. Your delicate orrery solar system is done, and it looks amazing!

Spellbooks of Dubious Origin

The celestial witch's spellbooks might've come from a bookstore or library, but it's probably best not to look too closely into their provenance. Suffice it to say, I've never seen books like this in my local library. How about you? One always wishes to have plenty of spellbooks on hand, since you never know when you'll need to reheat a cup of tea (with magic, of course), find a match to the single sock that came out of the dryer (again, with magic), or summon a fireball. You know, everyday magic things.

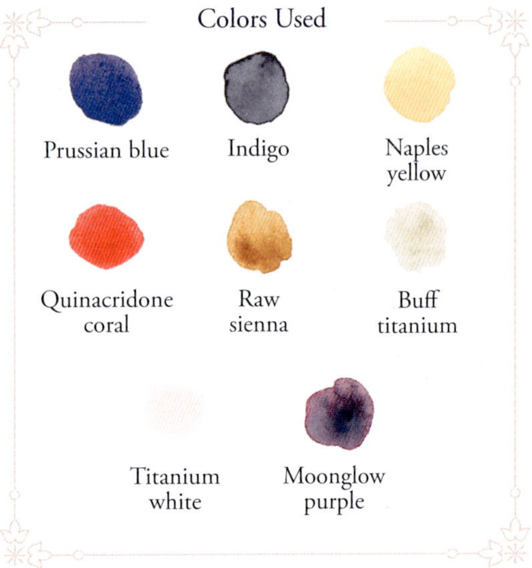

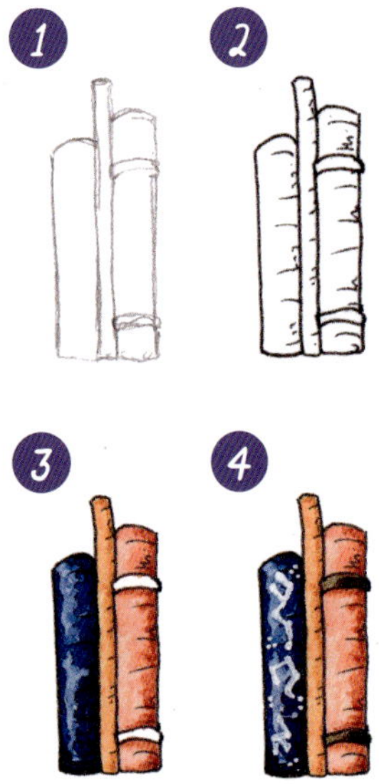

1 Sketch three rectangles, keeping the corners rounded to give the appearance of the curved spines of the books.

2 Trace your pencil outline with a waterproof pen, adding shading to the books and the lines for the leather bindings on the book farthest to the right. Once the ink is dry, gently erase the pencil layer.

3 Make sure to let each book dry before painting the one next to it so the colors don't bleed together. Start with your larger brush and a very watered-down Prussian blue with the tiniest hint of indigo on the left book. Build up several layers to make a dark, starry night color, adding more indigo to each layer to make deep shadows. Then fill in the center book with Naples yellow mixed with quinacridone coral, adding shadows towards the right side by adding a bit of raw sienna. Finally, add buff titanium combined with Naples yellow and quinacridone coral to the main body of the right book, adding shadows with raw sienna and the tiniest hint of indigo. Don't start on the details on the books until this layer is completely dry!

4 Now let's add stars and constellations to the book on the left with titanium white and your smaller brush. Add raw sienna mixed with Prussian blue, indigo, and moonglow purple to the bindings on the book on the right to make a nice, leathery brown—and you're all done!

Moonlight-Infused Amethyst Crystal

There's always space for more crystals on the celestial witch's shelf, and this moonlight-infused amethyst crystal is the perfect size to tuck between the enchanted pocket sundial and delicate orrery solar system. Are amethyst crystals not quite what you're dreaming of painting today? You could swap out the crystal in this tutorial for a geode, a rock, or any other small treasure you've collected.

Colors Used

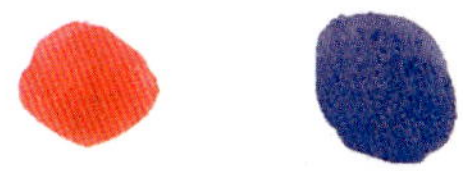

Quinacridone coral

Prussian blue

1

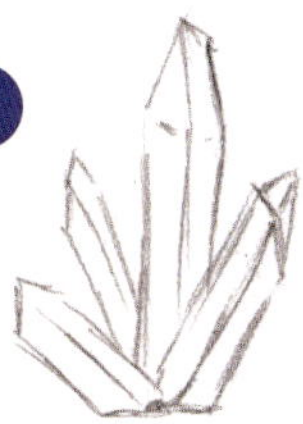

2

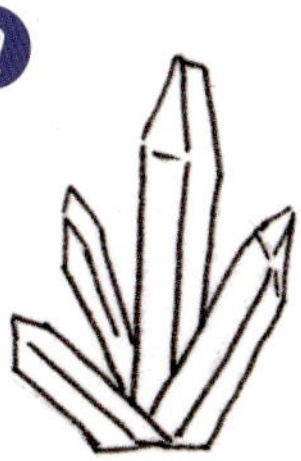

3

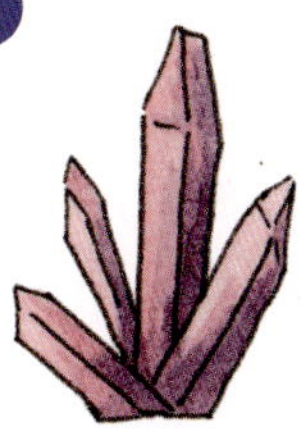

1 The size and number of crystal pieces can be easily modified to fit any open space on the shelf, but we'll start off with a pencil sketch of four rectangles with pointy ends.

2 Go over your pencil sketch with a waterproof pen, keeping the lines as straight as possible, and then once the ink is dry, erase the pencil.

3 Use your smaller brush to mix up some quinacridone coral and the tiniest hint of Prussian blue to make a bright purple, and use it to fill in the whole crystal. Let it dry, then add more Prussian blue to make a darker purple, and use that to fill in the faces that will be shadowed, building up a few layers towards the base where the shadows will be darker. And that's it—you're finished! The crystals are a fantastic place to incorporate your favorite colors, so if purple isn't your thing, you can swap the colors out for anything that makes you happy! One of the easiest ways to make your overall shelf (or painting in general) look cohesive is to use a color palette that repeats throughout the painting. (You'll notice that in this chapter, we've used a lot of Naples yellow and quinacridone coral, and that's on purpose to help tie everything together.) My point here is that, if you use a different color, I'd recommend finding other places on the shelf to incorporate it as well so it looks a little more grounded, but it's totally up to individual preference!

Maidenhair Fern that Grows in Moonlight and Sunlight

We all know how difficult it can be to get houseplants to grow happily, but the celestial witch doesn't need to worry about that. Why not? This beautiful maidenhair fern is enchanted to grow in both moonlight and sunlight, so it's always in peak condition. This example shows a plain, terra-cotta pot with some subtle pink highlights, but plant pots are one of my favorite ways to add extra personality to shelves. So if you're looking for something more colorful, you could swap it out for a tea tin or something like an ancient Roman pot.

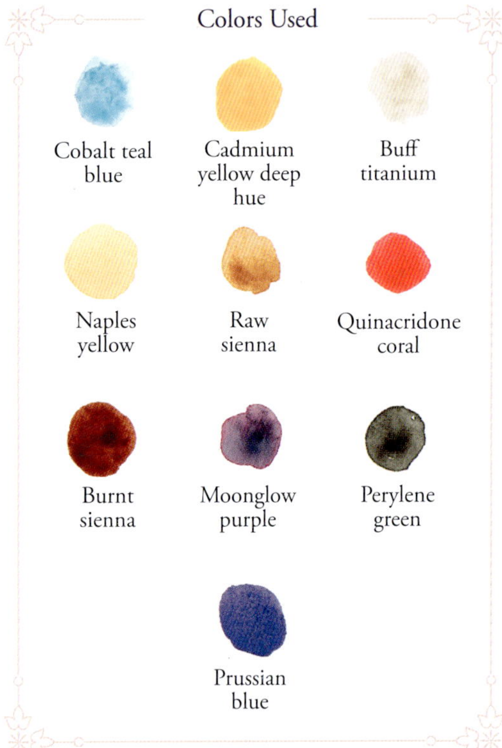

1

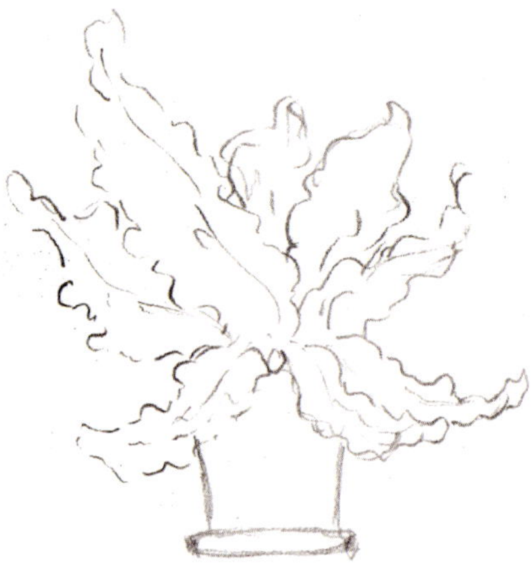

1 Sketch the outline of a terra-cotta pot with a base, and then draw some gently curving lines for the center lines of the leaves. Now, add some wiggly lines to indicate the outlines of the leaves, starting at the front and working backwards. Erase any areas of the pot that are covered by leaves so they don't get inked in the next step.

2

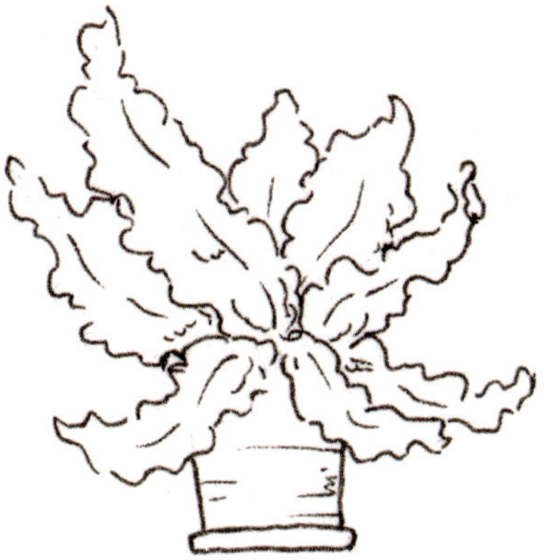

2 Go over your pencil outline with a waterproof pen, keeping the outline loose and focusing more on the overall movement of the plant as opposed to drawing each and every leaf accurately. Once the ink is dry, gently erase the pencil layer.

3

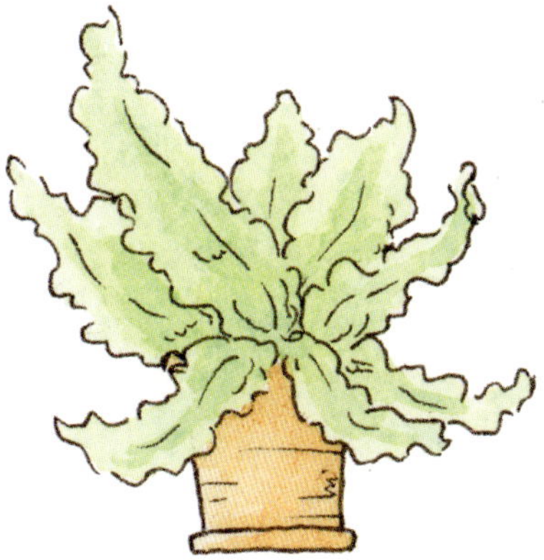

3 Using your larger brush, fill in the whole fern with a light layer of cobalt teal blue mixed with cadmium yellow deep hue and a smidge of buff titanium, building up the first few layers of shadows. Let it dry completely. Next, fill in the whole pot with Naples yellow mixed with raw sienna, building up several layers to begin the appearance of shadows.

4

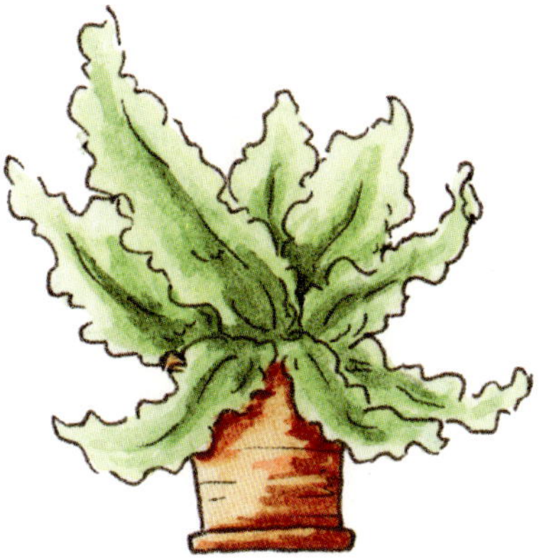

4 Once the prior layer is mostly dry, add some quinacridone coral highlights to the pot and build up layers of raw sienna combined with burnt sienna, quinacridone coral, and increasing amounts of moonglow purple until the shadows are as dark as you'd like them to be. Let that dry all the way, and then build up layers of cobalt teal blue combined with cadmium yellow deep hue and buff titanium. Also add hints of perylene green and Prussian blue on the leaves for texture, with perylene green near the base of the plant where the shadows will be the darkest. And you're finished with your beautiful fern!

Terrarium with an Ever-Blooming Moonflower

Flowers are beautiful to have around, but they often don't last as long as one might like. This ever-blooming moonflower in a beautiful, stained-glass terrarium is the perfect solution: a delightful pop of color that's so much fun to paint!

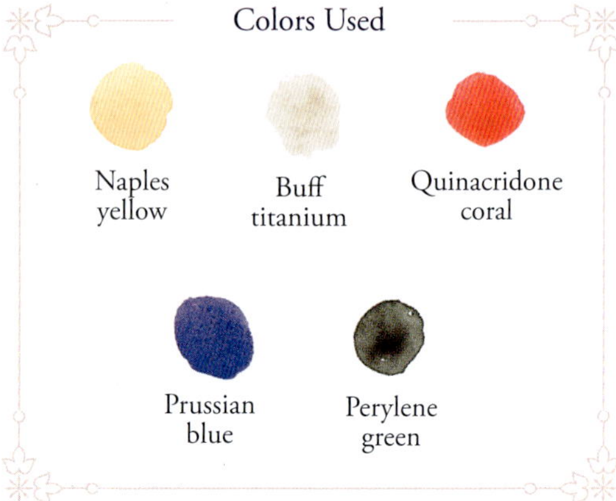

1

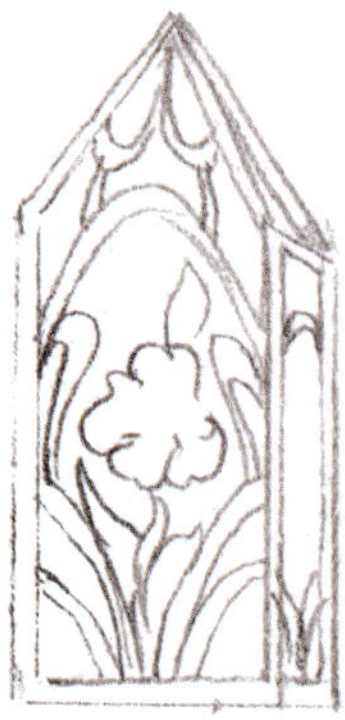

2

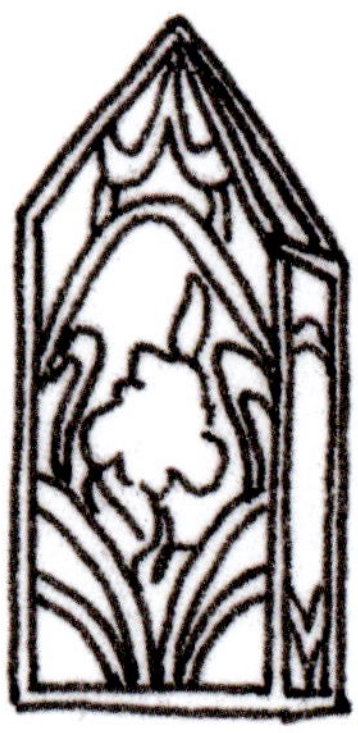

1 Start off your pencil sketch by drawing the outline of the overall terrarium, and then add the stained-glass shapes, and then the flower. If you prefer to simplify the design, you can change the shapes of the stained-glass pieces so there are fewer of them or draw the whole design slightly larger so the individual lines aren't as small. Feel free to adapt the tutorial so it works for you!

2 Use your waterproof pen to go over the pencil layer, and then once the ink is dry, gently erase the pencil. If you'd like the areas between the glass to be black, you can simply color them in here, but the tutorial in the next step will paint them a dark bluish-gray if you prefer that appearance.

3

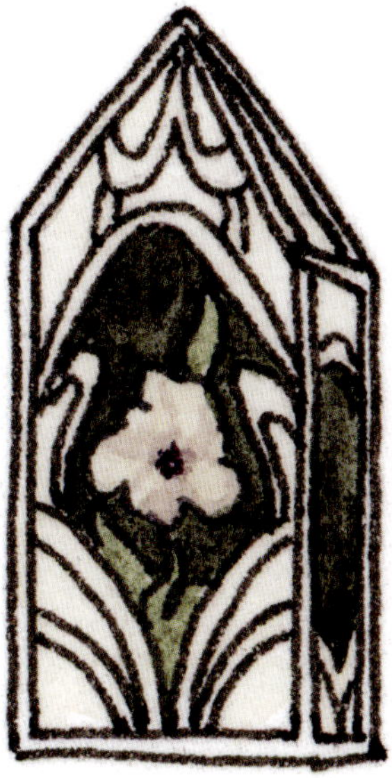

4

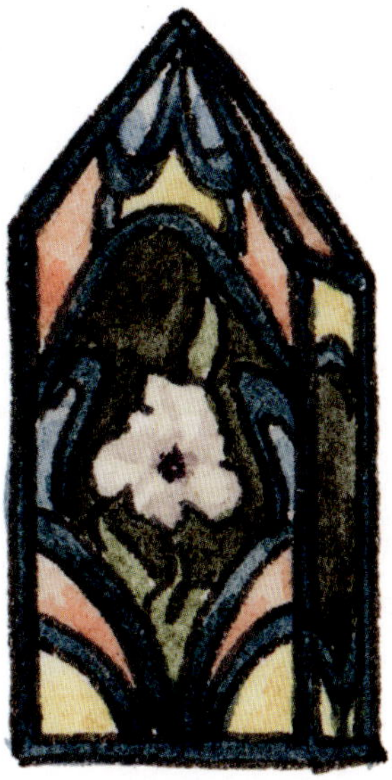

3 Use your smaller brush to paint all the stained-glass areas with a very, very light layer of Naples yellow, and allow that to dry. Add a bit of buff titanium to the flower and dab some quinacridone coral mixed with Prussian blue in the center to make a shadow. Smooth the shadow toward the edges of the petals to give your flower some depth. Give the flower a few minutes to dry so the edges don't bleed together, and then fill in the space between the flower and stained glass with perylene green mixed with varying amounts of Naples yellow. Build up several layers to imply a leafy texture.

4 Now for the stained glass, which is one of my favorite things to paint! Start off by painting the welds using a mixture of Prussian blue, buff titanium, and a bit of perylene green, and then allow this to dry all the way. For the yellow areas, add a second layer of Naples yellow, making the areas towards the bottom right of each section darker. Mix up some quinacridone coral, Naples yellow, and buff titanium, and fill in the pink sections with a few light layers, again making texture and shadows by allowing the layers to dry in between. Finally, use Prussian blue mixed with buff titanium to fill in the blue sections, and your moonflower is ready to admire!

Drawers for Bits and Bobs

It's easy for clutter to accumulate on a shelf, since there's such an interesting assortment of trinkets and magical objects in the celestial witch's cottage. To keep everything organized, let's paint some wooden drawers that can be filled with bits and bobs, which has the added bonus of keeping them safe from the cat's inquisitive paws!

Colors Used

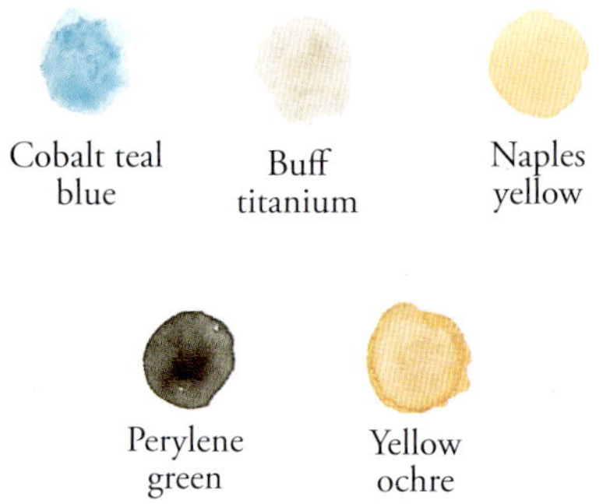

1

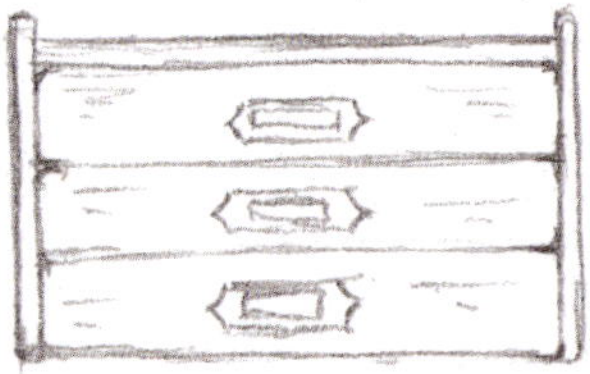

2

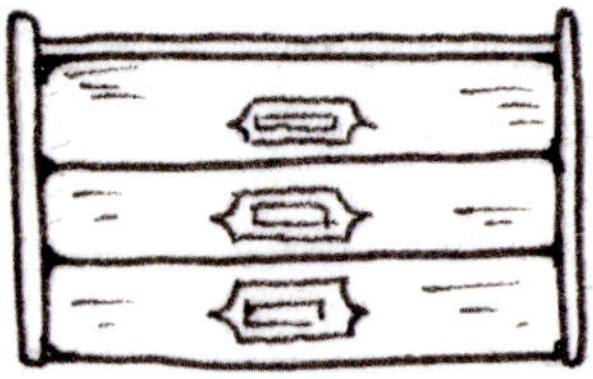

3

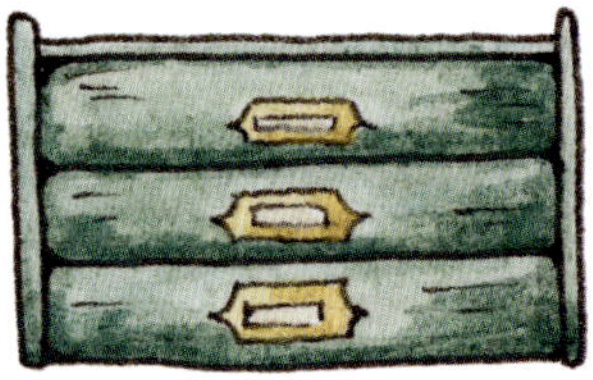

1 Use your pencil to draw a rectangle, and then add the drawers and other details—making the set of drawers as simple or as fancy as you'd like.

2 Trace your pencil outline with a waterproof pen, adding extra lines to indicate the wood grain on the drawers, and then once the ink is dry, gently erase the pencil.

3 Using your larger brush, mix up some cobalt teal blue, buff titanium, Naples yellow, and perylene green, and use it to fill in the whole set of drawers (other than the draw pulls). Build up shadows with additional layers with increasing amounts of cobalt teal blue and perylene green until you love the way it looks, and then let it dry completely. Then switch to your smaller brush and combine yellow ochre, buff titanium, and Naples yellow, and fill in the outside section of each drawer pull. Then use a bit of pure buff titanium to fill in the label on each drawer. If you'd like to make the labels dark instead of light, pure perylene green or indigo will give a slightly spookier effect. Another option, since this is, after all, the celestial witch, is to do a sunset or sunrise theme with purple on top, pink in the middle, and yellow for the bottom drawer's label. And now your drawers are ready to be filled with mysterious treasures!

The Celestial Witchery Shelf

Now it's time to work on the actual shelf for our celestial witch so there's a nice surface to arrange all the items on. Let's begin!

1

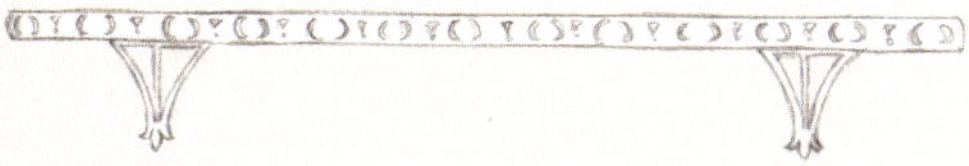

2

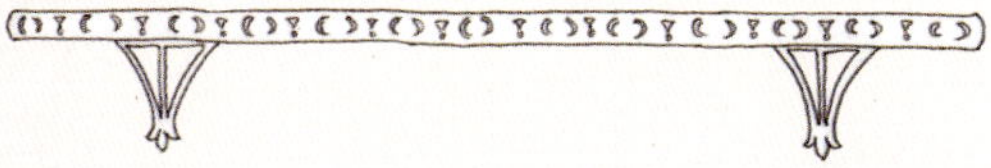

3

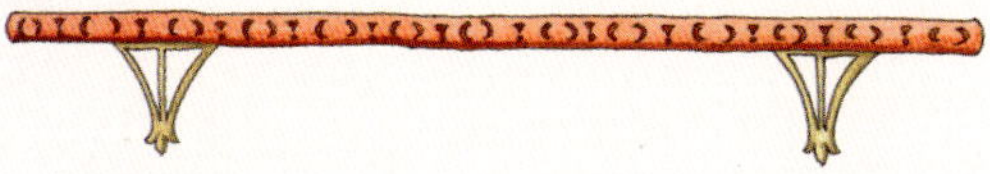

Colors Used

Quinacridone coral
Naples yellow
Buff titanium
Raw sienna
Burnt sienna
German greenish raw umber
Yellow ochre

1 First, sketch the two horizontal lines for the top and bottom of the shelf, using a ruler if you'd like perfectly straight lines or free drawing them for a more organic appearance. Add the edges of the shelf and the crescent moon and triangle design, and then sketch the brackets.

2 Before you add ink, make sure you know whether or not you'll have any items overlapping with the shelf. In the example shown at the beginning of this chapter (page 124), the cat's tail overlaps with the shelf, so you wouldn't want to ink the shelf where the tail will be. Once you sort that out, trace the pencil with a waterproof pen, and then once the ink is dry, gently erase the pencil.

3 Using your larger brush, fill in the whole shelf with a layer of quinacridone coral mixed with about an equal amount of Naples yellow as well as a hint of buff titanium, raw sienna, and an even tinier bit of burnt sienna. Build up three to five layers to indicate the rounded shape of the shelf. Add darker shadows to the shelf by mixing a bit of German greenish raw umber into your shelf base color (and make a good bit of this color as you'll need more once this shadow layer has dried). While that dries, fill in the brackets with a few layers of yellow ochre mixed with Naples yellow and buff titanium, adding shadows with German greenish raw umber. Let dry completely. Finally, fill in the crescent moon and triangle shapes on the shelf with the leftover shadow color, and admire your beautiful work!

Assembling Your Celestial Witchery Shelf

Let's put all these enchanting celestial witchery items together to make a beautiful shelf! You can arrange them exactly like the tutorial, rearrange them, mix and match between the various shelves, or add items of your own. So many options!

Colors Used for the Background

Naples yellow | Cadmium yellow deep hue | Yellow ochre

1

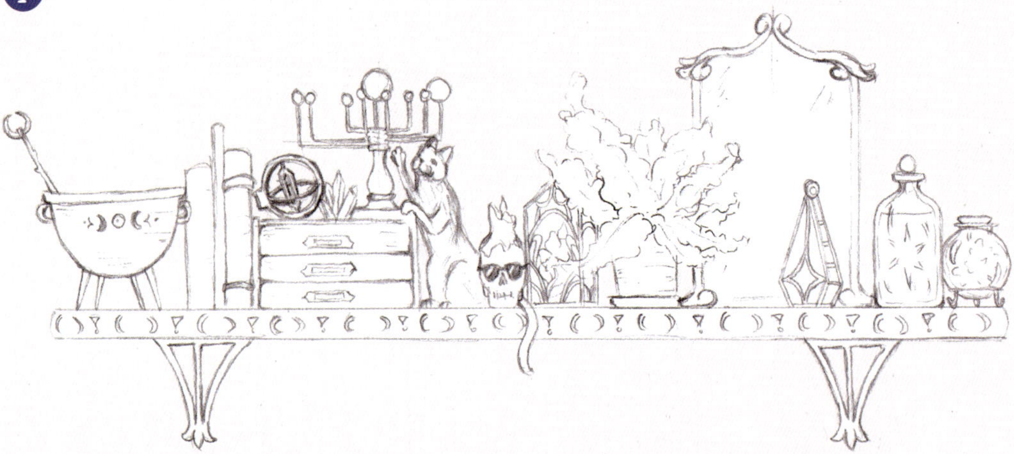

1 Start by sketching the shelf, and then mark the edges of each item so you can allocate enough space and nothing is squished off the end. Refer to The Celestial Witchery Shelf (page 149) for more guidance on sketching the shelf, and please refer back to each project's tutorial as needed for the sketches of the individual items.

2

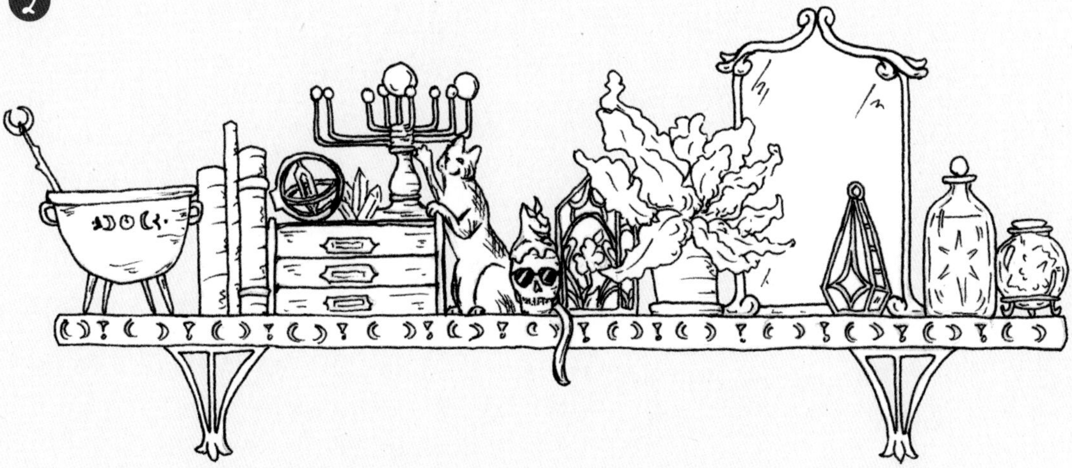

2 Using your waterproof pen, add ink to the Maidenhair Fern that Grows in Moonlight and Sunlight (page 144), Ever-Glowing Lantern (page 131), Haunted Skull with Sunglasses (page 128), Midnight-Colored Familiar (page 138), and Cauldron Full of Moonlight (page 126). Then ink the shelf and remaining items, referring to the individual instructions for any item that you'd like more detail on. Once the ink is dry, gently erase the pencil layer.

3 If you'd like to add a colored background to your painting like the one shown in the example, now is the easiest time to do it. So let's start off by choosing a color, and then we'll add it in the next half of this step. Swatch as many options as you'd like on some scrap paper, and then mix up a good amount of your chosen color—you won't want to try and mix more halfway through, since your wet edges will start to dry out and you can end up with some funny lines. If you'd like to make the yellow shown in the example, mix up some very watered-down Naples yellow with a hint of cadmium yellow deep hue and the tiniest little bit of yellow ochre. Keep in mind that this background is a very light yellow, and most of the items on the shelf are relatively dark, so if a little bit of background color gets inside the lines, it's not the end of the world. However, if you've chosen a darker background, you'll want to be much more careful when painting it in, since you won't be able to cover up any mistakes without gouache or other opaque paint.

Using either your smaller or larger brush, carefully outline your illustration with water to create the first part of your wet base layer, and then use a much larger brush (if you have one) to expand that layer of water to wherever you'd like your colored background to end. Once your water layer is complete, and while it's still wet, start building up a few layers of your yellow, making sure to work quickly (but carefully) so the first sections don't dry out completely before you're done. Build up as many layers as you'd like, and then set your shelf aside until it's completely dry.

4 We'll paint the shelf first, so refer back to The Celestial Witchery Shelf (page 149) for more detail as needed, and paint yourself a beautiful shelf. Remember to leave the cat's tail unpainted!

3

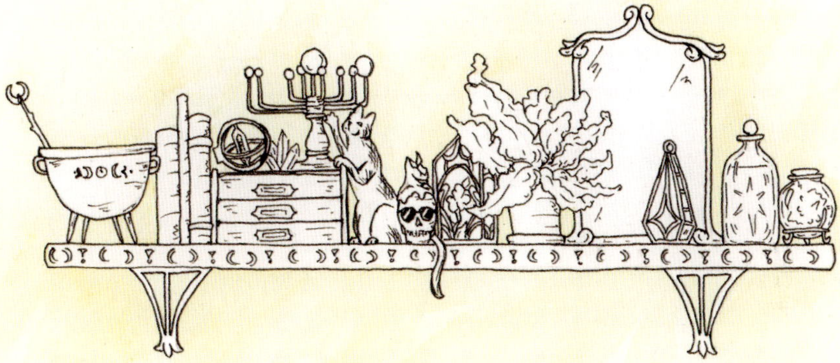

4

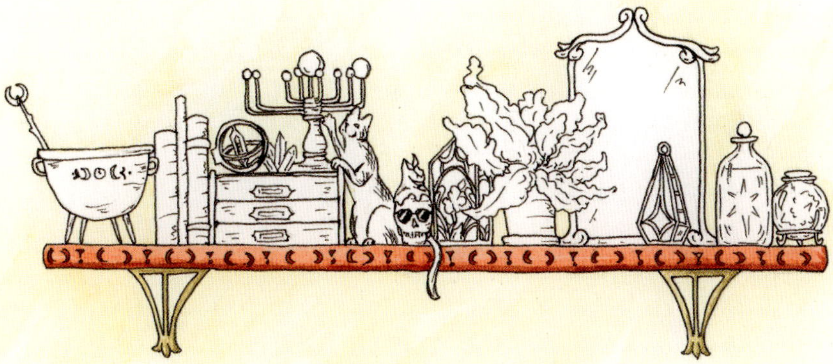

5

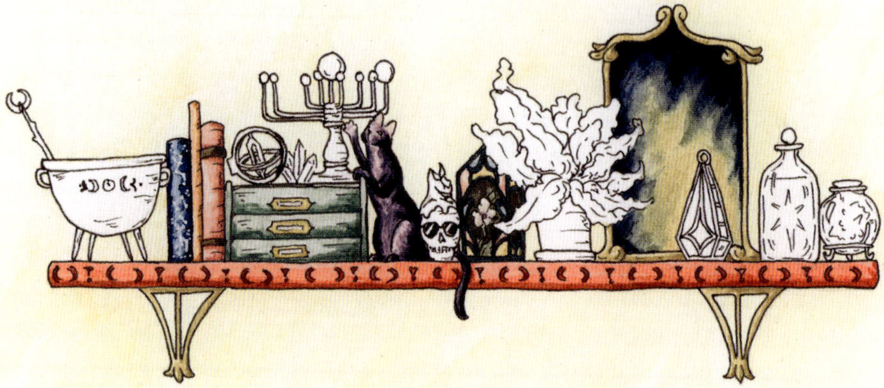

5 It's often easiest to avoid mistakes by painting items in the background of the shelf first, then the foreground. With that in mind, let's start off by painting the Spellbooks of Dubious Origin (page 142), Drawers for Bits and Bobs (page 148), Midnight-Colored Familiar (page 138), Terrarium with an Ever-Blooming Moonflower (page 146), and Ancient Spell Mirror (page 132). Whew! Take a break if you need to, you're making great progress!

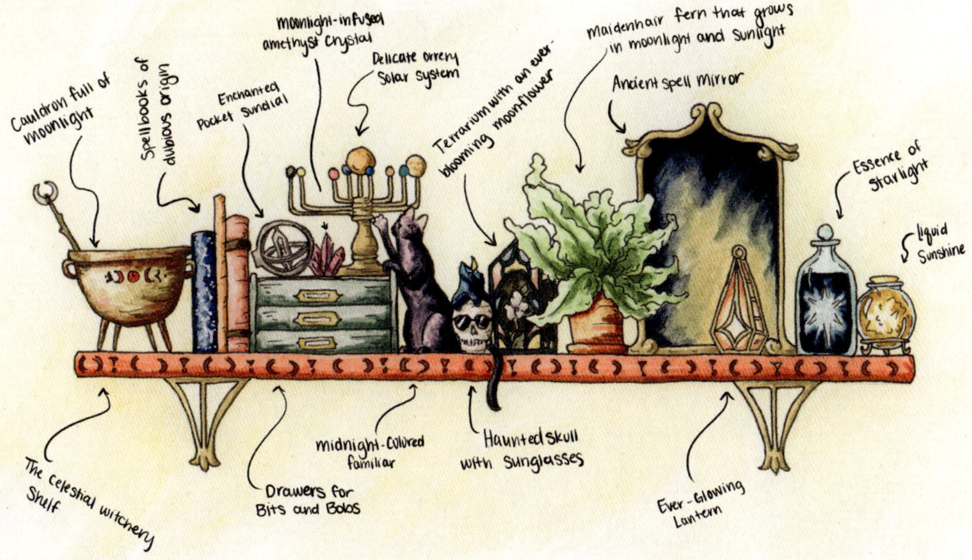

6 All right, we're in the home stretch! Now it's time to paint the Cauldron Full of Moonlight (page 126), Enchanted Pocket Sundial (page 130), Moonlight-Infused Amethyst Crystal (page 143), Delicate Orrery Solar System (page 140), Haunted Skull with Sunglasses (page 128), Maidenhair Fern that Grows in Moonlight and Sunlight (page 144), Ever-Glowing Lantern (page 131), Essence of Starlight (page 134), and finally, Liquid Sunshine (page 136). It looks amazing—your celestial witch's shelf is spectacular!

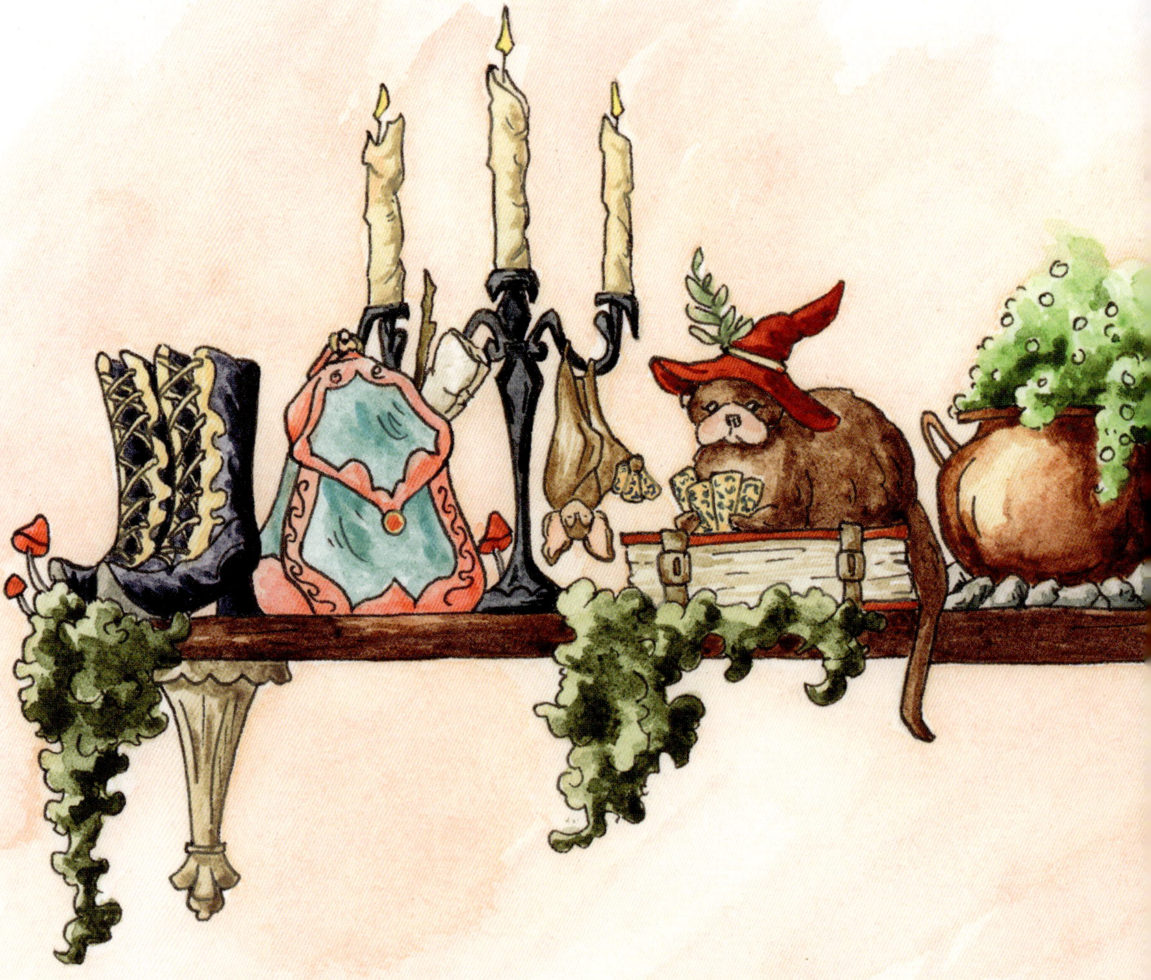

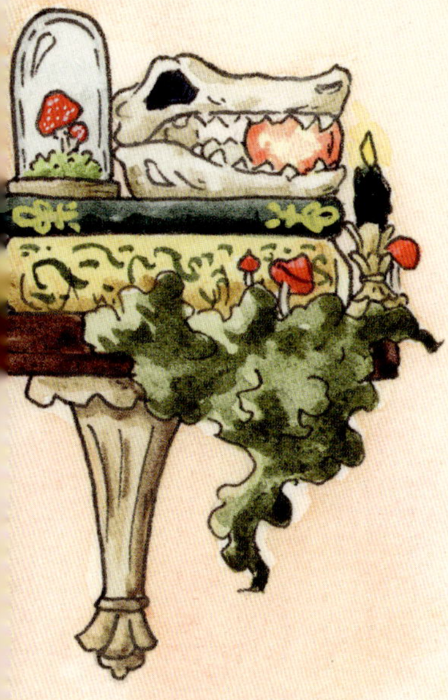

Swamp Witchery

Covered in climbing moss and full of mysterious items, the swamp witch's shelf has everything you'd need for an afternoon of adventuring, followed by an evening of reading and brewing potions. The otter, bat, and talking alligator skull are always nearby to provide commentary and ask endlessly for snacks and cookies, and they provide excellent book recommendations. With so many interesting things to paint, let's grab some art supplies and get painting!

Talkative Otter in a Pointed Hat

Every witch needs a companion to chat with, and the swamp witch keeps company with a talkative otter in a pointed hat and an inquisitive bat playing cards who love to play Go Fish, but between games they go on adventures and read books with the swamp witch.

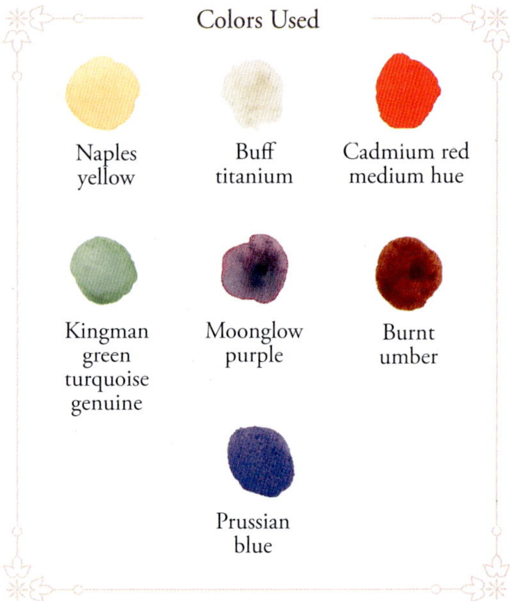

1

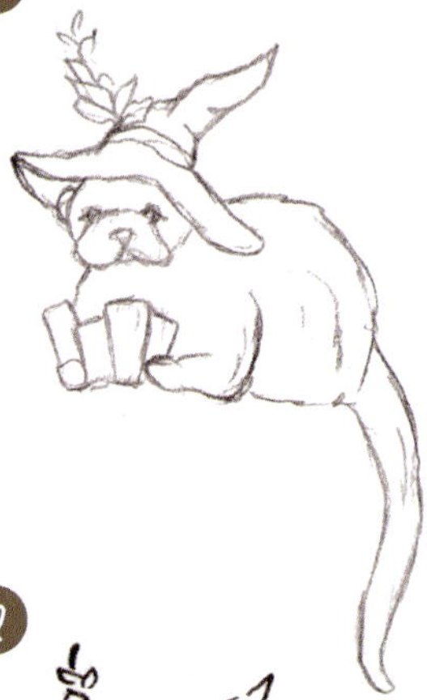

2

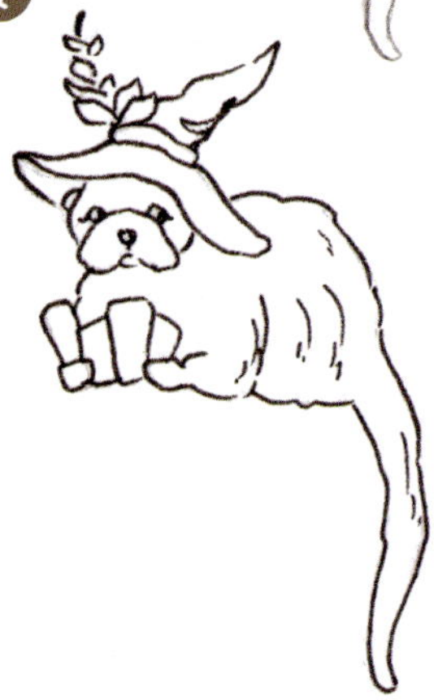

1 Start off with a light pencil sketch of the otter, beginning with an egg shape for the body before adding the head and face. Add in some playing cards being held in the otter's paws, a tail, and a hat with a jaunty stalk of leaves, erasing any parts of the head that are now covered by the hat so we don't accidentally add ink there in the next step.

2 Using your waterproof pen, go over the pencil sketch, adding shading and some extra lines to give the appearance of the otter's fur. Gently erase your pencil layer.

3

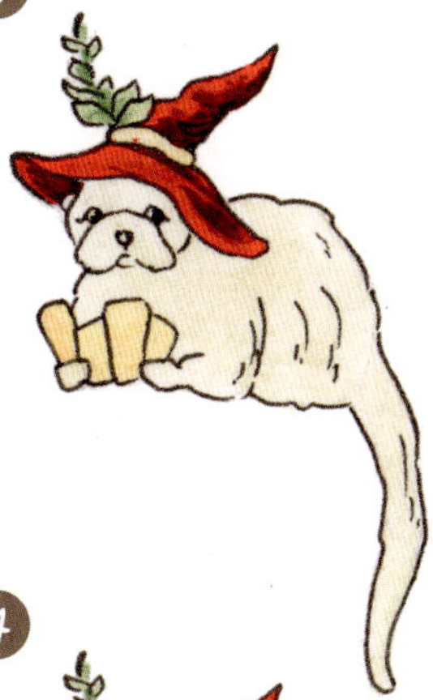

4

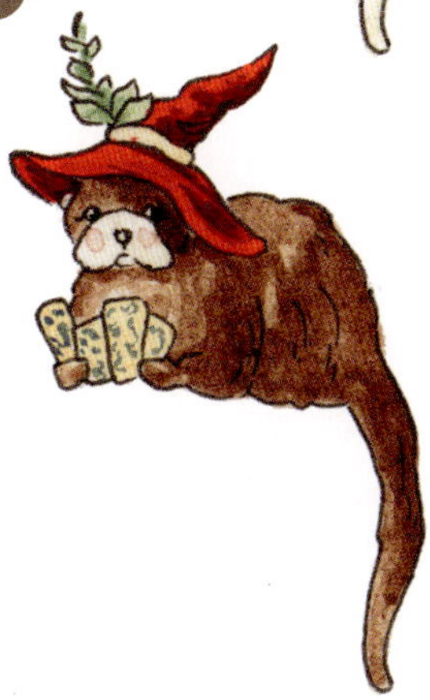

3 Using your larger brush, fill in the whole otter with a light mixture of Naples yellow mixed with buff titanium. Once that dries, use cadmium red medium hue to fill the hat, Naples yellow on the hat band, and Kingman green turquoise genuine mixed with Naples yellow on the leaves. While that layer is still wet, use moonglow purple and pure Kingman green turquoise genuine to add shadows and texture to the hat and leaves, respectively. Paint the playing cards with a light layer of Naples yellow, and allow that to dry completely before the next step. The playing cards are a fun spot to add more color to your painting, especially if you have a bit of gouache to work with so you're able to paint light on top of dark—as always, the tutorial is just an example, and you should make the shelf reflect your own unique personality however you'd like!

4 Add a light layer of Naples yellow, buff titanium, and the tiniest hint of cadmium red medium hue to the otter's face, and then add just a smidge more cadmium red medium hue to that mixture, and use it to dab some rosy highlights onto the otter's cheeks. Fill in the fur with layers of burnt umber mixed with Naples yellow, buff titanium, and moonglow purple, adding a larger proportion of moonglow purple for the shaded areas, building up the layers until you have nice shadows and a slight fur texture. Once the base color of the playing cards is completely dry, mix up some concentrated Prussian blue and buff titanium, and using your smallest brush, add a decorative design to the backs of the cards. Now your otter is ready to play Go Fish!

Pointed Boots for Traipsing in the Swamp

These fun, pointed boots are the perfect mix of fashionable and practical for traipsing in the swamp. How is that possible, given that the laces might let in water? Easy—the boots are enchanted to be waterproof but breathable, so the swamp witch's feet are always dry and not too hot or too cold. They really are the perfect shoes.

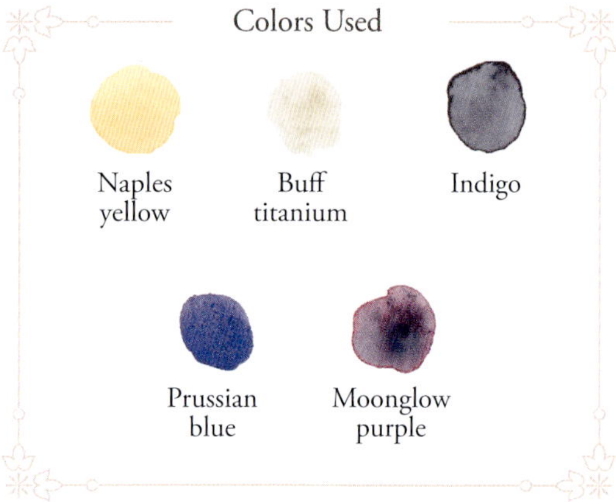

1

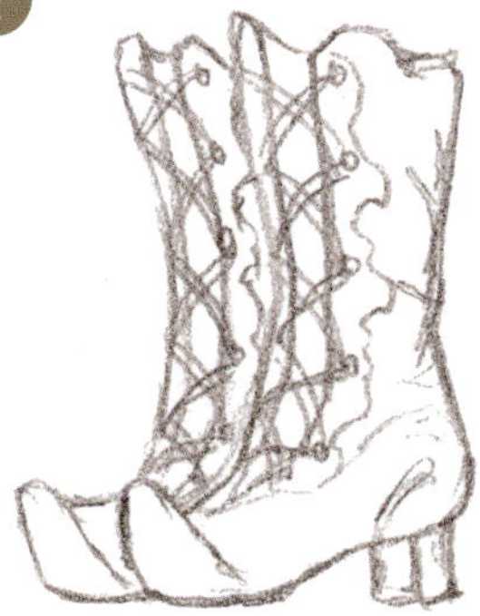

2

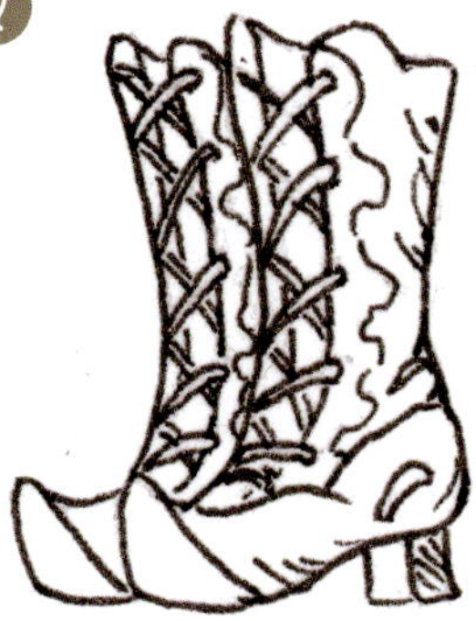

1 Lightly sketch the pencil outline for the boots, making them as tall and pointed, or as round and blocky, as you'd like, and then sketch in the laces and the edges of the decorative border. Shoes can be particularly hard to draw, so you can break the shape down into two perpendicular cylinders (the part for a foot and the part for a leg), sketch those lightly, and then add the other details.

2 Go over your pencil outline with your waterproof pen, adding extra shading near the bottom right edges of the boots where the light will cast shadows. Laces can be very fussy to draw, so if that's not your cup of tea, you can easily draw some squiggles and your boots will still look awesome. Once the ink is dry, gently erase the pencil layer.

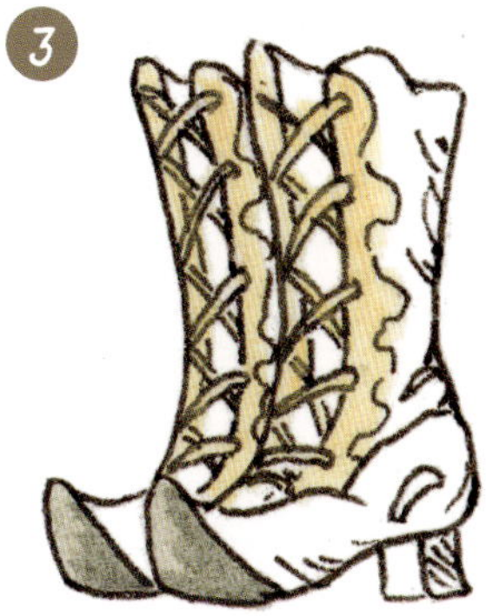 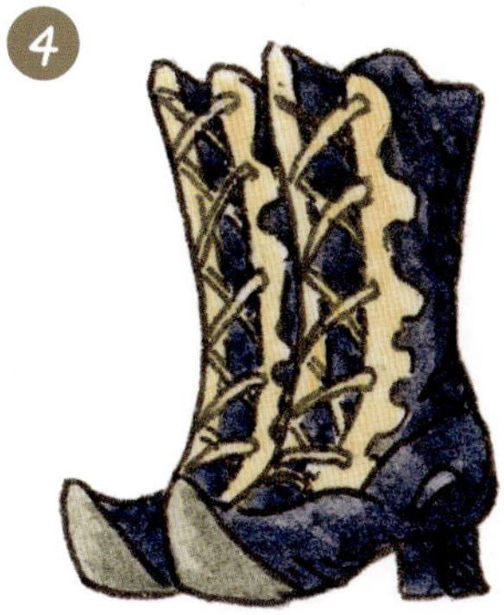 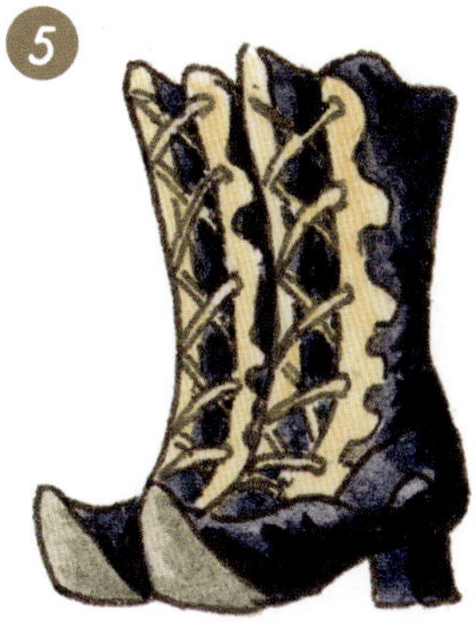

3 Use your smaller brush to fill in the decorative edges and laces with Naples yellow mixed with buff titanium, adding a bit more Naples yellow where you'd like to give the impression of shadows. Then combine Naples yellow and a bit of indigo, and use that to fill in the bits of the soles that are pointing up at the front of each boot. Let this layer dry completely—we don't want to take any chances of the dark blue in the next step bleeding into the decorative edges!

4 Once the yellow layer is completely dry, paint the rest of each boot with a layer of Prussian blue mixed with a bit of Naples yellow and a tiny hint of indigo and moonglow purple, adding a second layer to start the shadows. To make sure we get nice, rich shadows, let this layer of paint dry at least partially before continuing to add more layers.

5 Let's finish up those shadows! Add some light shadows to the decorative edges using pure Naples yellow and your smaller brush. Then build up three or four additional layers of your blue color, adding increasing amounts of indigo and moonglow purple, until you love the way the boots look!

Inquisitive Bat Playing Cards

Always found hanging around near the swamp witch and talkative otter, the inquisitive bat playing cards offers a unique perspective to every discussion. I absolutely love adding tiny bats to paintings. I find that they add so much whimsy and personality! If you'd like to have even more fun, you can add an itty bitty hat, scarf, or some tiny reading glasses or sunglasses!

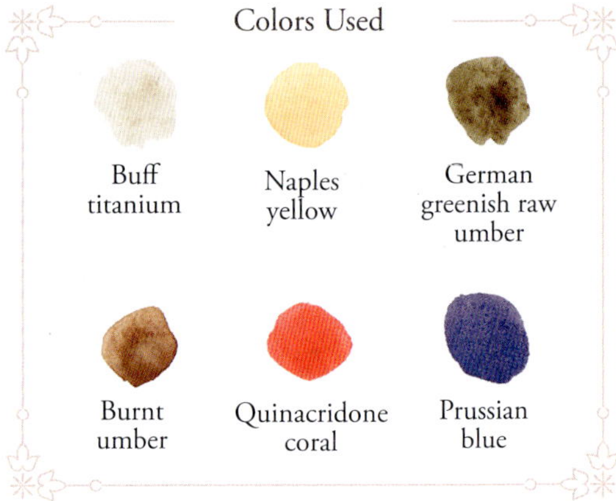

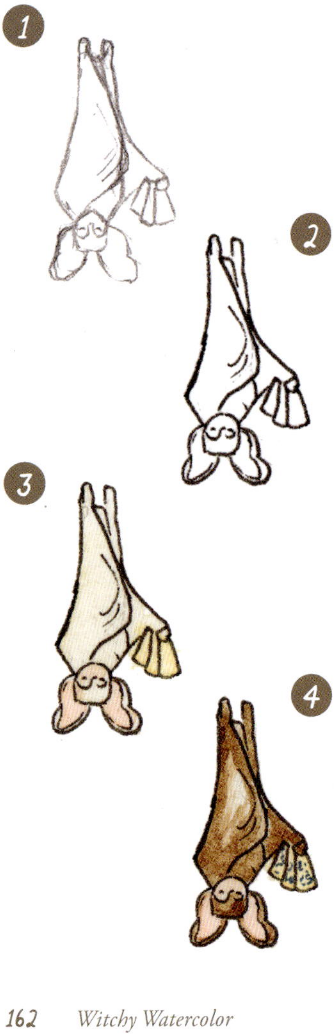

1 Sketch the outline of the bat, including some cute ears and an extended wing holding a set of playing cards. It can help to start by drawing a very light outline of the overall bat's shape (an upside-down diamond), and then fill in the details from there.

2 Using your waterproof pen, go over the pencil outline, adding extra lines for shadows and texture. Once the ink is dry, gently erase the pencil layer.

3 With your smaller brush, fill in the whole bat (other than the centers of the ears) with a light layer of buff titanium mixed with a hint of Naples yellow, German greenish raw umber, and burnt umber, and then fill in the playing cards with Naples yellow. Add a small dab of quinacridone coral mixed with buff titanium and Naples yellow to the ears and cheeks to help give the bat a friendly appearance. Then once the playing cards have dried completely, you can move to the next step.

4 Mix up some burnt umber, German greenish raw umber, Naples yellow, and buff titanium, and then use light layers to build up shadows and texture on the bat until you love the way it looks. Finally, mix up some concentrated Prussian blue and buff titanium, and use your smallest brush to add a decorative design on the cards, matching the design you did for the otter. Now, the bat would like to know if you have any threes?

Gothic Candelabra

Candelabras are one of my favorite things to paint since they're a great way to add lots of personality to a composition. The one in this tutorial is gently curving and symmetrical, but you can replace the curves with sharp angles to achieve a delightfully spooky look if that's what you prefer! You can also add a bit of moss or a climbing vine to give your shelf a mysterious, long-forgotten look.

Colors Used

Prussian blue
Deep sap green
Indigo
Naples yellow
Buff titanium
German greenish raw umber
Cadmium yellow deep hue

1

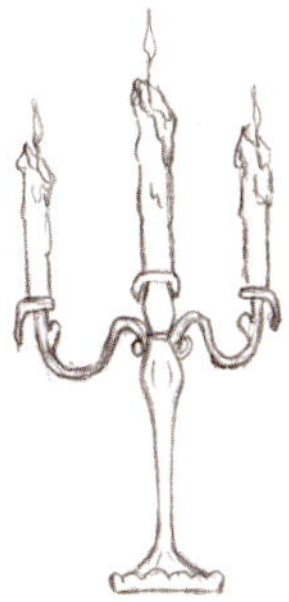

2

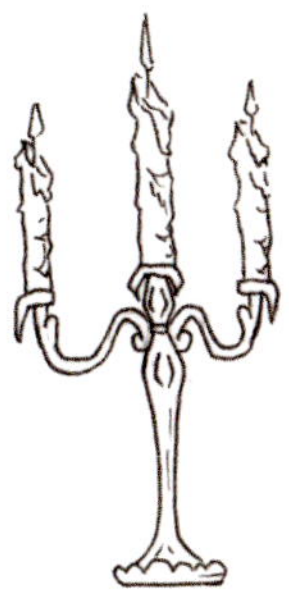

3

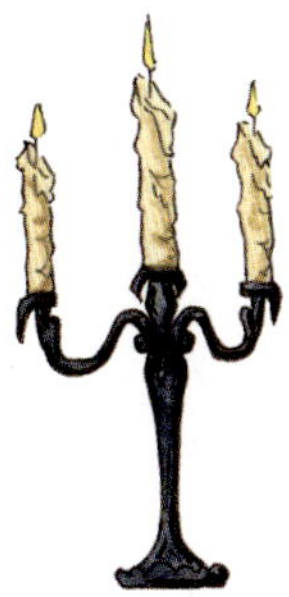

1 Draw a vertical center line with your pencil marking the top and bottom of your candelabra, and then sketch the candelabra along with its candles and their sparkling flames. You can add more candles to your candelabra or include dangling, glittering crystals—this is such a fun spot to add tons of personality, so let your imagination run wild!

2 Carefully trace your ink outline with a waterproof pen, adding shading and filagree for visual interest. Once the ink is dry, gently erase the pencil layer.

3 Mix together equal amounts of Prussian blue, deep sap green, indigo, and Naples yellow, and fill in the whole candelabra with the larger brush, building up two or three thin layers. Add a bit more deep sap green and indigo, and build up more layers to deepen the shadows. Paint the candles with Naples yellow mixed with buff titanium, adding shadows along the right edges with German greenish raw umber. Finally, take your smaller brush with cadmium yellow deep hue and paint the candle flames, and you're done!

Talking Alligator Skull with a Crystal Ball

Alongside the chatter of the otter and bat, you'll often hear clever quips and advice from the talking alligator skull. Aside from providing excellent companionship, the alligator skull also keeps track of the grocery list, so you never end up with a missing item after a quick run to the apothecary for more spell ingredients (and snacks). If you'd like your alligator skull to be a bit more whimsical, you can add a top hat or sunglasses (or both)!

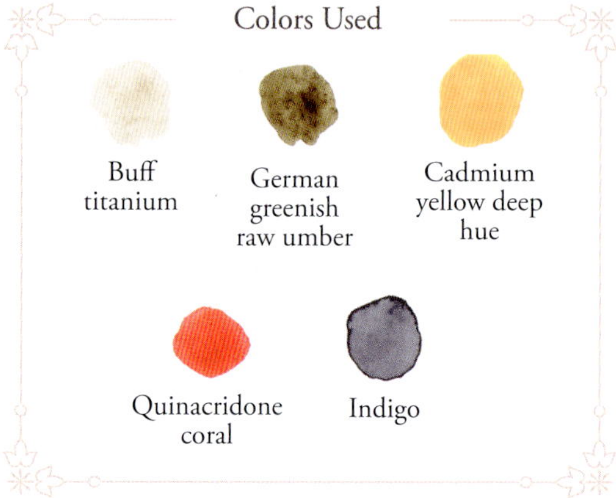

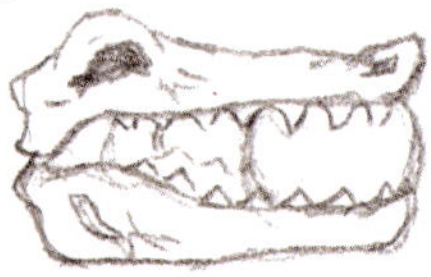

1 The alligator skull fits loosely within the outline of a rectangle, so start off by using your pencil to sketch a light rectangle, and use that to block in the general size and shape. Then fill in the remaining details, being sure to include some ferocious teeth! Depending on how large you'd like the crystal ball to be, you can also block in the overall shape of the skull as a pizza box—two rectangles connected at one end.

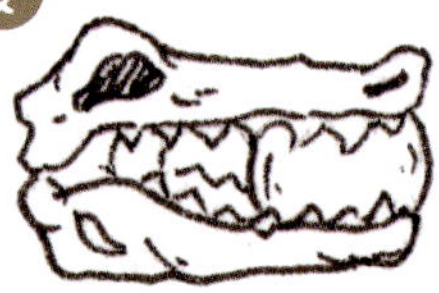

2 Use your waterproof pen to trace the outline of your skull, and then add the two visible edges of the crystal ball. Add some extra lines for details and shading. Once the ink is dry, gently erase the pencil layer.

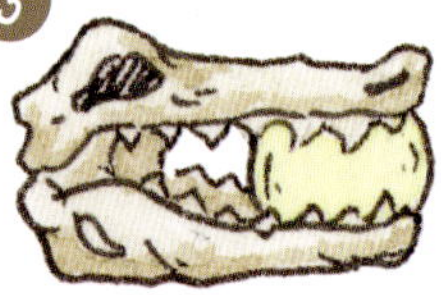

3 With your larger brush, cover the whole skull with a light layer of buff titanium. Then build up shadows and texture with two or three layers of German greenish raw umber. If you prefer a slightly warmer tone for your alligator skull, you can add a bit of Naples yellow and/or raw sienna to the shadows. Then add an initial layer of cadmium yellow deep hue to the crystal ball.

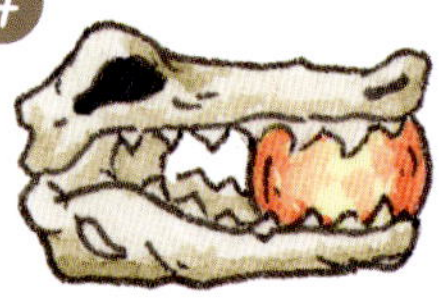

4 Once that layer is dry, use your smaller brush to add a second layer of cadmium yellow deep hue to the center of the ball, and add a ring of quinacridone coral around the outside, blending the two colors together so the ball appears to be glowing. Add more shadows to the skull as needed and fill in the eye with indigo. Your alligator skull is ready to chat!

Long-Lost Book of Perilous Spells

Some spellbooks contain spells far too interesting to be opened and read by just anyone, and our swamp witch certainly has all sorts of interesting books. Here, we'll paint a long-lost book of perilous spells, complete with a pair of sturdy locks to keep its contents safe from inquisitive eyes. If you'd like a fun, easy modification, you can add a mouth or eyes to your book, which will definitely make it more intimidating. People will think twice about picking it up to peruse its contents!

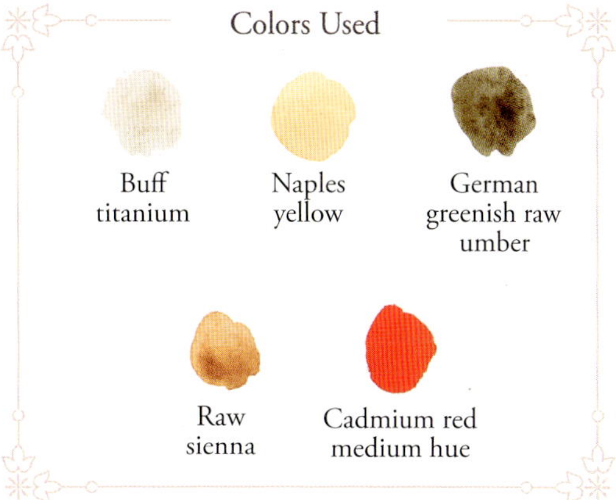

1

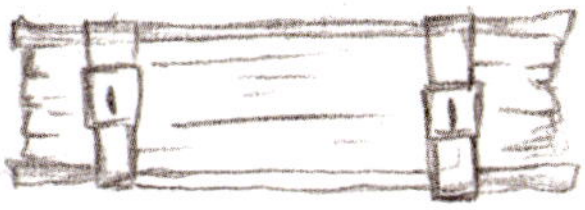

2

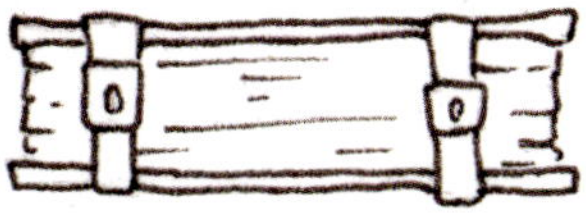

3

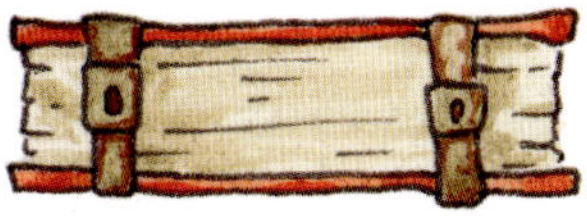

1 Start off with a light pencil sketch of a rectangle, and then add the top and bottom covers and the locks. You don't need to worry about making straight lines for the book covers—it's probably led an interesting life and looks a bit wonky, which just adds to its charm.

2 With your waterproof pen, trace that pencil outline, adding shading and some light lines to give the impression of worn pages, and then once the ink dries, gently erase the underlying pencil layer.

3 Use buff titanium combined with Naples yellow and a hint of German greenish raw umber to fill in the pages with the larger brush, adding shadows and texture with a few very light layers of German greenish raw umber. Once that's had a minute to dry, paint the covers with raw sienna mixed with cadmium red medium hue and your smaller brush. Finally, fill in the locks with German greenish raw umber, adding a bit of texture with German greenish raw umber mixed with a hint of raw sienna and cadmium red medium hue so they look old and worn. What secrets do you think the book holds?

Cauldron with a Bubbling Potion

You never know what kind of potion or concoction the swamp witch will be brewing up—perhaps a spell to keep mosquitoes off the porch or to keep books dry so she can read outside in the rain. Have fun with the shape and color of the cauldron. It's a great place to set the tone of the overall shelf—warm and friendly or spooky and mysterious!

Colors Used

- Raw sienna
- Buff titanium
- Naples yellow
- Quinacridone coral
- German greenish raw umber
- Moonglow purple
- Prussian blue
- Cadmium yellow deep hue
- Cobalt teal blue
- Deep sap green

1

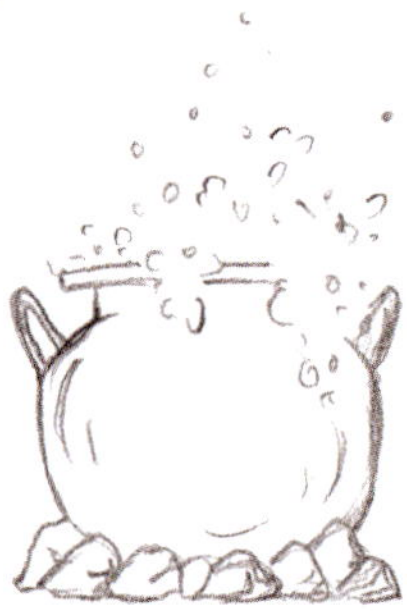

2

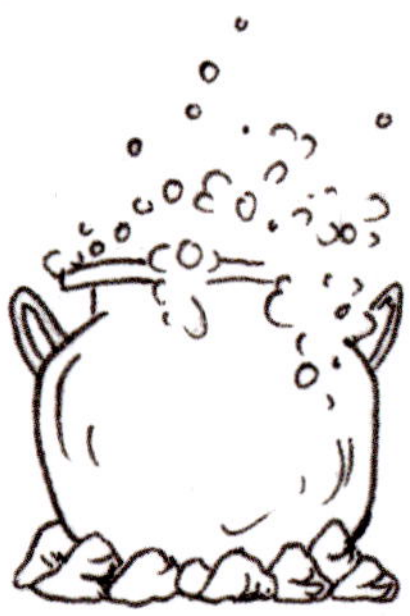

1. Lightly sketch a squished oval for the overall shape of the cauldron, and then add the rocks, handle, and bubbling potion—making it as large or as small as you like. We don't need to outline the entire bubbling portion at the top since we'd like it to look like the potion is bubbling up with billowing smoke. So add some circles and looping lines near the cauldron itself, and taper them off as you move away from the cauldron.

2. Using your waterproof pen, start off with the ink outline of the potion, and then the rocks, and finally the cauldron. Add some bubbles to the potion and lines to the cauldron. Once the ink is dry, gently erase the pencil layer.

3

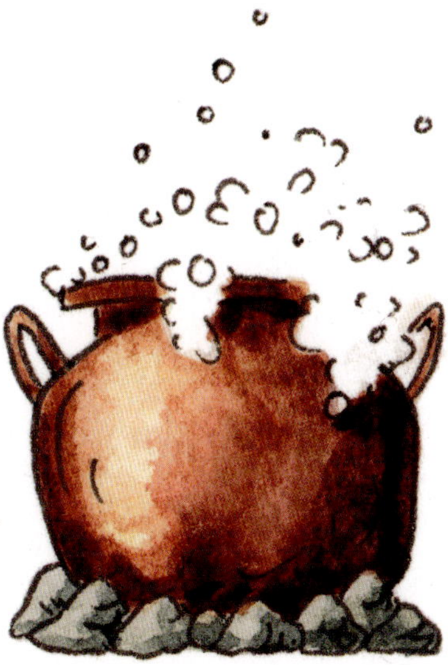

4

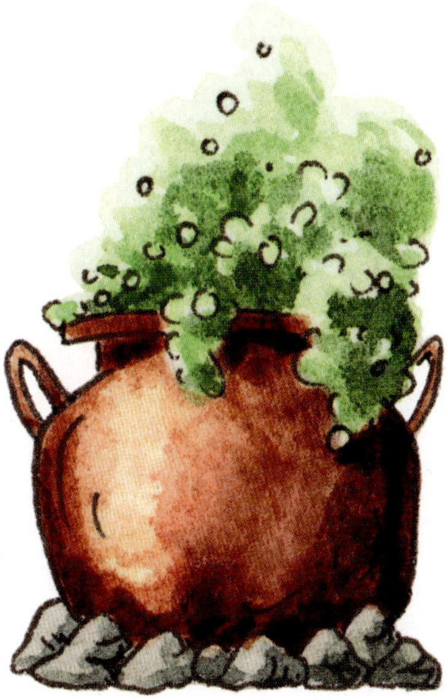

3 Grab your larger brush and fill in the whole cauldron with a layer of raw sienna mixed with equal parts buff titanium and Naples yellow. Then add shadows and depth with three to ten layers of that mixture, gradually adding in some quinacridone coral, German greenish raw umber, and moonglow purple until you have a nice contrast between the lightest and darkest portions of the cauldron. Mix up buff titanium, German greenish raw umber, and a hint of Prussian blue to make a gray color, and fill in the rocks. Add some shading by adding more Prussian blue to the mixture, and then we can get started on the potion!

4 Once the cauldron has dried, use your larger brush to fill in the whole potion with a very light, almost translucent layer of cadmium yellow deep hue mixed with cobalt teal blue. Then use a stronger mixture of those colors (more paint, less water), gradually adding some German greenish raw umber, deep sap green, and a tiny hint of Prussian blue to add depth and shadows, making sure to leave some light-colored bubbles! Keep building up three to five light layers of color until you've got nice, deep shadows and your potion looks ready to bubble right off the page!

Glass Terrarium with Poison Mushrooms

The swamp witch finds all sorts of interesting treasures and plants while trudging through the swamp and keeps some in glass terrariums to enjoy on her shelves. In this tutorial, we'll paint a glass terrarium with poison mushrooms, enchanted so the mushrooms always have exactly the right growing conditions.

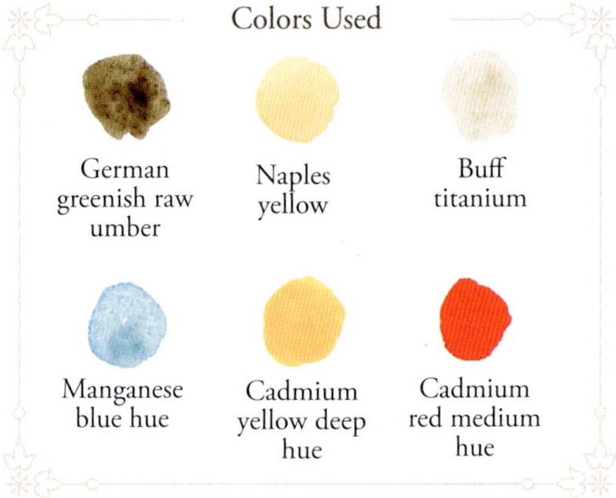

1

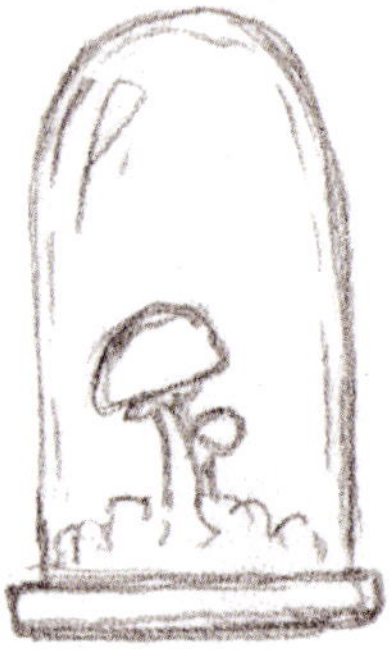

2

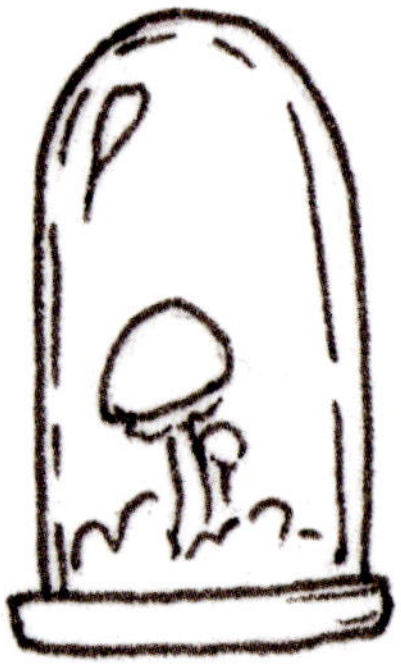

1 Start off by lightly sketching the terrarium's outline with a pencil, and then add the base, mushrooms, and a teardrop reflection. While the dome shape I've shown here is a very traditional shape for a terrarium, there are tons of beautiful options with a wide range of complexity, so you can have a lot of fun with the design of your terrarium if you'd like to experiment!

2 Using your waterproof pen, trace your pencil outline, and then once the ink dries, gently erase the underlying pencil and let's start painting!

3

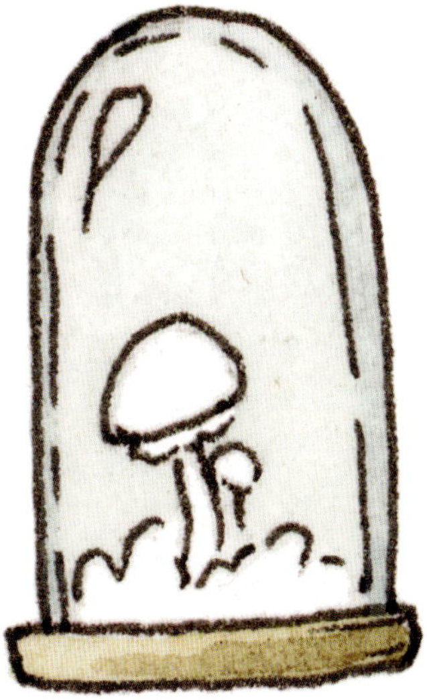

4

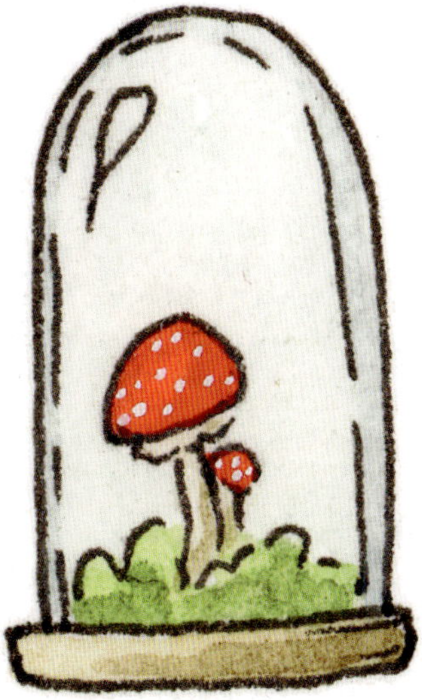

3 Mix up German greenish raw umber and Naples yellow, and with the larger brush, fill in the base of the terrarium, adding several layers towards the right side to make a shadow. Then mix buff titanium and manganese blue hue, and fill in the terrarium around the mushrooms, leaving those spots dry. With your smaller brush, add a second layer of that light blue color to the outer edge of the glass to define the edges.

4 Once that layer is dry, grab your smaller brush and start painting the moss and mushrooms! Mix up a nice, happy green color with manganese blue hue and cadmium yellow deep hue, and use it to fill in the moss, adding shadows to give it texture with a hint of German greenish raw umber. Use a very light layer of buff titanium to fill in the whole mushrooms—stems, tops, and all—and then add shadows to the stems using German greenish raw umber. Let that dry completely, and then add a light layer of cadmium red medium hue to the mushrooms, leaving the white polka dots blank (or plan to add them back in with a white pen or white gouache afterwards). Slowly build up layers of cadmium red medium hue until your mushrooms look round and glowing, and then you're done! Congratulations, they look awesome!

Sturdy Adventuring Knapsack

A sturdy adventuring knapsack is a staple of any afternoon of exploration, and our swamp witch has a colorful knapsack full of maps, supplies, and plenty of space to collect new treasures along the way. I love designing rucksacks for shelves—they add so much personality and visual interest, and they're such a fun place to incorporate extra colors and details. If you'd like to add a few more whimsical items, you could place some keychains on the knapsack or add extra plants and twigs peeking out of the pockets.

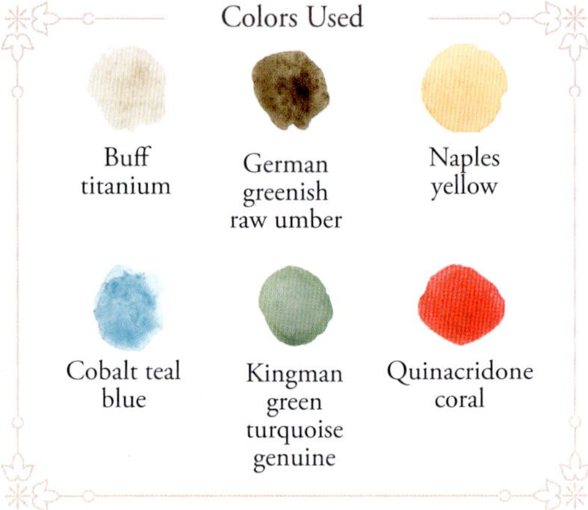

1

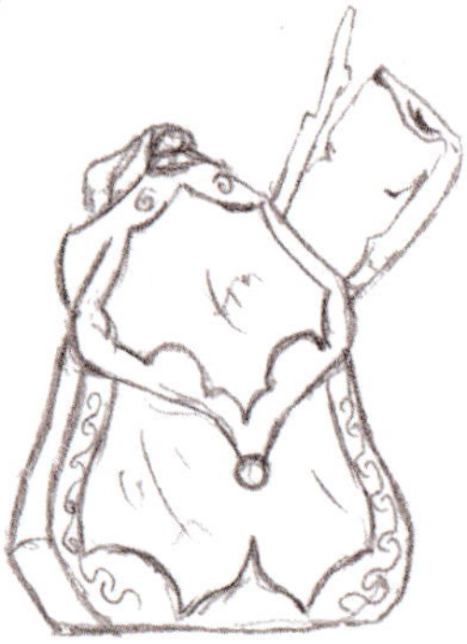

2

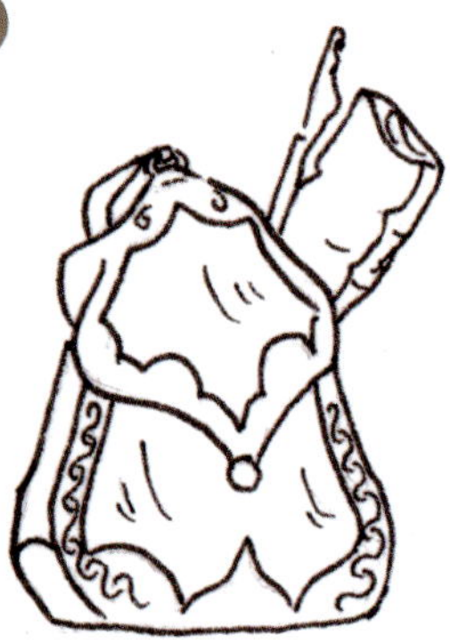

1 Start off with a pencil sketch of the knapsack's outline, making the base nice and rounded so it looks full of supplies and treasures. The example shown here includes a decorative border all around the knapsack's edges, but you could also add pockets or keep it plain—it's up to you!

2 Using your waterproof pen, trace that pencil outline, adding details along the border and the beginnings of some shadows. Once the ink is dry, gently erase the pencil layer.

3

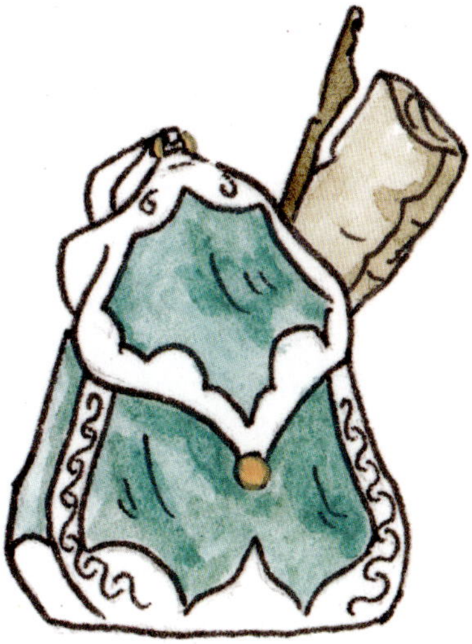

4

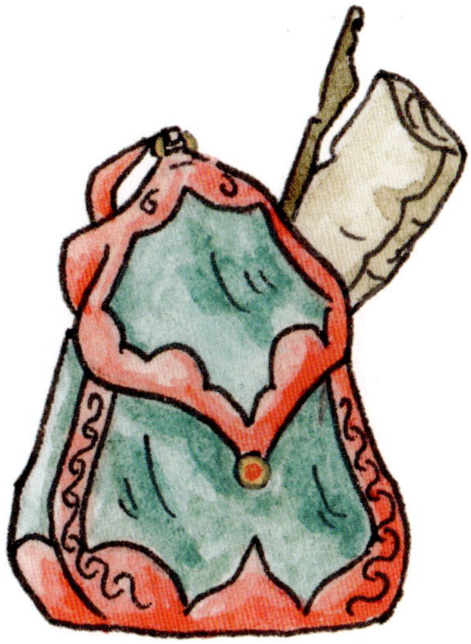

3 With your larger brush, mix up a light parchment shade using buff titanium and a tiny hint of German greenish raw umber. Then use this to fill in the scroll, adding some shadows with watered-down pure German greenish raw umber. Switch to your smaller brush and paint the stick with more German greenish raw umber, and then carefully fill in the gold hardware on the knapsack with Naples yellow. With your larger brush, mix up a beautiful teal-blue color by combining cobalt teal blue with a smidge of buff titanium and Kingman green turquoise genuine. Fill in the main sections of the knapsack with this mix. Add a bit more Kingman green turquoise genuine as you go along, adding shadows to the cloth, building them up until it looks three-dimensional.

4 Once that layer is dry, make a happy pink color with quinacridone coral and Naples yellow, and use it to fill in the decorative borders, using whichever brush you prefer. Finally, use some pure quinacridone coral to add shadows and details on the borders, and then fill in the center of the buckle so it looks like a jewel. You're now ready to go on adventures!

Mesmerizing Potion Bottle

With a cauldron full of bubbling potions, the swamp witch is going to need a plethora of magical potion bottles, so let's paint one! Potion bottles are a fabulous place to add tons of personality to your shelf by varying the shapes, arrangements, sizes, and colors to your heart's content! The dark glass of this bottle catches the lights from the candles and mysterious flames in the swamp witch's cottage, creating mesmerizing reflections and casting mysterious shadows . . . take a sip of the potion if you dare!

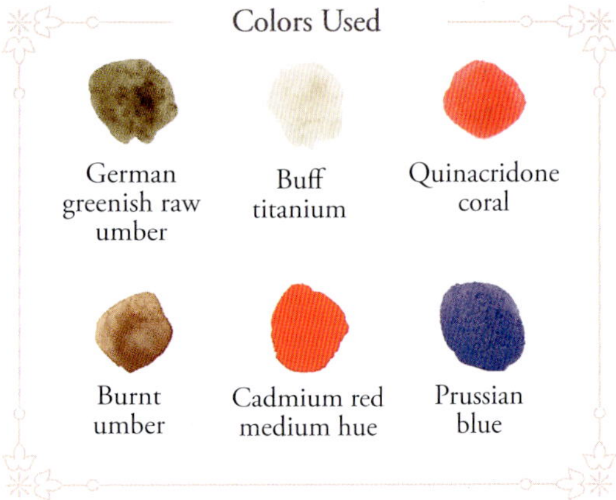

1
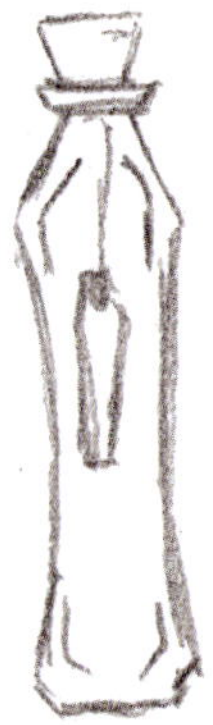

2
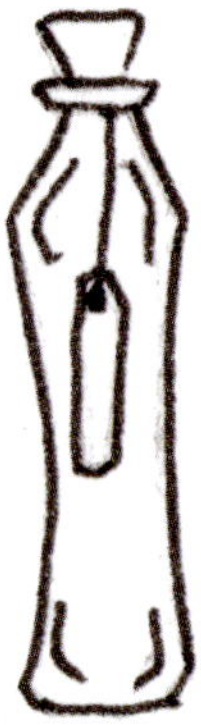

1 Start your pencil sketch by outlining the bottle, giving it some fun, angular edges, and then add the cork and paper label. Be mindful of what the bottle will be overlapping with (or what will be overlapping with the bottle) when it's on your final shelf—you don't want to paint a whole bottle to find yourself needing something else to be visible in front of it!

2 Go over your pencil sketch with a waterproof pen, adding lines for the reflections of light on the glass, and then once the ink dries, gently erase the pencil layer.

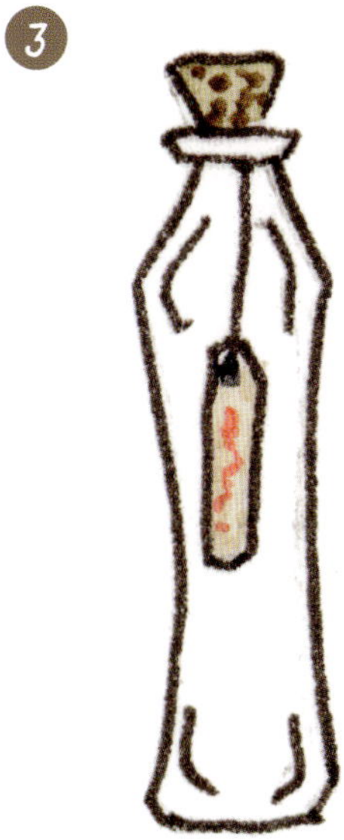

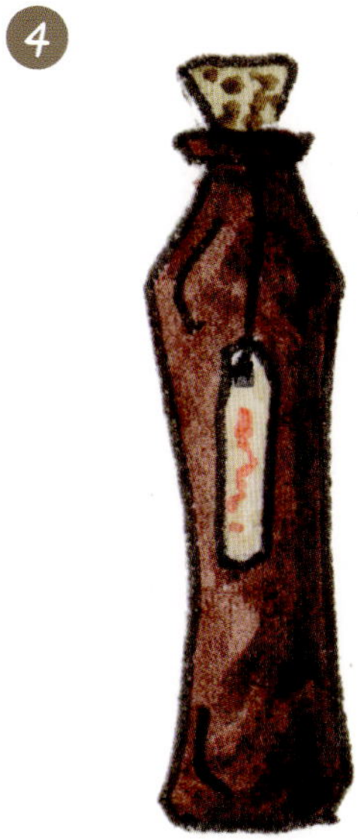

3 Using your smaller brush and German greenish raw umber, fill in the cork, and then add buff titanium to the paper tag. Build up a tiny bit of German greenish raw umber around the edges of the tag to give it a weathered appearance, and then allow it to dry completely. Use some concentrated quinacridone coral (or any other color you like) to add some tiny squiggles to the tag to give the impression of a handwritten label. (We'll pretend whoever wrote the label has some shockingly illegible cursive.) Finally, add some dots of concentrated German greenish raw umber to the cork to give it some texture.

4 Now, on to the actual potion part! Mix up a lovely, dark brown color using burnt umber, cadmium red medium hue, quinacridone coral, and a bit of Prussian blue, and then use several layers of it to fill in the bottle, and you're ready to brew up a storm (hopefully not literally)! Try building up more color towards the lower right edge of the bottle, leaving the upper left side a bit lighter to give the impression of light reflecting off of dark-colored glass. We're using a bunch of colors together here, which may seem like overkill, but we want a mysterious, deep, purply-brown color, and this is my favorite combination to achieve that particular effect. But if you'd like a simpler color combo, you can just use burnt umber and moonglow purple. And now your mesmerizing potion is ready to enjoy!

Enchanted Pink Potion

You never know when you'll need something glowing and magical to brighten your day, so this potion is something the swamp witch always keeps on hand. We'll slowly build up layers of color until the enchanted pink potion bottle appears to be glowing from within. You can use this technique with any color combination—you just want a strong contrast between the light inner color and the darker outer color.

Colors Used

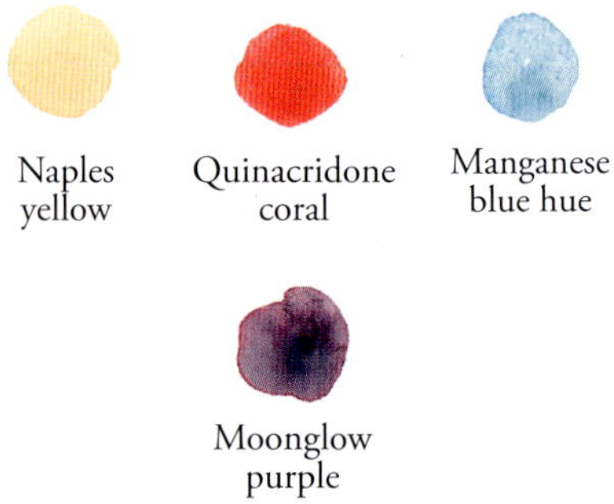

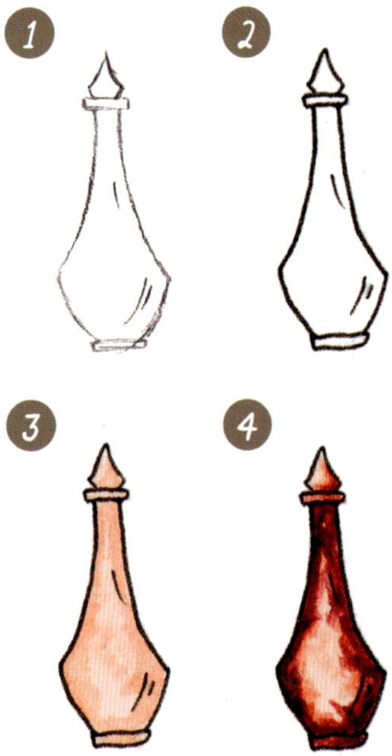

1 Use your pencil to sketch the outline of the bottle, giving it delicately swooping curves and a teardrop-shaped stopper in the top.

2 Grab your waterproof pen and use it to trace your pencil outline, making sure to include a bit of shading and a line or two to indicate the reflection of the light on the glass. Once the ink is dry, gently erase the pencil layer.

3 Using your smaller brush and Naples yellow combined with a hint of quinacridone coral, fill in the entire bottle, including the stopper, building up a few layers towards the outside of the bottle. Let this dry completely.

4 Again using your smaller brush, start building up ten or so light (very, very light) layers of your quinacridone coral and Naples yellow color combination, slowly (very, very slowly) adding increasing amounts of quinacridone coral, followed by manganese blue hue, and finally some moonglow purple. You'll start each successive layer a bit farther from the center, ultimately leaving a wobbly star shape untouched in the very center so the base color from the prior step glows through. Finally, mix together quinacridone coral and moonglow purple, and blend in a final layer at the very outer edge of the bottle and right edge of the cork to add the last bit of contrast. If any of the edges end up looking too harsh, you can take a barely damp brush and gently nudge them to blend the colors a bit more, but be careful not to blend the colors too much or you'll lose the glowing effect.

Dark Candle on a Golden Candlestick

A small, portable light source can be quite handy, especially living in a swamp. You never know when the swamp witch will need to investigate strange noises or stay up late into the night reading a particularly excellent book. The color of the candle will help set the tone for your overall shelf—the more warm colors you include, the cozier and friendlier your shelf will feel. Meanwhile, cooler colors will give a spookier, more haunting appearance.

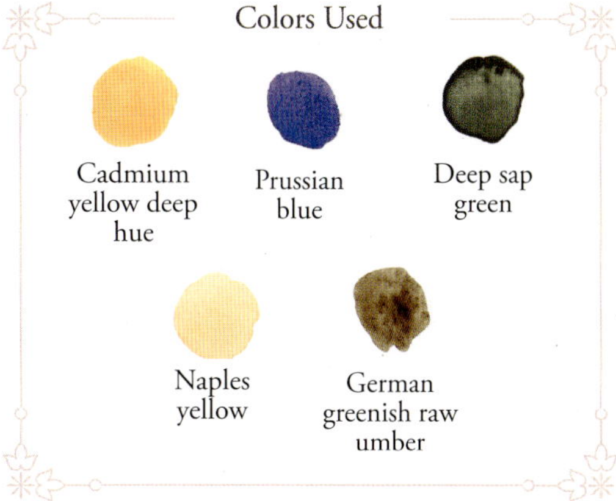

1

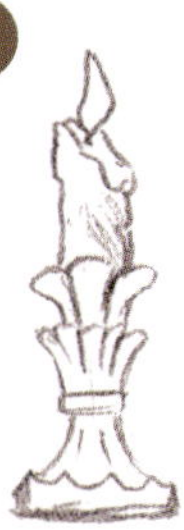

2

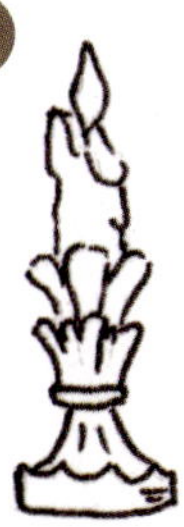

3

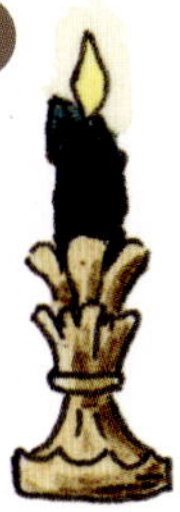

1 Using your pencil, lightly sketch the outline of the candle and its stand, starting off with a vertical center line so you can make sure it's symmetrical. This particular candlestick is quite small, but you can tinker with the size, color, and shape to best suit your particular tastes. One of my favorite candle shapes is short and squat, almost a square—something about that on a blocky little candlestick always feels very cozy on a shelf.

2 Draw over your pencil layer with a waterproof pen. Also, make sure to add some shading towards the lower right side of the candlestick to make shadows. Once the ink is dry, gently erase the pencil layer.

3 Let's work from the top down, for no particular reason, but we need to start somewhere! Fill in the flame with cadmium yellow deep hue, and then gently blend out the edges so it glows. Mix a very dark blue with equal amounts of Prussian blue and deep sap green, and then use several layers to fill in the candle. Finally, fill in the whole candlestick with Naples yellow mixed with German greenish raw umber, and then add shadows with German greenish raw umber. You're finished—it looks amazing!

Enchanted Books

One can never have too many books (until you have to move or rearrange them, but the swamp witch has spells for all that), so let's paint some enchanted books for our swamp witch to enjoy! If you wish to add titles to your books, you can modify the decorative designs or skip them entirely. If you have some gouache paint (which is opaque), you can use that to add titles or decorative designs on top of dark backgrounds, but keep in mind that it's difficult to paint light colors on top of dark areas if you're only using watercolors.

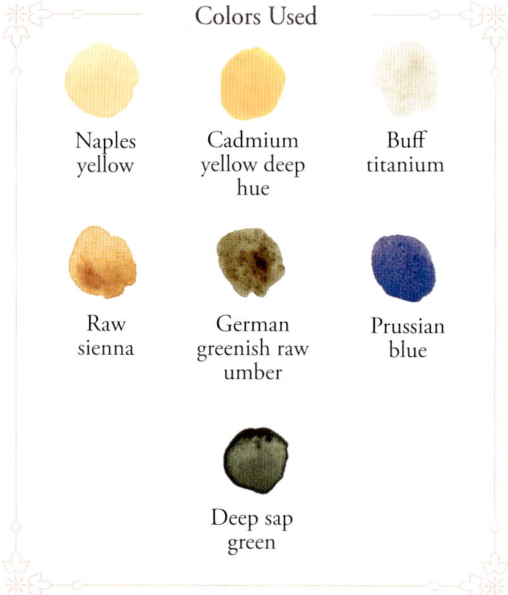

1

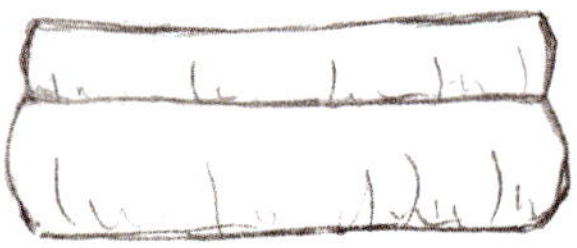

2

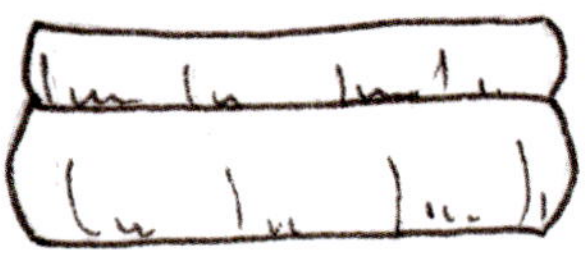

1 This step is nice and easy. Draw two rectangles with rounded edges with your pencil. You can use a ruler if you prefer perfectly straight lines, or free draw the lines for a more organic look.

2 Use your waterproof pen to go over the ink outline, and add some gently curving lines coming up from the bottom edge of each book to make the shadows cast by their spines. Once the ink is dry, gently erase the pencil layer.

3

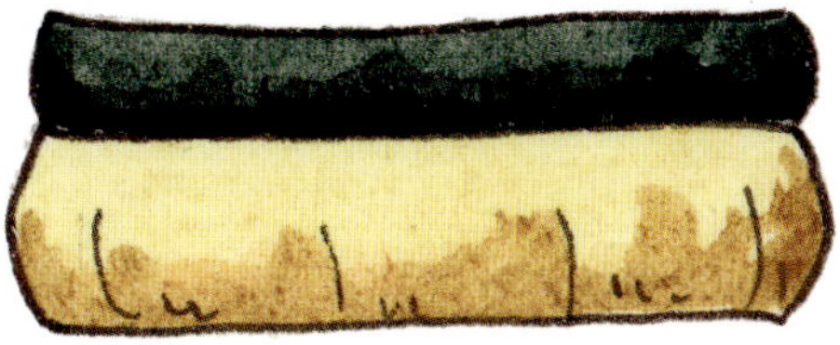

4

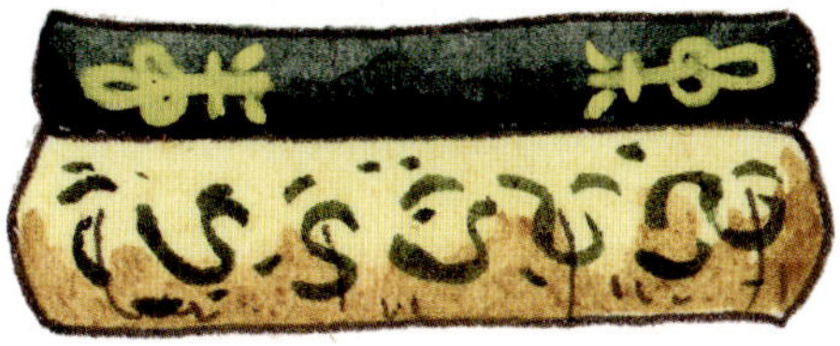

3 With your larger brush, mix up a nice, light yellow color with Naples yellow, cadmium yellow deep hue, and buff titanium, and use it to fill in the bottom book. Then add a bit of raw sienna and German greenish raw umber, and add a layer of this slightly darker yellowish brown at the bottom of the book where you drew shadows in the previous step. Let the yellow book dry, then repeat the process with the top book, mixing Prussian blue, Naples yellow, buff titanium, and a whisper of deep sap green initially, and add more Prussian blue and deep sap green for the shadow. It's super important to let this layer dry completely before moving to the lovely decorations, so now's a great time for a quick break!

4 Now that your books are totally dry, mix up some concentrated Prussian blue and raw sienna with your smaller brush, and use it to paint a decorative design on the bottom book. Then mix up some concentrated cadmium yellow deep hue and buff titanium and add a design to the upper book. If you prefer, you can also use gouache or a colored gel pen to add these decorative designs. Gouache is a particularly useful option if you'd like to add a light-colored design on top of a darker book. If you don't want to invest in a lot of gouache colors, you can get a white tube of gouache and simply mix little dabs of it with whatever color of watercolor you'd like to use. You can also paint the whole book with whatever light color you'd like the decorative design to be (in this case yellow), and then carefully add the darker spine color around the decorative design; I find that it can be very frustrating, so I personally avoid that option. And now you're ready for some enchanted reading!

Delicate Moss and Mushrooms

Since our witch lives deep in a mysterious, magical swamp, her shelf will be covered in delicate, draping moss and brightly colored mushrooms. These botanical details are a fabulous place to add lots of personality to your shelf. You can make it as overgrown and colorful or as simple and subtle as you like, so grab your painting supplies and let's get started!

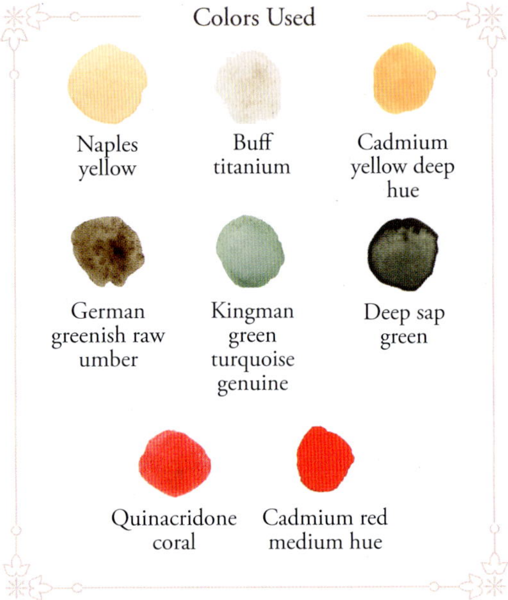

1

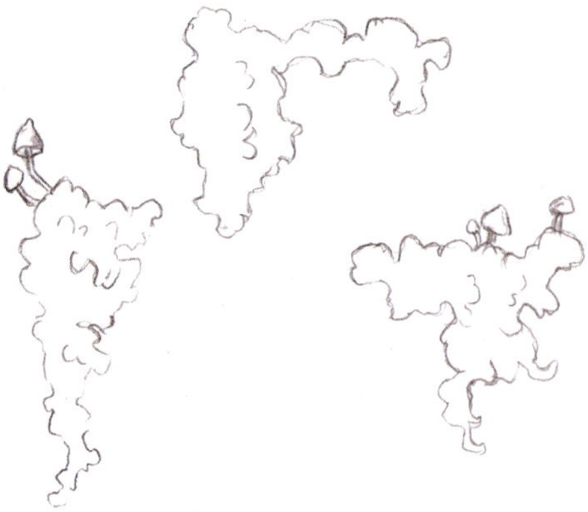

1 You'll need to have The Swamp Witchery Shelf (page 180) already sketched out to add the moss and mushrooms. It'll also help to have an idea of where to place the various items on your shelf so we can make sure the greenery fits naturally around all the items. Start off with a light pencil sketch for the moss, and then add the mushrooms wherever suits your fancy. Keep in mind that we don't need a full outline of the moss—focus more on adding small lines to give a wispy appearance.

2

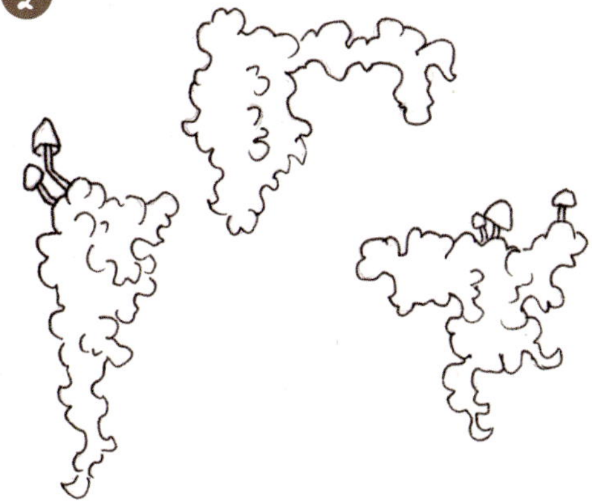

2 Using your waterproof pen, go over the pencil layer, making sure to keep your strokes light so the moss looks like it'll sway softly in the breeze. Once the ink is dry, gently erase the pencil layer.

3

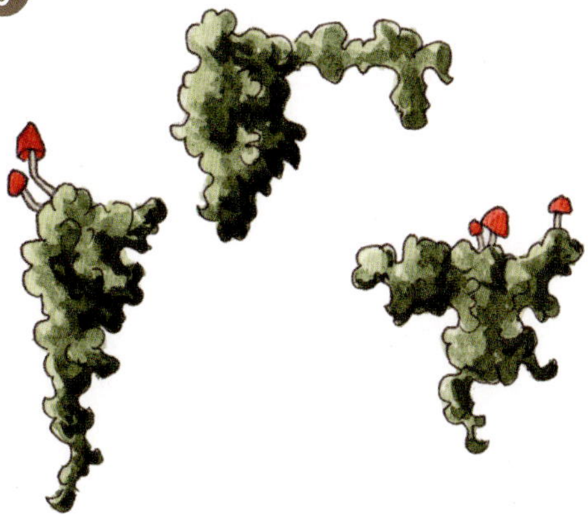

3 We'll build up several layers of greens to give the moss depth, so with the larger brush, fill in all the moss with a light layer of Naples yellow, buff titanium, cadmium yellow deep hue, and German greenish raw umber, with a teensy bit of Kingman green turquoise genuine and deep sap green. While that's still wet, add gradually increasing amounts of Kingman green turquoise genuine and deep sap green to build up three to five layers of shadows and texture on the moss. (Keep in mind that you can always go back and add more later if needed.) Then use your smaller brush to fill in the stem of each mushroom with buff titanium and the tops with quinacridone coral, adding a bit of cadmium red medium hue to make shadows on the right side of each mushroom top. Now your moss and mushrooms are ready to admire!

The Swamp Witchery Shelf

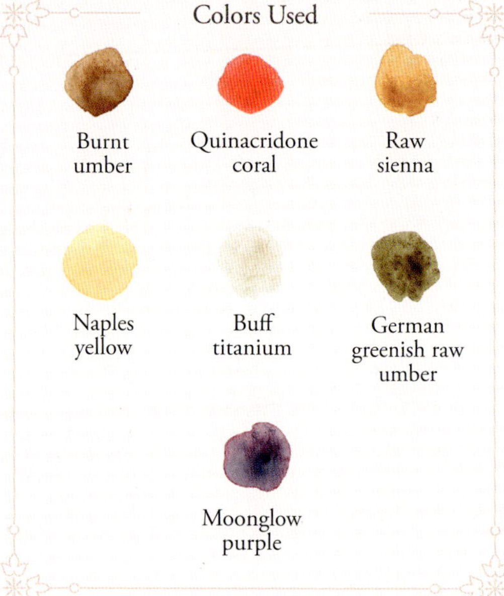

Now let's paint a shelf so we can arrange all the charming swamp witchery items! As we chatted about for the other shelves, you won't want to add ink and paint to your shelf until you've decided where to arrange all the items, since some things will overlap with the shelf—and you'll want to make sure you leave space for those!

1

1 The first step here is to decide how big or small you'd like the shelf to be, and then draw a thin rectangle that size. You can use a ruler if you'd like perfectly straight lines, or free draw it for a more organic look. My preferred method is to use a ruler for this pencil sketch step, and then freehand the ink drawing in the next step—but you should always do whatever works best for you! Next, sketch the shelf supports, making them as detailed or as simple as you'd like.

2

3

2 Go over your pencil sketch with a waterproof pen, making sure you've left space for anything that will overlap with the shelf in the final illustration. Once the ink is dry, gently erase the pencil layer.

3 Using your larger brush, fill in the whole shelf with burnt umber combined with quinacridone coral, raw sienna, and Naples yellow. Fill both brackets with buff titanium, combined with Naples yellow and German greenish raw umber. Allow that layer to dry for a few minutes, and then start building up a woodgrain texture with light strokes of your wood color with increasing amounts of burnt umber and moonglow purple, still using your larger brush, but with a fine point. (This can most easily be achieved by gently rotating the brush as you pull it through the paint.) Add several layers of shadows to the right side of each bracket using German greenish raw umber with slowly increasing amounts of moonglow purple, and your shelf is finished!

Assembling Your Swamp Witchery Shelf

Now that we've talked about how to paint each of the individual swamp witchery items, let's put the pieces together to make a finished shelf! If you enjoy the way the items are arranged in this tutorial, feel free to follow along exactly the way it's shown. But if you'd prefer to rearrange the items, mix and match between the witches, or add items of your own, please do so!

Colors Used for the Background

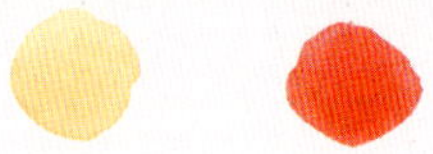

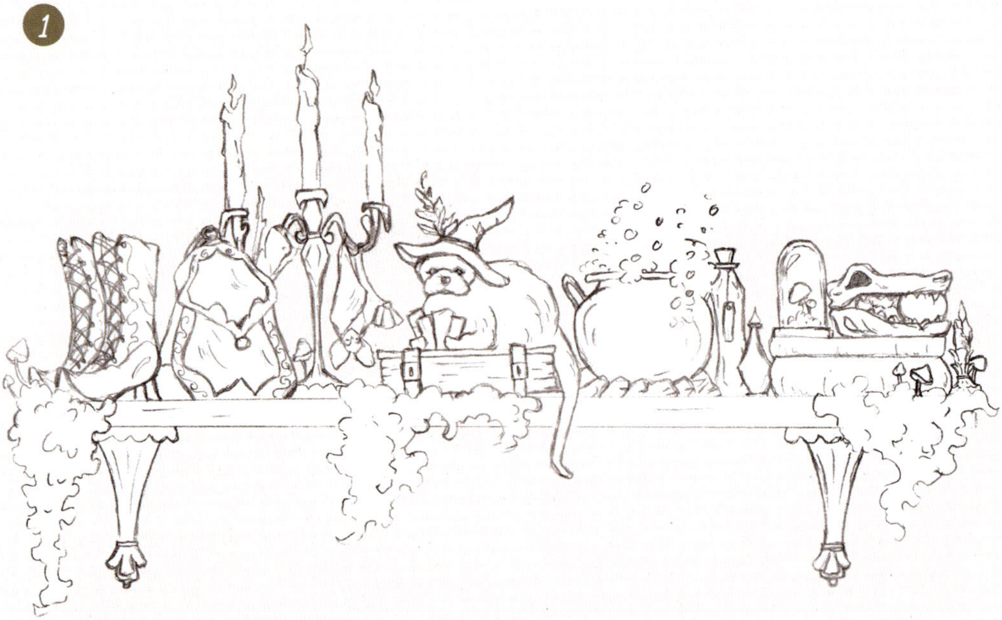

1 Start off with a very light pencil sketch of the shelf, and then go along it and mark the edges of each item so you can make sure everything has enough space. If you're not sure about the layout, I'd recommend using a digital sketching program to try different arrangements until you have something you love. Refer to The Swamp Witchery Shelf (page 180) for details on sketching the shelf, and please refer back to each project's tutorial as needed for the instructions on drawing the individual items.

2

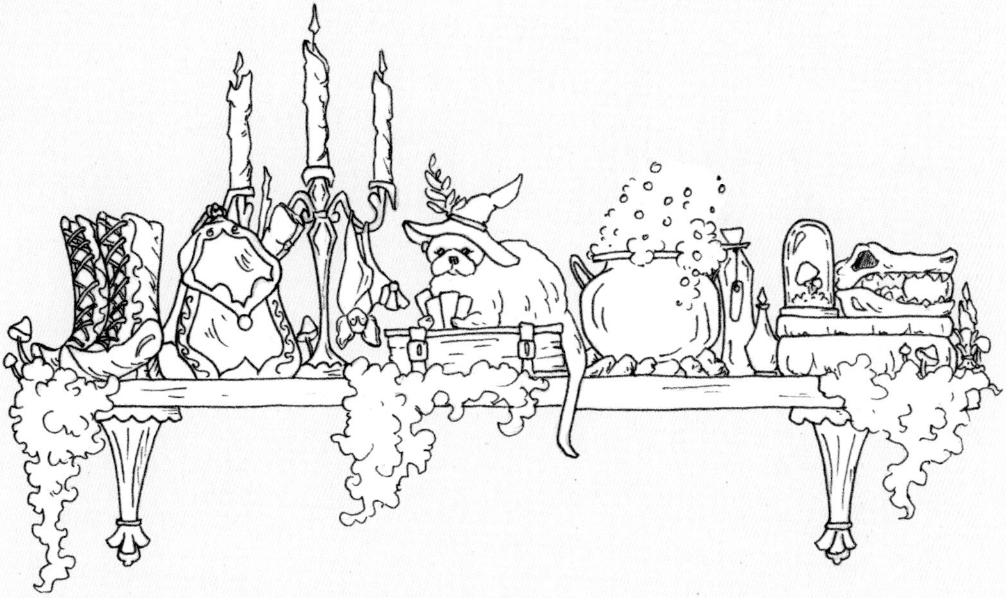

2 Now, grab your waterproof pen and let's add ink to the pencil sketch! Start off by inking the Delicate Moss and Mushrooms (page 178) and the Talkative Otter in a Pointed Hat (page 158), since those items are in the "front" and overlap with other things. Then add the rest of the ink and, once it's dry, gently erase the pencil layer.

3

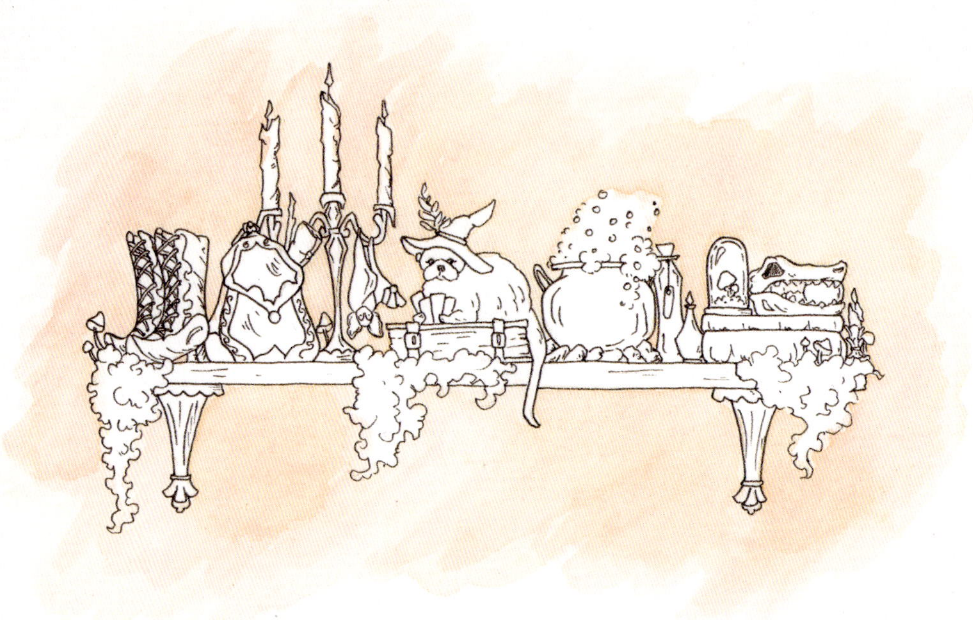

3 Before we get started on the actual shelf, let's paint a light watercolor wash in the background. You can use any color you'd like, but in this example, I've used a light wash of Naples yellow combined with quinacridone coral applied with an extra-large brush. First, take a brush with a relatively fine point, and using a small amount of water, carefully trace the ink outline from the prior step. Try not to get any water onto or inside the lines—we just want a damp surface on the background. Then take an extra-large brush (or whatever size you have), and add a light layer of water everywhere you'd like to add the background color.

While the water layer is still wet, make a diluted mixture of Naples yellow combined with quinacridone coral, and apply it gently in layers with your extra-large brush, using your slightly smaller brush to make sure the edges where the color meets the ink outline stay crisp and neat. Build up as many layers as you'd like, and then let it dry completely before moving to the next step. The nice thing about using a light-colored background like this one is that we don't have to worry too much about it bleeding into the areas we'll be painting next. But if you choose to use a dark background color, you'll need to exercise a bit more caution.

4

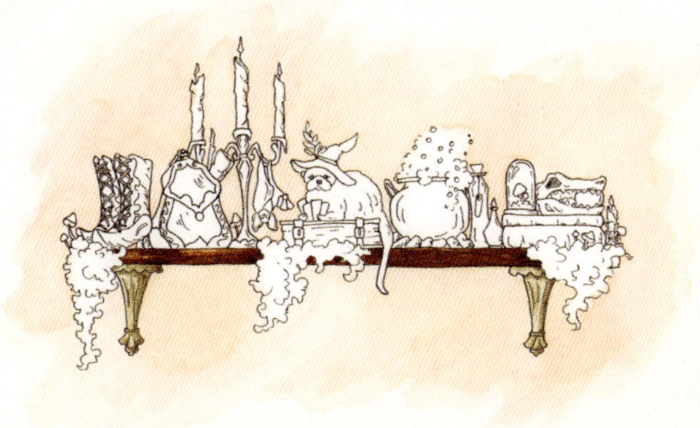

5

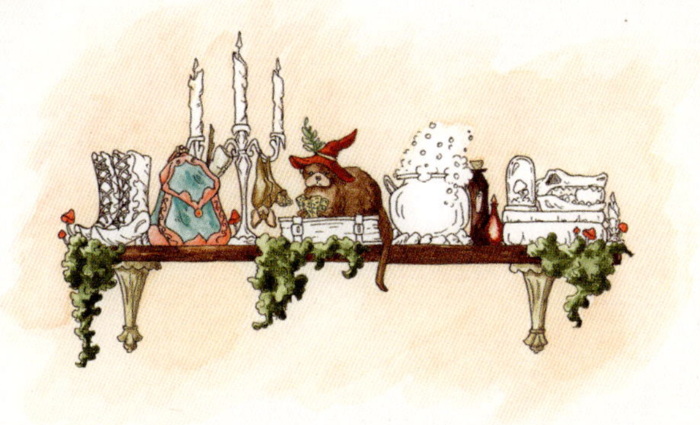

4 Let's start off by painting the shelf to set the tone for the other items. Turn to The Swamp Witchery Shelf (page 180), and paint yourself a lovely shelf, making sure you let it dry before moving on to the next step. If you're not sure exactly what color to paint your shelf, you can always paint the items first, and then go back and do the shelf—feel free to experiment and find what works best for you!

5 You can, of course, paint the items on the shelf in any order you'd like—left to right, front to back, totally random—there's no wrong answer! If you'd like to paint the items in the front first, start off by painting the Delicate Moss and Mushrooms (page 178), Sturdy Adventuring Knapsack (page 170), Inquisitive Bat Playing Cards (page 162), Talkative Otter in a Pointed Hat (page 158), Mesmerizing Potion Bottle (page 172), and Enchanting Pink Potion (page 174). You're almost there, and it's looking awesome! Take a break if you need to, and then let's finish up your beautiful shelf!

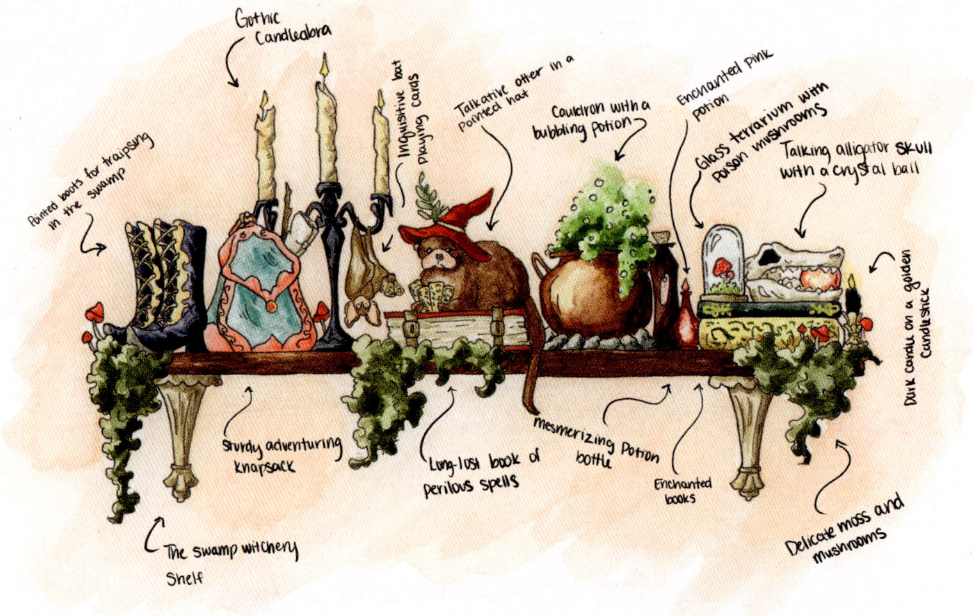

6 Now let's paint the remaining items: the Pointed Boots for Traipsing in the Swamp (page 160), Gothic Candelabra (page 163), Long-Lost Book of Perilous Spells (page 165), Cauldron with a Bubbling Potion (page 166), Enchanted Books (page 176), Glass Terrarium with Poison Mushrooms (page 168), Talking Alligator Skull with a Crystal Ball (page 164), and finally, Dark Candle on a Golden Candlestick (page 175). Now step back and admire your beautiful Swamp Witchery shelf. It looks amazing!

Acknowledgments

Thank you so much to everyone who made this magical book possible! I can hardly believe I get to wake up every day to paint, write, and find magic in the world, and it wouldn't be possible without each and every one of you. So thank you, truly, for making dreams come true and for sticking around on this magical adventure.

The wonderful team at Page Street, especially my lovely editors Krystle and Sarah, made the process so smooth, and I couldn't have done it without you! Your ideas, feedback, suggestions, and patience in answering my endless questions made this book what it is, and I'm so thankful for you!

Thank you to my husband, Zach, for patiently looking at every sketch and painting, making a million cups of coffee, and always being so supportive.

To my family and friends, for teaching me to see magic in everyday life and always finding a bit more room on the walls to hang another painting, thank you. Endless hikes, adventures, science experiments, and trips to the library made both the foundation for this book and a lifetime of fond memories.

Special thanks to all my lovely friends on the internet, especially all the wonderful people on Instagram. It's been such a treat to share my love of painting with you and make so many sweet friends! I'm always so thankful to you for following along on my artistic adventures and for your kind encouragement and helpful feedback. I hope you love this book and find all sorts of magic and inspiration within its pages—I wrote it for you to enjoy, and I can't wait to see what you create!

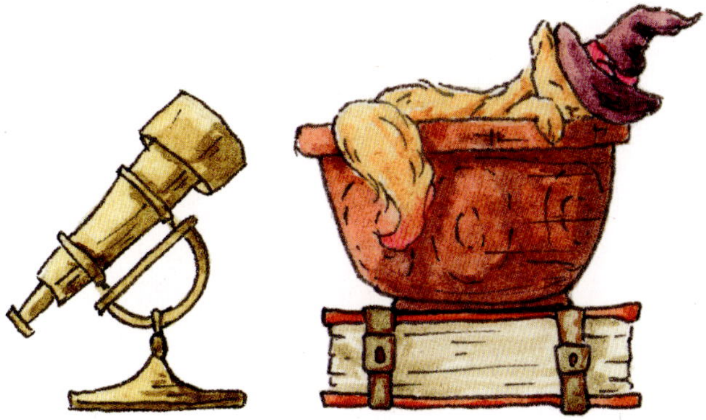

About the Author

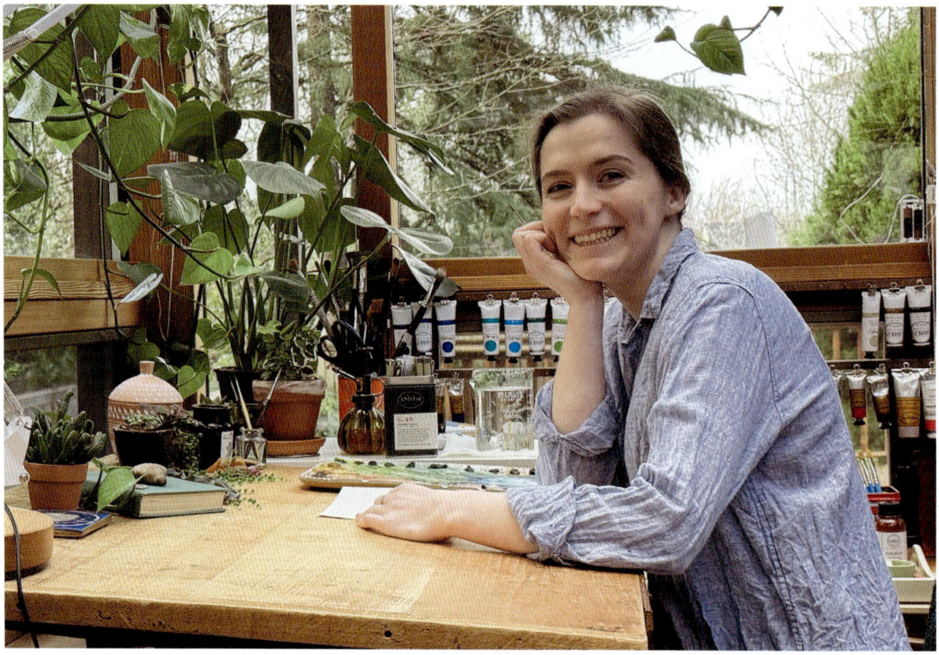

Lizzy is a painter who uses watercolor and gouache to create fantastical worlds and capture treasured memories. With a background in chemistry and nursing, she blends her love of science, fairy tales, and the outdoors to create whimsical and detailed paintings that encourage the viewer to step into a new world or glimpse snippets of magic in the everyday. Her work is inspired by a childhood spent reading fanciful stories and sci-fi novels, building forts, and playing in the woods. She hopes to evoke a sense of enchantment through her art, eliciting thoughts of raindrops and wildflowers, cups of tea, and reading books by a cozy fire. When she's not painting, Lizzy enjoys hiking in the beautiful Pacific Northwest, where she lives with her husband, Zach, a sweet golden retriever, and two mischievous cats. She also loves baking, woodworking, knitting, and reading every book she can get her hands on.

Index

A

Adventuring Knapsack, Sturdy, 170–71
Amethyst Crystal, Moonlight-Infused, 143
Ancient Spell Mirror, 132–33
animals
  Cat Napping with Spelled Knitting, 60–61
  Clever Mouse Hiding from the Cat, 73
  Distinguished Seagull with a Witch's Hat, 94–95
  Feline Familiar Napping in a Mixing Bowl, 18–19
  Fishbowl with a Brightly Colored Fish, 99
  Inquisitive Bat Playing Cards, 162
  Midnight-Colored Familiar, 138–39
  Octopus Familiar in a Magical Cauldron, 92–93
  Talkative Otter in a Pointed Hat, 158–59
  Talking Alligator Skull with a Crystal Ball, 164
Armillary Stargazing Sphere, 111

B

Basil, Charming Potted, 28–29
Beautiful Seashells, 113
Blue and White China Teacup, 41
books
  Books of Magic Spells and Recipes, 74–75
  Enchanted Books, 176–77
  Enchanted Spellbooks, 97
  Long-Lost Book of Perilous Spells, 165
  Romantic Paperback Books, 80–81
  Spellbooks of Dubious Origin, 142
  Witchy Cookbooks, 34–35
Books of Magic Spells and Recipes, 74–75
Boots, Pointed, for Traipsing in the Swamp, 160–61
Boots, Sturdy, for Seaside Adventures, 98
Bottled Weather Spells, 100–101
bottles
  Bottled Weather Spells, 100–101
  Enchanted Pink Potion, 174
  Essence of Starlight, 134–35
  Liquid Sunshine, 136–37
  Magical Ship in a Bottle, 96
  Magic Potion Bottles, 40
  Mesmerizing Potion Bottle, 172–73
Bright Red Coral, 112
brushes, 11

C

Cake, Magical Frosted, 36–37
Candelabra, Gothic, 163
Candle, Dark, on a Golden Candlestick, 175
Candle for Late-Night Reading, 108
Candlestick, Dark Candle on a Golden, 175
Cards, Inquisitive Bat Playing, 162
Cat Napping with Spelled Knitting, 60–61
Cauldron Full of Moonlight, 126–27
cauldrons
  Cauldron Full of Moonlight, 126–27
  Cauldron with a Bubbling Potion, 166–67
  Mysterious Cauldron, 20–21
  Octopus Familiar in a Magical Cauldron, 92–93
Cauldron with a Bubbling Potion, 166–67
celestial witchery, 125–55
  Ancient Spell Mirror, 132–33
  Cauldron Full of Moonlight, 126–27
  Celestial Witchery Shelf, 149
  Delicate Orrery Solar System, 140–41
  Drawers for Bits and Bobs, 148
  Enchanted Pocket Sundial, 130
  Essence of Starlight, 134–35
  Ever-Glowing Lantern, 131
  Haunted Skull with Sunglasses, 128–29
  Liquid Sunshine, 136–37
  Maidenhair Fern that Grows in Moonlight and Sunlight, 144–45
  Midnight-Colored Familiar, 138–39
  Moonlight-Infused Amethyst Crystal, 143
  Spellbooks of Dubious Origin, 142
  Terrarium with an Ever-Blooming Moonflower, 146–47
Celestial Witchery Shelf, 149
  assembling, 150–55
Charming Potted Basil, 28–29
Cherry Pie in a Red Pan, 33
China Teacup, Blue and White, 41
China Teapot, Delicate, 72
Clever Mouse Hiding from the Cat, 73
Climbing Potted Vine, 44–45
clothing
  Cozy Witch's Hat, 66–67
  Pointed Boots for Traipsing in the Swamp, 160–61
  Sturdy Boots for Seaside Adventures, 98
  Wellies for Traipsing in the Garden, 71

Colorful Stained-Glass Lamp, 22–24
color selection and mixing, 12–13
Cookbooks, Witchy, 34–35
Copper Teakettle, Shining, 30–31
Coral, Bright Red, 112
cottage witchery, 59–89
  Books of Magic Spells and Recipes, 74–75
  Cat Napping with Spelled Knitting, 60–61
  Clever Mouse Hiding from the Cat, 73
  Cottage Witchery Shelf, 82–83
  Cozy Stained-Glass Lamp, 64
  Cozy Witch's Hat, 66–67
  Delicate China Teapot, 72
  Floral Teacup, 77
  Magical Crystals, 78
  Magical Springtime Flowers in a Tea Tin, 62–63
  Mysterious Crystal Ball, 70
  Pumpkin from the Witch's Garden, 65
  Romantic Paperback Books, 80–81
  Three-Tier Tower of Treats, 68–69
  Tiny House for Fairy Visitors, 79
  Wellies for Traipsing in the Garden, 71
  Wooden Trinket Shelf, 76
Cottage Witchery Shelf, 82–83
  assembling, 84–89
Cozy Stained-Glass Lamp, 64
Cozy Witch's Hat, 66–67
Crystal, Moonlight-Infused Amethyst, 143
Crystal Ball, Mysterious, 70
Crystal Ball, Talking Alligator Skull with a, 164
Crystal Ball with a Driftwood Stand, 114
Crystals, Magical, 78

D

Dark Candle on a Golden Candlestick, 175
Decorative Tea Towel, 42–43
Delicate China Teapot, 72
Delicate Dried Herbs and Flowers, 25–27
Delicate Moss and Mushrooms, 178–79
Delicate Orrery Solar System, 140–41
Distinguished Seagull with a Witch's Hat, 94–95
Drawers for Bits and Bobs, 148
Dried Herbs and Flowers, Delicate, 25–27
Driftwood Stand, Crystal Ball with a, 114

E

Enchanted Always-Warm Teacup, 106
Enchanted Books, 176–77
Enchanted Hourglass Timer, 32
Enchanted Kitchen Utensils, 38–39
Enchanted Pink Potion, 174
Enchanted Pocket Sundial, 130
Enchanted Spellbooks, 97
Essence of Starlight, 134–35
Ever-Glowing Lantern, 131

F

Fairy Visitors, Tiny House for, 79
Feline Familiar Napping in a Mixing Bowl, 18–19
Fern, Maidenhair, that Grows in Moonlight and Sunlight, 144–45
Fishbowl with a Brightly Colored Fish, 99
Floral Teacup, 77
Flowers, Delicate Dried Herbs and, 25–27
Flowers, Magical Springtime, in a Tea Tin, 62–63
food
  Cherry Pie in a Red Pan, 33
  Magical Frosted Cake, 36–37
  Pumpkin from the Witch's Garden, 65
  Three-Tier Tower of Treats, 68–69
  Warm and Gooey Chocolate Chip Cookie, 105
Frosted Cake, Magical, 36–37

G

Glass Terrarium with Poison Mushrooms, 168–69
glazing, 12
Golden Candlestick, Dark Candle on a, 175
Gothic Candelabra, 163

H

Hand-Carved Wood Storage Rack, 46–47
Hat, Cozy Witch's, 66–67
Hat, Talkative Otter in a Pointed, 158–59
Haunted Skull with Sunglasses, 128–29
Herbs, Mortar and Pestle with Spelled, 48
Hourglass Timer, Enchanted, 32

I

Inkwell with Phoenix Feather Quill, 110
Inquisitive Bat Playing Cards, 162

K

Kitchen Utensils, Enchanted, 38–39
kitchen witchery, 17–57
  Blue and White China Teacup, 41
  Charming Potted Basil, 28–29
  Cherry Pie in a Red Pan, 33
  Climbing Potted Vine, 44–45
  Colorful Stained-Glass Lamp, 22–24
  Decorative Tea Towel, 42–43
  Delicate Dried Herbs and Flowers, 25–27
  Enchanted Hourglass Timer, 32

Enchanted Kitchen Utensils, 38–39
Feline Familiar Napping in a Mixing Bowl, 18–19
Hand-Carved Wood Storage Rack, 46–47
Kitchen Witchery Shelf, 49–50
Magical Frosted Cake, 36–37
Magic Potion Bottles, 40
Mortar and Pestle with Spelled Herbs, 48
Mysterious Cauldron, 20–21
Shining Copper Teakettle, 30–31
Witchy Cookbooks, 34–35
Kitchen Witchery Shelf, 49–50
assembling, 51–57
Knapsack, Sturdy Adventuring, 170–71
Knitting, Cat Napping with Spelled, 60–61

L

Lamp, Colorful Stained-Glass, 22–24
Lamp, Cozy Stained-Glass, 64
Lantern, Ever-Glowing, 131
Liquid Sunshine, 136–37
Long-Lost Book of Perilous Spells, 165

M

Magical Crystals, 78
Magical Frosted Cake, 36–37
Magical Ship in a Bottle, 96
Magical Springtime Flowers in a Tea Tin, 62–63
Magic Potion Bottles, 40
Maidenhair Fern that Grows in Moonlight and Sunlight, 144–45
Mesmerizing Potion Bottle, 172–73
Midnight-Colored Familiar, 138–39
Mirror, Ancient Spell, 132–33
Moonflower, Terrarium with an Ever-Blooming, 146–47
Moonlight-Infused Amethyst Crystal, 143
Moon Phases Chart, Weathered, 109
Mortar and Pestle with Spelled Herbs, 48
Moss and Mushrooms, Delicate, 178–79
Mouse Hiding from the Cat, Clever, 73
Mushrooms, Delicate Moss and, 178–79
Mushrooms, Glass Terrarium with Poison, 168–69
Mysterious Cauldron, 20–21
Mysterious Crystal Ball, 70
Mysterious Treasure Box, 115

O

Octopus Familiar in a Magical Cauldron, 92–93
Orrery Solar System, Delicate, 140–41
Otter, Talkative, in a Pointed Hat, 158–59

P

paints, 11, 12
paper, 11
warped, 15
pencils, 11
pens, 11
Phoenix Feather Quill, Inkwell with, 110
Pie, Cherry, in a Red Pan, 33
Pink Potion, Enchanted, 174
plants
Charming Potted Basil, 28–29
Climbing Potted Vine, 44–45
Delicate Dried Herbs and Flowers, 25–27
Glass Terrarium with Poison Mushrooms, 168–69
Magical Springtime Flowers in a Tea Tin, 62–63
Maidenhair Fern that Grows in Moonlight and Sunlight, 144–45
Mortar and Pestle with Spelled Herbs, 48
Pumpkin from the Witch's Garden, 65
Terrarium with an Ever-Blooming Moonflower, 146–47
Pocket Sundial, Enchanted, 130
Pointed Boots for Traipsing in the Swamp, 160–61
Poison Mushrooms, Glass Terrarium with, 168–69
Potion, Enchanted Pink, 174
Potion Bottle, Mesmerizing, 172–73
Potted Basil, Charming, 28–29
Potted Vine, Climbing, 44–45
Pumpkin from the Witch's Garden, 65

Q

Quill, Inkwell with Phoenix Feather, 110

R

Romantic Paperback Books, 80–81

S

Seagull, Distinguished, with a Witch's Hat, 94–95
Seashells, Beautiful, 113
sea witchery, 91–123
Armillary Stargazing Sphere, 111
Beautiful Seashells, 113
Bottled Weather Spells, 100–101
Bright Red Coral, 112
Candle for Late-Night Reading, 108
Crystal Ball with a Driftwood Stand, 114
Distinguished Seagull with a Witch's Hat, 94–95
Enchanted Always-Warm Teacup, 106
Enchanted Spellbooks, 97
Fishbowl with a Brightly Colored Fish, 99
Inkwell with Phoenix Feather Quill, 110
Magical Ship in a Bottle, 96

Mysterious Treasure Box, 115
Octopus Familiar in a Magical Cauldron, 92–93
Sea Witchery Shelf, 116–17
Shelf with Stained-Glass Details, 102–3
Silver Filagree Teapot, 107
Stargazing Telescope, 104
Sturdy Boots for Seaside Adventures, 98
Warm and Gooey Chocolate Chip Cookie, 105
Weathered Moon Phases Chart, 109
Sea Witchery Shelf, 116–17
assembling, 118–23
Shelf with Stained-Glass Details, 102–3
shelves
Celestial Witchery Shelf, 149–55
Cottage Witchery Shelf, 82–89
Hand-Carved Wood Storage Rack, 46–47
Kitchen Witchery Shelf, 49–57
Sea Witchery Shelf, 116–23
Shelf with Stained-Glass Details, 102–3
Swamp Witchery Shelf, 180–86
tips and tricks for creating, 14–15
Wooden Trinket Shelf, 76
Shining Copper Teakettle, 30–31
Ship, Magical, in a Bottle, 96
Silver Filagree Teapot, 107
Skull, Haunted, with Sunglasses, 128–29
Solar System, Delicate Orrery, 140–41
Spellbooks, Enchanted, 97
Spellbooks of Dubious Origin, 142
Spell Mirror, Ancient, 132–33
Stained-Glass Lamp, Colorful, 22–24
Stained-Glass Lamp, Cozy, 64
Stargazing Sphere, Armillary, 111
Stargazing Telescope, 104
Starlight, Essence of, 134–35
Sturdy Adventuring Knapsack, 170–71
Sturdy Boots for Seaside Adventures, 98
Sunshine, Liquid, 136–37
supplies, 11
swamp witchery, 157–86
Cauldron with a Bubbling Potion, 166–67
Dark Candle on a Golden Candlestick, 175
Delicate Moss and Mushrooms, 178–79
Enchanted Books, 176–77
Enchanted Pink Potion, 174
Glass Terrarium with Poison Mushrooms, 168–69
Gothic Candelabra, 163
Inquisitive Bat Playing Cards, 162
Long-Lost Book of Perilous Spells, 165
Mesmerizing Potion Bottle, 172–73
Pointed Boots for Traipsing in the Swamp, 160–61
Sturdy Adventuring Knapsack, 170–71
Swamp Witchery Shelf, 180–81
Talkative Otter in a Pointed Hat, 158–59
Talking Alligator Skull with a Crystal Ball, 164
Swamp Witchery Shelf, 180–81
assembling, 182–86

T

Talkative Otter in a Pointed Hat, 158–59
Talking Alligator Skull with a Crystal Ball, 164
teacups and teapots
Blue and White China Teacup, 41
Delicate China Teapot, 72
Enchanted Always-Warm Teacup, 106
Floral Teacup, 77
Shining Copper Teakettle, 30–31
Silver Filagree Teapot, 107
Tea Towel, Decorative, 42–43
techniques, 12–13
Telescope, Stargazing, 104
Terrarium, Glass, with Poison Mushrooms, 168–69
Terrarium with an Ever-Blooming Moonflower, 146–47
Three-Tier Tower of Treats, 68–69
Timer, Enchanted Hourglass, 32
Tiny House for Fairy Visitors, 79
Treasure Box, Mysterious, 115
Trinket Shelf, Wooden, 76

V

Vine, Climbing Potted, 44–45

W

Warm and Gooey Chocolate Chip Cookie, 105
warping, 15
watercolor techniques and paints, 12–13
Weathered Moon Phases Chart, 109
Weather Spells, Bottled, 100–101
Wellies for Traipsing in the Garden, 71
wet-on-dry, 12
Witch's Hat, Cozy, 66–67
Witch's Hat, Distinguished Seagull with a, 94–95
Witchy Cookbooks, 34–35
Wooden Trinket Shelf, 76
Wood Storage Rack, Hand-Carved, 46–47